MW01147645

The Corrie Herring Hooks Series

Texas Mushrooms A Field Guide

BY SUSAN METZLER AND VAN METZLER

ORSON K. MILLER, Jr., Scientific Advisor

University of Texas Press, Austin

Copyright © 1992
by the University of Texas Press
All rights reserved
Printed in Japan

First Edition, 1992

Requests for permission to reproduce material from this work should be sent to Permissions, University of Texas Press, Box 7819, Austin, Texas 78713-7819.

∞ The paper used in this publication meets the minimum requirements of American National Standard for Information Sciences—Permanence of Paper for Printed Library Materials, AMSI Z39.48-1984.

LIBRARY OF CONGRESS
CATALOGING-IN-PUBLICATION DATA

Metzler, Susan.
Texas mushrooms : a field guide / by Susan Metzler and Van Metzler. — 1st ed.
p. cm.
Includes bibliographical references and index.
ISBN 0-292-75125-7 (alk. paper). — ISBN 0-292-75126-5 (pbk. : alk. paper)
1. Mushrooms—Texas—Identification.
2. Mushrooms—Texas—Pictorial works.
I. Metzler, Van. II. Title.
QK617.M49 1992
589.2'22'09764—dc20 91-2239
CIP

FRONTISPIECE PHOTO: VM
Leucocoprinus birnbaumii

Contents

Figures

Tables

Acknowledgments

This project would never have been undertaken had it not been for the members, past, present, and future, of the Texas Mycological Society. From its founding in 1977 the society's Annual Mushroom Forays have brought professional mycologists and interested amateurs together in combined pursuit of knowledge, fungi, and fun. From beginners to advanced students, from those who are interested only in learning to identify edible mushrooms to those who want to become experts, from children to grandparents, no one could ask for a better group of friends. And we thank them all for their enthusiasm and encouragement for this project.

One person deserves special credit—David P. Lewis of Vidor, Texas, who has been studying Texas mushrooms since the early 1970s and who has always been ready when we said, "Let's hunt mushrooms!" Dave is probably the most knowledgeable person on Texas mushrooms, and he has generously reviewed this manuscript and made suggestions and comments that have greatly improved its content.

A special thanks also goes to all our photographer friends. This project was carried out during three years of drought, and we were simply unable to get many of the photos we needed. Without photos contributed by Alan Bessette, Joe Liggio, Don Gray, Donald Smith, Clark Ovrebo, David Lewis, Cynthia Young, and Heinz Gaylord, this project would have been much more difficult.

We are also deeply grateful to Charles "Chuck" Barrows, now deceased, of Santa Fe, New Mexico, who set an example of the contributions amateurs can make to mycological knowledge by collecting and identifying mushrooms for nearly fifty years; Pat Brannen, also of New Mexico, who brought new meaning to "dyeing with mushrooms"; Gene Heitzman, deceased, the first person who encouraged us to write this book; and all our friends and fellow members of mycological societies all over the United States and all those who have hunted mushrooms with us over the years. And a special thanks to one more person, Ruth Taber of Texas A&M University, without whom this book would never have happened.

For all of you, we have tried to write the book we wish we had had when we were beginners!

Photo credits are indicated by initials:

AB	Alan Bessette
HG	Heinz Gaylord
DG	Don Gray
DL	David Lewis
JL	Joe Liggio
VM	Van Metzler
OM	Orson Miller
CO	Clark Ovrebo
DS	Donald Smith
CY	Cynthia Young

1. Mushroom Hunting in Texas

Mushroom hunting in Texas can be a year-round activity. Given sufficient rainfall, many types of mushrooms can be found at almost any time of year. Other mushrooms are seasonal, but only during prolonged periods of freezing weather will no mushrooms be found.

Texas offers a number of ecological areas in which to search: the desert and semiarid areas of West Texas, the Hill Country with its alkaline soil, and the acid soils in the forested areas of East Texas. Each of these areas supports its own fungus communities, and the results ("fruiting bodies" or "mushrooms") can readily be found by a sharp-eyed observer.

And here's the good news: virtually all the choice edible mushrooms and fungi occur in some part of Texas at some time of the year; many enjoy an extended growing season and are plentiful. By the same token, the deadly poisonous, the toxic (those that cause gastric or other upset, but from which one normally survives), and the unpalatable also occur. Fortunately for the beginner, several of the best-known edibles (oyster mushrooms, puffballs, chanterelles) are easy to learn and to distinguish from potentially harmful species. After all, you don't have to know the dahlias from the daisies to be able to pick the roses in the garden!

For the more advanced student, Texas (and especially East Texas, including the Big Thicket) offers a fascinating combination of species known from diverse areas—the tropics, South America, and Malaysia, as well as species known from other parts of the United States and Europe. Another challenge to the advanced student is working with species "complexes": the gradual intergrading between species that are normally distinct. The desert and semiarid regions offer a special challenge complicated by short, unpredictable periods of rainfall followed by an almost immediate fruiting of species.

A great deal of study remains to be done on the fungi of Texas. In 1899, L. M. Underwood stated: "When area is considered, probably this state [Texas] presents the best example of a region practically unknown to the mycologist. [A few reports] constitute our entire knowledge of the fungi of one of the most interesting regions in the entire country."* Since that time, only a

*Lucius M. Underwood, *Moulds, Mildews, and Mushrooms* (New York: Holt & Co., 1899), p. 193.

handful of mycologists have worked here, and a few people cannot adequately sample and categorize the diversity of fungi found throughout the year. It has been estimated that as many as eight thousand to ten thousand species of fungi are to be found in Texas, but at the present fewer than one thousand have been identified to the species level. Thus, mycology is a field in which amateurs can make significant contributions to science.

What's special about mushroom hunting in Texas? The fun you'll have! You can walk new trails or the same trails and see something different every time. Enjoy our beautiful state from an entirely different angle—and double your enjoyment with chanterelles for dinner! Take the entire family—kids are great "spotters" as they have sharp eyes and are built low to the ground; seniors will enjoy walking at a leisurely pace; you'll learn more about your natural surroundings, and all will sleep well after a peaceful day in the woods.

FIGURE 1. Regions of Texas

What This Book Is and Isn't

This book is a pictorial guide to common Texas mushrooms and fungi. Some of the species pictured here are included in other field guides; many are not. No species are shown that do not occur in Texas. The term "common," unless stated otherwise, is used here to mean "common in Texas." Every attempt is made to picture our species accurately. Mushrooms that are smaller, larger, or differently shaped or colored here compared to those found in other places are accurately depicted. The book relies heavily on photographs that illustrate the key features of each species rather than lengthy technical descriptions. You should read the descriptions with care and look for the key features illustrated in the color photographs.

Orson Miller has been studying mushrooms throughout North America for thirty years. He has also carried out fieldwork in Europe, Asia, and Australia. The Metzlers have been hunting, photographing, and trying to identify Texas mushrooms since their college days. They are active in both the North American Mycological Association* and the Texas Mycological Society† (TMS), a nonprofit educational and social group based in Houston whose purpose is to identify and enjoy the mushrooms of our state. To this end, they teach classes, lead "nature walks," and talk to garden clubs (and anybody who'll listen) in order to spread the word about Texas mushrooms. This book evolved out of frustration at trying to use field guides from other parts of the country and the world to identify Texas mushrooms.

We prefer to recognize and cover distinctive species that can be clearly distinguished by field characteristics, and we encourage any novice mushroom hunters to take this approach. We made the assumption that you have no microscope available to look at spores and tissue samples; thus, where such examination is the only way to distinguish between closely related species, we provided the name of the most commonly found form.

---

*North American Mycological Society, Kenneth Cochran, Executive Secretary, 3556 Oakwood, Ann Arbor, Mich. 48104-5213.

†Texas Mycological Society, 7445 Dillon, Houston, Tex. 77061.

We have also avoided technical terms wherever possible and have defined those terms for which there are no simple substitutes. For readers with a microscope some technical data, such as spore size, is provided in the appendix, but no attempt is made to describe all the microscopic parts of the mushroom. Technical works are listed for those who wish to become more fully involved with the microscopic features of mushrooms.

This book is *not* intended to be used as a guide to what you can eat safely without expert confirmation, and neither the authors nor the publisher accept responsibility for any problems encountered by readers who try to use it as such.

This book is *not* a substitute for having a mycologist (professional or amateur) available to help you with your identification. This is especially true for those who want to eat wild mushrooms. After all, if you put a wrong name to a mushroom you suffer no great consequences, but if you eat the wrong mushroom and end up in a hospital, it can be a matter of (*your*) life or death.

If your aim is to be able to eat wild mushrooms safely, try to take a class or go on nature walks with someone knowledgeable. Best of all, join a mycological society, such as TMS,* and attend the Annual Mushroom Foray! Most mycological societies sponsor a weekend of mushrooming—field trips, identification seminars, beginners' workshops, preparing and tasting sessions, lectures, and talks. In addition, over the course of the weekend, as many as three hundred mushrooms will be identified, labeled, and displayed for you to study.

We hope that you will take time to see the mushrooms, appreciate their beauty and diversity, and experience enough success at identifying the ones you find that you will meet your goals, whether they are to enjoy a panful of edible mushrooms or to pursue the study of mushrooms using this as well as the other technical books and guides available.

---

*There is also a New Mexico Mycological Society, 332 Tulane NE, Albuquerque, N.M. 87106, which holds annual forays in the mountains of New Mexico and is perhaps more convenient for people living in West Texas.

VM

About Mushrooms and Fungi

A LITTLE ABOUT FUNGI

Fungi are placed in a separate kingdom called the Myceteae. They are separated from the plant kingdom because they do not contain chlorophyll like green plants, which make their own food through a process called *photosynthesis.* Fungi do not make their own food but rather obtain nutrients by breaking down organic matter or by obtaining it directly from higher plants. If the organic matter is dead, such as dead leaves, sticks, logs, and cones, the fungi are called *decomposers,* or *saprophytes.* However, many other fungi attack living plants and animals and may kill part or all of the host. These fungi are called *parasites.* A third group of fungi, which include many of our edible and poisonous mushrooms, grow around and into the small rootlets of green plants. The fungi obtain carbon (sugar) made by the green plant and in turn provide the green plant with phosphorus and nitrogen. These fungi form part of a mutually beneficial relationship and are called *mycorrhizal fungi* (*myco*= fungi; =*rhizal* = root). The mycorrhizal fungi are often associated with forest trees, such as oaks, birches, beeches, pines, hemlocks, spruce, and fir, as well as shrubs, such as blueberries.

The body of the fungus is called the *mycelium,* or *spawn,* by the commercial mushroom grower. It is usually a white or light-colored mass of minute, stringlike cells called *hyphae.* The individual cells are microscopic. However, you may expose the intricate network of mycelium if you kick a rotting log or clear away wet leaves or needles. As the mycelium grows, the hyphae secrete enzymes, which break down the complex organic molecules and release simpler ones that can be absorbed and utilized by the fungus as food. In this way, the fungus plays a vital role in releasing nutrients for higher plants and animals to use. Recent studies have shown that significant increases in growth and nutrient uptake accrue to the tree and that such trees possess distinct advantages over nonmycorrhizal ones when confronted with shortages of nutrients or water. Therefore, fungi play a significant role in the maintenance and growth of trees and other vegetation.

After a period of vegetative growth of the hyphae under optimal growing conditions, which may vary from fungus to fungus, each species will produce its characteristic fruiting body. A wide variety of fruiting bodies from typical mushrooms with a cap and gills, boletes with a cap and pores, fungi that resemble sea corals, called the coral fungi, and the spongelike morels, all arise from very similar-looking mycelium. Fungi can be found fruiting at any time. Some fungi fruit during very specific times each year while others only require good moisture conditions. In summary, a knowledge of the period of the year when a mushroom fruits, the substrate on which it fruits, and the plant community with which it is associated is an essential part of successful mushroom hunting.

TERMS

Fungus is a name given to any member of the fungi kingdom and may refer to the hyphae or to the fruiting body, such as the mushroom. *Mushroom* is a common term that can be applied to the fruiting body of a fungus, usually one that has a distinct cap and stalk. However, the term is often applied in a general way to the fruiting bodies of the larger fungi even if they do not show the typical cap and stalk features. The term *toadstool* refers more specifically to the mushrooms with a distinct cap and stalk. Some people use it to mean only poisonous mushrooms, while others use it as a general term for all mushrooms. The ambiguity makes *toadstool* an undesirable term to use.

CLASSIFICATION

The fleshy fruiting fungi are divided into "classes" based on how and where they produce their spores. Members of the subdivision Ascomycotina, the "ascos," generally produce eight spores contained in a saclike structure called an *ascus.* The microscopic ascus (pl., asci) contains the spores and looks much like a pea pod containing peas. The spores function in much the same way as seeds do in that they germinate and reproduce the organism. They are the results of meiosis, the sexual process. Members of this group feature a fertile layer of asci, which contain thousands of ascospores capable of being widely dispersed by wind or other means in order to ensure the establishment and growth of new individuals. Members of the subdivision Basidiomycotina typically produce their spores on club-shaped cells called *basidia,* which appear to have four baseballs attached to the end of a bat. These are the spores that are born on the club-shaped cell. The gills or pores of a mushroom contain the fertile layers of these club-shaped cells. These features can be seen only with a microscope. There is some correlation between these classes of fungi and the methods of producing spores as well as the general kinds of fruiting bodies that each class produces. Within the Basidiomycotina, one class, the Gasteromycetes, also produces spores on basidia, but the spore-bearing structures are enclosed by the fruiting body, and the basidia are surrounded by a structure called a *peridium.*

The scientific names given to mushrooms are required to follow the rules of the binomial system of nomenclature and are in Latin or are "Latinized." The genus name is given to a group of mushrooms that have many similar characteristics. In this book, many of the major genera are briefly described to help you grasp their characteristics so that with practice you will recognize a genus even though you may not know which species it is. The species name is given to those mushrooms in the genus that are capable of mixing or interbreeding. This

TABLE 1. Classification of the Groups Included in the Kingdom Myceteae (Fungi) Covered in This Book

DIVISION AMASTIGOMYCOTA

SUBDIVISION BASIDIOMYCOTINA:
spores borne on club-shaped structures called basidia

Class Hymenomycetes:
spores borne externally on gills or in tubes, not enclosed in a sac

Order Agaricales:
mushrooms with a cap, and basidia located on gills or in tubes on the underside of the cap; with or without a stalk

Family Amanitaceae: white spore print, with free gills, universal veil present

Family Lepiotaceae: white spore print, with free gills, without universal veil

Family Hygrophoraceae: white spore print, attached, waxy gills

Family Russulaceae: white spore print, attached gills, brittle tissue

Family Tricholomataceae: white spore print, attached gills

Family Pluteaceae: pink spore print, gills free from the stalk

Family Entolomataceae: pink spore print, gills attached to the stalk

Family Cortinariaceae: bright rust, orange-brown, or grayish brown spore print, with a veil

Family Bolbitiaceae: rusty brown to dark brown spore print

Family Agaricaceae: dark brown spore print, gills free from the stalk

Family Strophariaceae: dark brown spore print, gills attached to the stalk

Family Coprinaceae: black to blackish brown spore print

Family Boletaceae: fleshy mushrooms with a cap and stalk and basidia located in tubes on the underside of the cap; usually on the ground

Order Aphyllophorales:
fungi with basidia located on spines, pores, or wrinkled surfaces; with or without a distinct cap; stalk central, lateral, or absent

Family Cantharellaceae: chanterelles—mushrooms with cap and stalk, with basidia located on wrinkled spore-bearing ridges on the underside of the cap

Family Clavariaceae: coral and club fungi

Family Hydnaceae: tooth fungi—mushrooms with basidia located on spiny teeth; cap and stalk may be present, or fruiting body may consist of a mass of spines

Family Polyporaceae: poroid fungi typically tough to woody, usually on wood; with basidia located in tubes

Miscellaneous genera

Orders Tremellales, Auriculariales, and Dacrymycetales (jelly fungi): fungi with amorphous shapes, often resembling a blob or extrusion of jelly

Class Gasteromycetes: spores enclosed by the fruiting body; spores borne on basidia within a fruiting body that is enclosed by an outer cover called a peridium

Order Lycoperdales (puffballs):
ball-shaped fungi whose spores "puff" from an opening at the top

Order Nidulariales (birds' nest fungi):
small fungi with spores in egglike packages resting in a cup-shaped structure that resembles a thimble-sized nest filled with eggs

Order Sclerodermatales (earthballs):
ball-shaped fungi with tough, thick outer covering that breaks open to release spores

Order Phallales (stinkhorns):
a group of colorful fungi, many of which are shaped like horns, with a very strong, distinctive odor

Other Gasteromycetes (stalked puffballs)

SUBDIVISION ASCOMYCOTINA:
spores enclosed in a saclike structure called an ascus

Class Pyrenomycetes (flask fungi):
fruiting bodies may have many different shapes, but all have a roughened, "pimply" surface from the flask-shaped structures that contain the spores

Class Discomycetes (cup, brain, and sponge fungi):
fruiting bodies that resemble cups, brains, or sponges, that have their spores produced in the ascus

---

NOTE: The classification of the Agaricales closely follows *Mushrooms of North America* by Orson K. Miller (New York: E. P. Dutton Press, 1981); the classification of the Gasteromycetes follows *Gasteromycetes: Morphological and Development Features with Keys to the Orders, Family, and Genera* by Orson K. and Hope H. Miller (Eureka, Calif.: Mad River Press, 1988); and the overall classification is as presented in *Fundamentals of the Fungi* by Elizabeth Moore-Landecker (3d ed., New York: Prentice-Hall, 1990).

doesn't necessarily mean that all members of a species look exactly alike; all people are of the same genus and species, *Homo sapiens,* yet almost no two are identical, and many are quite unique.

The rules of nomenclature give the person who first recognizes a new species the right to bestow the species name. He or she may honor the person who discovered it, the place where it was found, its colors, any notable characteristics, or perhaps the trees or other plants with which it associates. Thus, in the genus *Lactarius* (the milk mushrooms, those that produce droplets of liquid when the gills are nicked or scratched), you will find the species *peckii* (for Charles Peck, an early New York botanist, who has been called the Father of American Systematic Mycology); *yazooensis* (which was first collected along the Yazoo River in Mississippi); *indigo* (for the distinct blue coloring); *corrugis* (the cap edges look as if they are "corrugated"); and *paradoxus* (paradoxical or confused), among others.

Hoping to end some of the confusion that surrounds Texas mushrooms, we have used the scientific names in this book. We have translated the Latin throughout to help you remember what the names mean and have included "common names" only where they are actually in common usage. In Texas, so little is known about mushrooms by the average person that "common" names are not common. The reader who collected morels (*Morchella esculenta*) in Michigan as a child will recognize them from the photos in this book, even though he or she may have called them "houbys," "merkles," "roons," or "sponge mushrooms."

Don't worry if you have a problem pronouncing the Latin names. We have heard these names pronounced every possible way, and all of them are "correct." You can use classical Latin pronunciation or just "sound them out." The "alternate Texas pronunciation" has a little twang and drawl, long *i*'s and *o*'s, short *a*'s and *e*'s—that's the way we say them!

How to Collect Mushrooms

First, always get permission. Whether you want to pick mushrooms on federal land, such as national parks, forests, or preserves, or state property, including state parks, and state forests, or on private property, get the owner or caretaker's permission before you start. Written permission is best. Failure to do this can be, at minimum, embarrassing and, at worst, can result in your arrest for trespassing or for collecting without a permit.

The gear you need is simple and inexpensive—all you need is a sturdy basket for carrying your mushrooms, a supply of paper or waxed-paper bags (plastic bags are not recommended as the mushrooms quickly become "goopy"), or a roll of waxed paper, a knife for cutting mushrooms off stumps or wood, and a small digging tool to dig mushrooms completely out of the ground. A compass to help you find your way out of the forest, a whistle to alert others in your party if you get separated, and some insect repellent are also highly recommended. In addition, if you plan to sit on the ground or lie down to take photographs, we suggest that you also carry a plastic garbage bag to keep a layer between you and the chiggers, ticks, fire ants, poison ivy, mud, and other hazards of outdoor life.

You should also dress properly: wear a hat or scarf to keep spiders and ticks out of your hair, long sleeves and long pants to minimize scratches from brush, and closed-in shoes. Hiking shoes or rubber boots offer ankle support and protection from snakebite and insect attack. Cotton clothing is preferable to polyester because it is cool and helps to minimize snagging as you walk through the woods. The same rainfall and humidity that bring mushrooms also bring mosquitoes and ticks, so a liberal application of repellent is recommended. (When we go mushroom hunting in the summer, we spray our bodies with repellent before getting dressed, then reapply as needed in the field.) Some mushroomers recommend sprinkling powdered sulfur (available at drug stores) in your socks to discourage chiggers. Ignore this advice at your peril!

When you arrive at your mushroom-hunting destination, take a few minutes to orient yourself to directions. Does the road run north and south, and are you going off to the east? Once you are in the woods, running around from mushroom to mushroom, it is easy to get turned around, and this orientation will help you make your way back to the car.

Look closely along the path or ground for mushrooms. Your eyes will sharpen for this task in time. When you find a mushroom, carefully dig it up, making sure to collect the entire base. Replace the dirt and leaves over the hole you leave so that the mycelium will not dry out and die. Place the mushroom in a paper or waxed-paper bag, or roll it up in a sheet of waxed paper, twisting the ends to hold the mushrooms in place. Put only like specimens in a single bag. If you find a large number and suspect they may be edible, make two collections: one for identification, containing a representative sample of age and size, and a second for the table, containing firm, young, bug-free specimens. You may "field trim" (cut the dirty bases off and clean the mushrooms a little with your knife) specimens in this second collection to minimize cleaning when you get home. Be sure to confirm your identification and your mushrooms' edibility before you eat them. Follow the mushroom hunter's first rule, "When in doubt, throw it out!" as well as the second rule, "Save a sample for the poison center, and take it with you to the emergency room."

We encourage you to attend the Annual Mushroom Foray, or take a class, or get a group of people together to look for mushrooms. You'll find that the friends you make, the pleasures of a day in the woods finding, discussing, and learning about fungi, and the enjoyment of a dinner featuring fresh wild mushrooms will make any amount of frustration worthwhile.

2. How to Use This Book to Identify Your Mushroom

The Challenge of Identification

Mushroom identification can be one of the most challenging hobbies you ever undertake. If you take up bird watching or wildflower identification, you have the advantage of already knowing the difference between a duck and a mockingbird and between a bluebonnet and an Indian paintbrush. Few beginners in mycology know an *Amanita* from an *Agaricus.* To illustrate the inherent challenges, consider the following example.

You have never before seen a head of lettuce or a head of cabbage, but today you found a head-shaped, green plant with shiny leaves that overlap each other. You pick it, take it home, and begin to consult your "Field Guide to Common Plants" to try to find out what you have found. Luckily for you, there is an introductory section in your book that allows you to turn to the section on "plants with short stems that form headlike structures of overlapping leaves." There, you find photos of iceberg lettuce and common cabbage. The photos look quite similar and, in reading the descriptions, you find in the comments section that "cabbage is much denser than lettuce, and the leaves are shiny and more compact." You lift your "head"; it seems quite dense to you, but how can you judge "more dense" with nothing to compare it to? And suppose that what you have is actually a bok choy, Chinese cabbage, which is not pictured or even referred to in your book. Or, perhaps, the lettuces and cabbages are in completely different sections of the book, and no reference is given from one group to the other. By now you would be frustrated, disgusted, and ready to pitch out your "head" and give up on trying to determine what you have found. But, if you take your "head" to a vegetable gardener and expert, he or she can show you both, let you weigh them in your hands, and smell and taste them. Then, you'll know a lettuce from a cabbage!

Mushroom identification is like that. There are more than ten thousand species of the larger fungi that have been identified in the world, and several thousand species are estimated to occur in Texas. The Texas Mycological Society has recorded nearly seven hundred species since 1977 at their Annual Mushroom Foray. And even if we could include great photos of all those species, with each photo showing all the important identification features, both young and old specimens, and the complete range of size, color, and form that each species could take, we still wouldn't even begin to cover all the species that occur *anywhere* in the state, and at any time of the year.

In this book, we have limited our scope to a little over two hundred species. We have included many of the most commonly found mushrooms and those that have the most widespread range. We have also included some species that are indigenous but which have not been pictured in other field guides.

An Approach to Identifying Mushrooms

Traditionally, most field guides use one of two methods to help you identify your mushroom. The most common method is the use of dichotomous keys in which you choose a series of two alternatives. You should arrive at the correct species name for your specimen if you use the key correctly and if the key is designed to include the mushroom you have. When we were beginners, we had a great deal of trouble getting to the correct name using keys, and now that we are teachers of other beginners, we have found our students to have great difficulty with them also. The second method that is often used to identify a mushroom is "picture matching"; that is, you sit down with your mushroom and your book and turn the pages, looking at the pictures until you find a photo that "matches" (or until you give up in frustration).

This book takes a different approach to helping you identify your specimen, and we think the book will work best for you if you'll follow our system. When you first use this book to identify the specimens you have found, select one group in which you have several specimens collected. Your best success will be from working with a collection that has young, old, and in-between specimens. This will help to minimize the differences in form that occur as a mushroom opens and matures.

Step 1. Start by comparing your specimens to the divisions listed in Table 2, "Quick Chart for Fungi Classification." The first two categories listed, mushrooms with gills (slender, leaf-like plates underneath the cap) and boletes (mushrooms with pores on the underside, looking like a well-used pin cushion) contain over two-thirds of the species listed in this book.

If your specimen resembles those of any *other* categories, turn directly to the section of the book listed and you can begin comparing your specimen to the general and specific descriptions listed until you have it identified.

Step 2. If your specimen is a mushroom with gills or pores under the cap, the next thing you must do is take a spore print. To make an accurate determination of what group your mushroom belongs in, you will have to know the color of the spores in deposit (not the color they appear under the microscope). Remove the stalk or cut it off just below the level of the gills or pores and place the cap, gill- or pore-side down, on white paper or a glass slide. Optionally, you may invert a glass or cup over the cap to prevent drafts from blowing the spores. In four to twelve hours, enough spores should have fallen that an accurate spore color can be determined. (We carry white slips of paper in the field and often start our spore print as soon as the mushroom is collected, wrapping the paper and mushroom cap in waxed paper and placing it flat on the bottom of the collecting basket.) At times, no spores will be deposited: this is usually due to the age of the specimen, but occasionally some mushrooms are sterile.

Step 3. Knowing the color of the spores from your specimen, you are ready to proceed to Tables 3–10 for mushrooms with gills, or to Table 11 for boletes, to determine which family of mushrooms is likely to contain your specimen. The families are grouped within the Tables by spore color. Locate the Table or Tables that cover mushrooms with the spore color you have determined. The first column on the left side of each Table contains a list of the parts of the mushroom: cap, gills, stalk, ring, etc. Note the characteristics of these parts of your mushroom and compare them to those listed in the charts. For instance, your white-spored mushroom with gills may have a red cap and a short, brittle white stalk, and you may have found it on the ground near a pine tree. As you work your way through the Tables, you discover that you can match these characteristics with the members of the *Russula* or *Lactarius* genera in the Family Russulaceae. Turn to the page listed for the family and begin comparing your specimen with the descriptions of the major genera in this family.

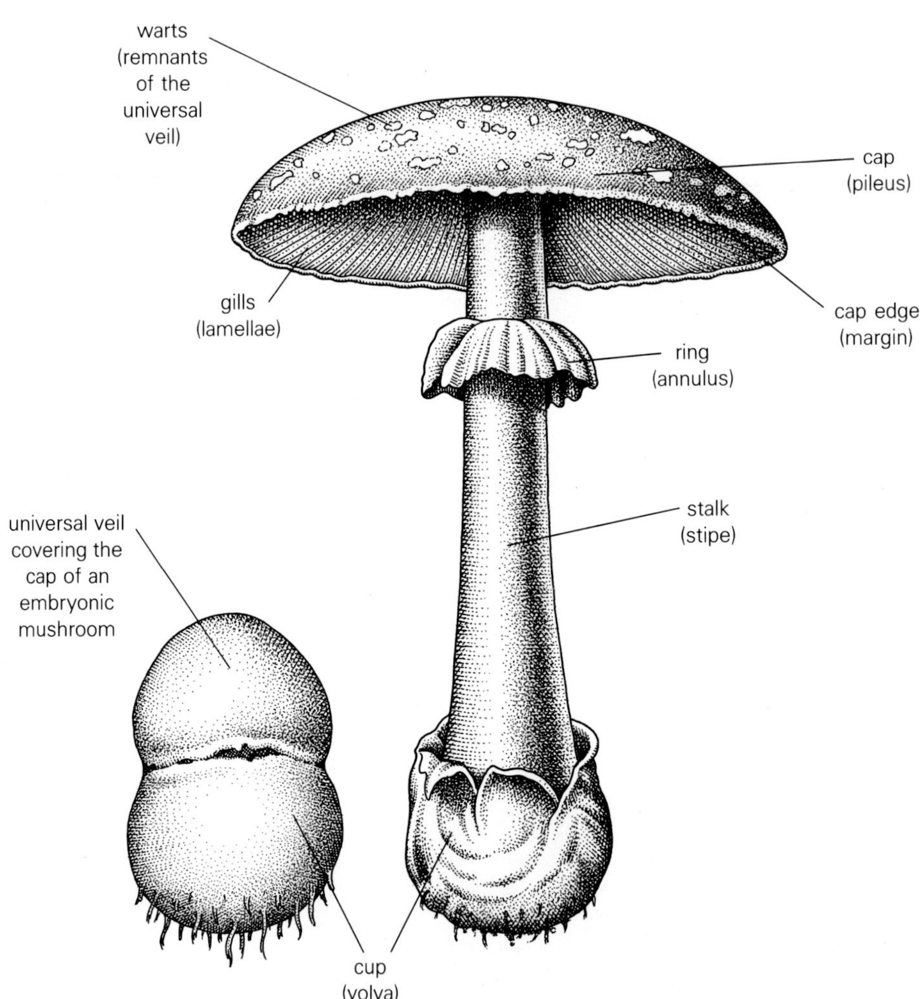

FIGURE 2. The parts of a mushroom

Terms not in parentheses are used in this book; those in parentheses are the technical terms used in other reference works.

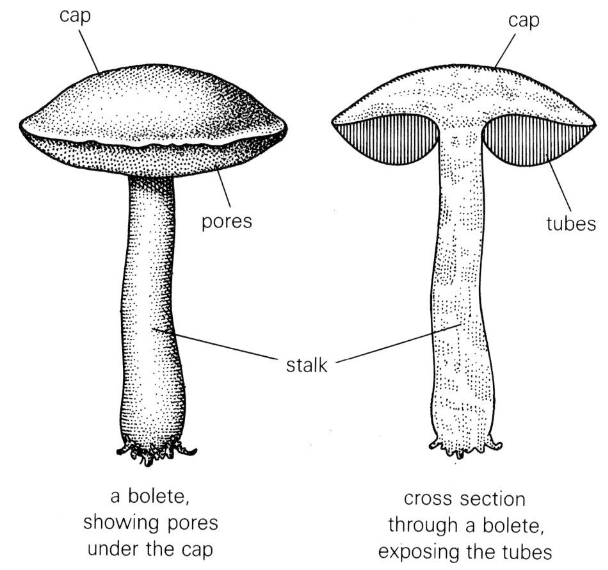

FIGURE 2A.

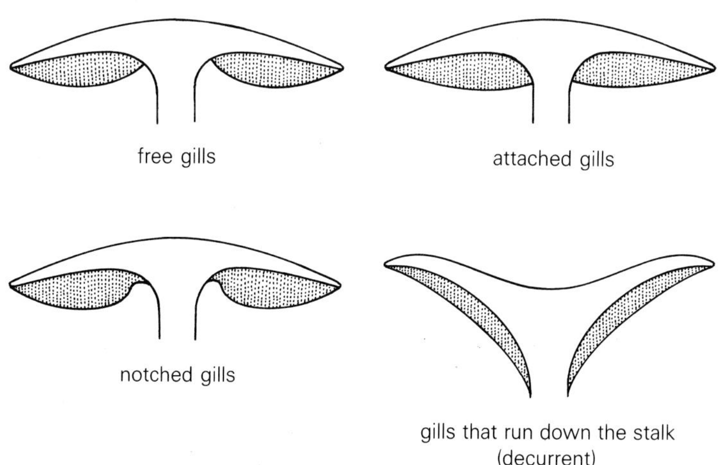

FIGURE 2B. Gill attachment

Step 4. At this point, stop and make some written notes about your specimen and its characteristics. You will want to write down the color of the spore print, the shape of the cap and stalk and other parts of your mushroom, and take a few measurements, including its height and width. Then note the presence of and any special characteristics of the gills, pores, stalk, and so forth. Cut one mature specimen down the center, and include in your notes the interior features, including any color changes that may occur. You should also note whether your fungus was found on the ground or on wood, grass, or some other place. Only when you have a complete written description are you ready to begin trying to "match" your specimen to those in the book.

Step 5. Read the descriptions carefully, compare the notes you took to the descriptions, and compare your specimen to the photos. Think of identification as a process of, first, determining which major group of fungus you have, then to which family it belongs. When you are comfortable that you are on the right track, try to determine your mushroom's genus, comparing your specimen closely to our descriptions. Then, when you are confident about the genus of your mushroom, compare your description to the species in that genus. If you don't find any species that match your mushroom either in written description or in a photograph, at least congratulate yourself on having arrived at the correct genus.

Once, a woman who had never tried to identify mushrooms came to the Texas Mushroom Foray, attended a beginners' workshop, went on a collecting trip, and participated in the identification session. At the end of the foray, she was heard to say, "I really learned a lot. I can look at a mushroom and tell if it's an *Amanita,* or a bolete, or something else. I couldn't do that when I got here!"

The point is, don't let yourself get frustrated and give up if identifying mushrooms is difficult for you. In this book, we have tried to make it as easy as possible. We have written our descriptions in "English," avoiding technical terms. Each time you try to identify a specimen you find, it will become easier for you. But there will always be mushrooms you just can't identify. We hope this book will give you enough success to continue to try.

TABLE 2. Quick Chart for Fungi Classification

MUSHROOMS Fruiting body with a cap, with or without a stalk, with spores borne on gills under the cap		Go to the charts for the mushroom families, PAGES 22–36
BOLETES Fruiting body with a cap and stalk, with spores borne on tubes under the cap		Go to the charts for the Bolete families, PAGES 202–203
CHANTERELLES Fruiting body with a cap and stalk, with spores borne on ridges on the underside of the cap		Go to section titled "Family Cantharellaceae: The Chanterelles," PAGE 236
CORAL AND CLUB FUNGI Fruiting body resembling a sea coral or small clubs, with the spores borne along the outside surfaces		Go to section titled "Family Clavariaceae: The Coral and Club Fungi," PAGE 242
TOOTH FUNGI Mushroom with or without a cap, with or without a stalk, with spores borne on spines or "teeth"		Go to section titled "Family Hydnaceae: The Tooth Fungi," PAGE 251

TABLE 2. Quick Chart for Fungi Classification (*continued*)

POLYPORES Mushroom with a cap, usually lacking a stalk, tough and woody, growing on wood, with spores borne on very short tubes visible as pores under the cap		Go to section titled "Family Polyporaceae: The Polypores," PAGE 258
JELLY FUNGI Fruiting body resembling a blob or extrusion of jelly, with spores borne along the body		Go to section titled "Orders Tremellales, Auriculariales, and Dacrymycetales: The Jelly Fungi," PAGE 277
PUFFBALLS Fruiting body resembling a small ball, without a stalk, usually on wood or on the ground, with spores produced inside the ball and emitted through a hole at the top		Go to section titled "Order Lycoperdales: The Puffballs and Earthstars," PAGE 285
BIRDS' NESTS Fruiting body resembling a thimble-sized birds' nest filled with tiny eggs; spores produced inside the egglike structures		Go to section titled "Order Nidulariales: The Birds' Nest Fungi," PAGE 293
EARTHBALLS Fruiting body resembling a ball with thick, rindlike skin; often found wholly or partly underground; spores produced in the center of the ball but are not extruded through a hole at the top		Go to section titled "Order Sclerodermatales: The Earthballs," PAGE 296

STINKHORNS Fruiting body resembling a horn, lattice, or other shape, emitting a foul odor, usually with a dark slimy layer that contains the spores		Go to section titled "Order Phallales: The Stinkhorns," PAGE 302
FLASK FUNGI Fruiting bodies may be of many different shapes but have in common a "pimply" surface with flasks imbedded that contain the spores	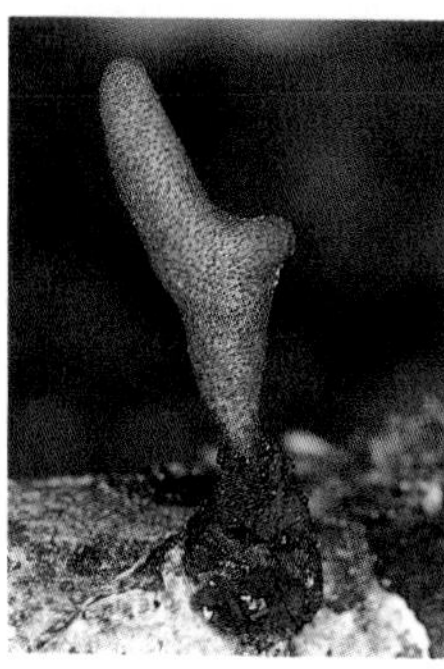	Go to section titled "Class Pyrenomycetes: The Flask Fungi," PAGE 314
CUP, BRAIN, AND SPONGE FUNGI Fruiting body resembling a cup (with spores borne along the inside), a brain (with spores produced along the folds), or a sponge (with spores produced inside the "pits"); some on wood, others on ground		Go to section titled "Class Discomycetes: The Cup, Brain, and Sponge Fungi," PAGE 322

TABLE 3. Major Genera in the Families of Mushrooms with White or Light-Colored Spore Print (Mostly Growing on the Ground)

Family	Amanitaceae (See page 59)	Lepiotaceae (See page 87)
Genus	*Amanita*	*Lepiota, Macrolepiota, Leucocoprinus, Chlorophyllum*
Spore print	White	Generally white; green in *Chlorophyllum*
Cap	Warts (usually white) often remain	Scales (often colored) usually present
Gills	Do not touch the stem (free)	Do not touch the stem (free)
Stalk	Tall and slender, broader at base	Tall and slender, often scaly
Ring	Present (distinct or along stem or cap edge)	Present: frequently moveable in age
Base, habit, habitat	Enlarged, and some have a cup at the base; usually single to several on ground	No cup at the base; single to several, some in fairy rings on ground or mulch
Comments	A very common genus: deadly members are common in wooded areas; membranous veil encases immature "button"; later becomes warts and cup	The "scales" on cap and stem do not wash or wipe off
Edibility	Includes deadly species; this genus is the most common cause of fatal poisonings in the U.S.	Includes edible and toxic species

TABLE 3

Hygrophoraceae (See page 97)	Russulaceae (See page 102)	
Hygrophorus	*Russula*	*Lactarius*
White	White, pale cream, or yellow	White
Brightly colored, often conical when young	Smooth, often colored	Many show concentric color zones
Thick and waxy when rubbed between finger and thumb	Usually attached, close or distant	Fresh specimens exude latex (milk) when cut
Frequently translucent; sometimes long	Short, often white and hollow, usually brittle	Short and usually white
Usually absent	None	None
No cup at the base; stem terminates in the ground; often in clusters on the ground	No cup at the base; often scattered on the ground or in grass	No cup at the base; usually single or in small groups under trees or in floodplains
A very colorful group; bright reds, greens, yellows, and oranges abound	One of the most common genera; texture brittle, like a stick of chalk or celery	A common genus; texture also brittle, like chalk
Some species edible; others not	Avoid those that are bitter and those that stain brown or red	Many good edibles—avoid those with latex that is bitter or stains yellow or lilac

TABLE 4. Common Genera of Tricholomataceae: Mushrooms with White or Pale Spore Prints (Species That Form Shelves, Growing on Wood)

Family	Tricholomataceae (See page 131)	
Genus	*Pleurotus*	*Panus*
Spore print	White to yellow, pale lilac	White or pale yellow
Cap	Smooth, white, gray or tan, often several inches across	Small to medium caps, often with many fine "hairs" on the cap; shelving species often have reddish color
Gills	Large and widely spaced; attached directly to the stalk or growing directly off wood	Gills are white and closely spaced
Stalk	Off-center, very short, or lacking altogether	Tough and fibrous if present; often lacking
Ring	None	None
Base, habit, habitat	Always growing on wood, often emerging from stumps and downed logs; often found in great shelving clusters	Found on decaying wood; often found in long, shelving rows
Comments	Look up for this fungus; it is often found on trunks of living trees as well as dead wood	Entire fruiting body may be covered with fine hairs; some species do not form "shelves" and are listed with the larger Tricholomas
Edibility	Edible and choice; a good group for beginners	Too tough to eat

TABLE 4

Tricholomataceae (See page 131)	
Anthracophyllum	*Phyllotopsis*
White	Pinkish, fading to white
Small, smooth, shelving caps, usually light brown	Medium to large, densely hairy, bright orange-yellow fan-shaped caps fading to dull yellow
Bright red, and ridgelike	Bright orange-yellow or yellow, distinct gills
Very short or lacking	Very short or lacking
None	None
Growing in clusters of many caps forming shelves	Growing, often in large shelving clusters, on wood
The bright red, widely spaced gills under a tan cap and lack of a stalk make this genus unmistakable	These fuzzy bright orange shelving mushrooms are easy to spot and have a distinct, foul odor to them
Not known, not recommended	Not edible

TABLE 5. Common Genera of Tricholomataceae: Mushrooms with White or Pale Spore Prints (Larger Species, Mostly Growing on Wood, Some on Ground)

Family	Tricholomataceae (See page 137)		
Genus	*Armillaria*	*Clitocybe, Omphalotus*	*Tricholoma*
Spore print	White	White, pink, or pale yellow	Usually white, but can be pale pink, lilac, buff, or yellow
Cap	May be smooth or covered with tiny hairs	Texture like kid leather; edges inrolled when young; center depressed at maturity	White or colored, smooth
Gills	Attached directly to stem	Extending down the stalk; white, or orange in *Omphalotus*	White, nonwaxy, notched at stalk
Stalk	Covered with fine scales	Thick, smooth, even diameter	Fibrous
Ring	Some with; some without	No ring	No ring
Base, habit, habitat	A tree-killing genus on dead or injured wood; in clusters	On the ground; or on wood (often buried); appearing singly, several, or in clusters	Generally on ground; many are mycorrhizal; usually single or scattered
Comments	At times prolific on wood	*Omphalotus* (the "jack-o'-lantern") glows in the dark and is toxic	Common cold-weather genus
Edibility	Edible, but cook long and thoroughly	A large and complex group; *Clitocybe nuda* is best edible	This group contains many fine edibles; a large and complex group

TABLE 5

Tricholomataceae (See page 137)

Hohenbuehelia	*Panus, Lentinus*	*Oudemansiella*
White	White or pale yellow	White
Shell or fan shaped; often rubbery in texture, smooth to scaly, caps white to brown	*Panus* has many fine hairs on cap, giving "fuzzy" texture; *Lentinus* is generally smooth	Rounded, with edges turned under in youth, flat, with a rise in the center at maturity
White to grayish and attached to the stalk	Extending down the stalk	Notched or directly attached, white, broad, widely spaced
Short, stocky, usually at the side	Short, thick and tough, sometimes off-center	Very long, slender and brittle
No ring	*Lentinus* may have a ring in youth; no ring in most species	No ring
Even diameter, found on the ground or on decaying wood	Growing on wood; often several to many, sometimes in clusters from a common base	With a long, rooting base often 4 inches or more into the soil
Often seen on mulch in wet weather	Entire fruiting body may be covered with fine hairs	Very common in East Texas woods in fall and winter
Edible when young and fresh; texture can be rubbery in age	Not generally considered edible	Edible

TABLE 6. Common Genera of Tricholomataceae: Mushrooms with White or Pale Spore Prints (Smaller Species, Mostly Growing on Wood, Some on Ground)

Family	Tricholomataceae (See page 149)		
Genus	*Laccaria*	*Marasmiellus*	*Collybia*
Spore print	White to pale pink	White	White to cream
Cap	Average 1 inch in diameter; depressed in center; cap margin turns under	Depressed cap, noticeable radial striations; often translucent	Smooth, rounded in youth, with edges rolled under, opening to nearly flat
Gills	Widely spaced, thick, pink, not waxy to the touch	Widely spaced, white; attached to or running down the stem	Attached, notched, or nearly free
Stalk	Tough and quite long; frequently bent near ground level	Tough, wiry, cartilaginous	Narrow, usually tough or pliant, often covered with fine fibers
Ring	None	None	None
Base, habit, habitat	Usually single, on the ground; some species have cottony mycelium at the base	Growing on ground or wood; usually single or several on small twigs	Even, usually on soil, humus, or leaf litter
Comments	Very common; often in sandy soil	The first mushrooms to appear after rains are often in this group	Can be difficult to identify for the inexperienced
Edibility	Generally edible, though small	Some are edible, but most are too small to bother with	Not recommended, especially for beginners

TABLE 6

Tricholomataceae (See page 149)

Strobilurus	*Xeromphalina*	*Mycena*
White	White	White
Smooth, very small, rounded, cream color	Small and smooth; flat, with inrolled edges; cap color commonly yellow or brown	Very thin fleshed; caps conical and parasol-like when young
Attached, and well spaced	Running a short distance down the stem	Closely spaced, very fragile
Often covered with downy fibers above the base	Tough, usually dark, short; pad at base often yellow-brown	Thin and easily broken; may be long
None	None	None
Rooting, and found on woody cones of conifers and magnolia	Growing directly on downed conifers; usually many fruiting bodies present on a stump or downed log	Several may emerge from the same base; usually single or several, often on leaves or small twigs
The most common species in Texas is found on magnolia cones	A common "trooping" mushroom; found in great numbers	"Fragile" and "tiny" describe this group; very common on leaves and sticks after rains
Not recommended; too tiny for appeal	Bitter; of no value as edibles	Of no value as edibles

TABLE 7. Genera of Mushrooms with Pink Spore Prints

Family	Pluteaceae (See page 158)	
Genus	*Pluteus*	*Volvariella*
Spore print	Pink to pale tan	Salmon to pink
Cap	Smooth, white to pale tan	Pale tan with minute radial hairs; "fringe" may appear along rim
Gills	Not attached to the stalk (free); become pink as spores ripen	Not attached to the stalk (free); color is pink when young, deepens to light brown
Stalk	Smooth, white, slender with even diameter	Smooth, white, slender with even diameter
Ring	None	None
Base, habit, habitat	Always growing on wood, often emerging from stumps; often several growing from one point of attachment	A large and obvious cup present at the base generally is fibrous and dark; usually single or several
Comments	Usually single, or a few growing together; slight "radishlike" odor; found year round	On wood, chips, or logs; usually single (though several may be on a single log); occasionally on corn cobs and other plant remains
Edibility	Edible, though not especially delicious	Edible and choice; closely related "straw mushroom" is used in oriental cooking

TABLE 7

Entolomataceae (See page 161)	Tricholomataceae (See page 141)
Entoloma	*Clitocybe*
Deep pink to salmon pink	Pale pink to buff
Rounded to pointed; one species may not expand or open in its "aborted" form	Tan with wavy margins when mature; edges may be inrolled when young
Attachment varies; color usually pink to light brown	Attachment is difficult to determine because they break away from the stem as the mushroom matures
Often twisted, sturdy, tough	Smooth; *Clitocybe nuda* is lavender and widens toward the base
None	None
Always on ground; usually several to many in small groups	On wood chips, mulch during cool seasons; short, squatty stature; usually single, though a number may be found in a small area
Often many specimens in one location, although specimens are single	Scattered on ground
Generally inedible or poisonous—caution!	Contains some edible species—*Clitocybe nuda* is the best edible

TABLE 8. Common Genera of Mushrooms with Yellow-Brown to Rusty Brown Spore Prints

Family	Bolbitiaceae (See page 166)	Cortinariaceae (See page 169)
Genus	*Conocybe*	*Galerina*
Spore print	Reddish to cinnamon brown	Rusty brown
Cap	White, tan or brown, usually conical (cone shaped)	Smooth and slightly slimy when moist; odor mild
Gills	Pale tan in youth, darkening as the spores mature	Attached in youth; yellowish to brown in age
Stalk	Equal diameter, slim, fragile, drab	Thin, slightly enlarged at base, dry, hollow
Ring	A ring is usually absent, but may be present in some species	A ring is usually present in species on wood; it may be gone at maturity in species on moss
Base, habit, habitat	Slightly enlarged in some species; usually scattered on lawns	Occur singly or in clusters on wood and moss
Comments	On grass, in lawns, in dung, and along roadsides	This genus contains deadly toxins!
Edibility	Caution: species are difficult to distinguish; some are toxic	Deadly poisonous! Be certain of your identification

TABLE 8

Cortinariaceae (See page 169)	
Gymnopilus	*Cortinarius*
Yellow-brown	Rusty brown
Orange-yellow; frequently very meaty	Usually colored: violet, brown yellow, red; may be dry or viscid
Yellow-brown	Rusty brown; covered with a fine, cobweblike veil when young
Usually yellow to brown; thick	Usually thick, same color as cap
No ring	A "color zone" may be present due to the cobweblike veil that catches the rusty spores
Most species grow on dead wood, often buried; a cluster of mushrooms may arise from a common base	Often swollen; some species are equal; usually occur singly or several on ground
Frequent in floodplains in late fall; many species are difficult to distinguish	A very common fall and winter genus
Inedible to toxic; one species is hallucinogenic	Caution: all contain toxins except *C. violaceous*

TABLE 9. Common Genera of Mushrooms with Dark Brown to Purple-Brown Spore Prints

Family	Strophariaceae (See page 179)	
Genus	*Psilocybe*	*Stropharia*
Spore print	Purple-brown in most species	Purple to purple-brown
Cap	Broad, bell shaped, notably peaked when young, often with golden "sunburst" centers	Rounded in youth; smooth, often cream, brown, or reddish
Gills	Close, deepening from gray to purple as spores mature	Notched or directly attached to the stalk, pale at first, darkening to the color of the spores
Stalk	Even, staining blue to purple when bruised	Even, thick or thin, and fairly brittle
Ring	Membranous, often colored purple by spores	Membranous veil present
Base, habit, habitat	Base is generally not enlarged; common on cattle manure, mulch, and rich soil	Even base; often found on soil, dung, decaying wood or sawdust, in forests and meadows
Comments	The purple-brown spores, growth on dung, and blue-staining reactions are the best identification characteristics	This is a common genus on dung of livestock
Edibility	Not recommended; hallucinogenic and toxic, occasionally causes severe reactions	Not recommended: some species are hallucinogenic and toxic

TABLE 9

Strophariaceae (See page 179)	Agaricaceae (See page 184)
Naematoloma	*Agaricus*
Purple-brown	Chocolate brown in most species
Color varies from red to brown to yellow	Rounded, light brown; some are smooth, others covered with fine hairs
Close, often notched at stem, darkening in age	Close, changing from pink to chocolate brown as spores mature
Often has an area of small fibers near base, a remnant of the veil	Short, even
Young species show a veil, but no ring forms	Membranous veil, often nearly unbroken in young specimens
Stalk may be fairly long and curved at base; common cool-weather mushroom, often growing on exposed roots	Base is often somewhat enlarged; common in lawns and grassy areas
Large groups of this mushroom are common in fall and winter	Beware of yellow-staining species and those with a chemical or creosote odor
Generally inedible to toxic	A variable genus, containing both choice edibles and toxic species

TABLE 10. Common Genera of Mushrooms with Black or Very Dark Brown Spore Prints

Family	Coprinaceae (See page 188)	
Genus	*Panaeolus*	*Coprinus*
Spore print	Black	Black
Cap	Bell shaped to conical, smooth, dry	Frequently bullet shaped when young
Gills	Gray to brown, sides often mottled	Deliquescing (dissolving) in age
Stalk	Thin and brittle, white to gray, hollow, fibrous	White, fibrous, hollow
Ring	Disappearing at maturity if present	Most species have none; some species have fibrous rings near the base in youth
Base, habit, habitat	Equal or enlarged; several to many, common on mulch, humus, and rich soil	On wood, humus, dung, or rich soil; several species have a fibrous mat at the base
Comments	The mushrooms often dry out and remain for a time, with their caps developing deep "bricklike" cracks	Many species have gills that deliquesce (dissolve) in age
Edibility	Generally toxic or not edible due to small size or insipid flavor	Some species are edible, but exercise caution: one species is toxic when combined with alcohol

For Boletes (Table 11) see pages 202–203

3. Mushroom Toxins

ROBERT HARVEY, M.D.

Eating wild mushrooms can be a treat; however, the mycophagist ("mushroom eater"—from *myco-*, mushroom, and *-phage,* eat) must know exactly what is being eaten, as there can be adverse reactions to eating wild mushrooms. These adverse reactions include mild to serious respiratory symptoms, such as a runny nose with itchy, watery eyes; mild to severe attacks of asthma; nausea and vomiting (which can be quite severe); and irreversible damage to such vital organs as the liver and kidneys, which can result in death. It is therefore of the utmost importance that the mycophagist know which mushrooms cause the various intoxications and avoid eating any mushrooms that could possibly contain any of these toxins. There is no room for experimenting. A common quote heard in mycological circles is, "There are old mycophagists and there are bold mycophagists, but there are no old, bold mycophagists."

Discrete mushroom intoxication presents in one of seven patterns. Should one be unfortunate enough to eat two mushrooms with different toxins, there can be overlap syndromes with symptoms of each toxin ingested. The general breakdown of fatal versus nonfatal reactions involves the time duration between ingestion of the toxin and when symptoms of illness first occur. The earlier the symptoms occur after ingestion the less the chance of fatal outcome. Symptoms occurring more than four to six hours after ingestion are associated with severe poisoning and possibly death. Ingestion of large amounts of deadly toxins may result in the earlier appearance of initial symptoms.

Types of Intoxication

1. Cyclopeptide or amanitin poisons cause death in 25 percent of patients who ingest them. Symptoms occur six to eight hours or more after ingestion and include nausea, abdominal pain, vomiting, bloody diarrhea, convulsions, coma, and death. Initial symptoms frequently subside for a number of hours, but on occasion remissions for up to four days have been reported. These toxins are contained in *Amanita* species (*A. phalloides, A. verna, A. virosa, A. bisporigera, A. ocreata*), *Galerina* (*G. autumnalis, G. marginata, G. venenata*), and some *Conocybe* and *Lepiota* species. There is no certain

antidote. The toxin attacks and irreversibly damages the liver and kidneys. Liver transplantation has been performed successfully in a limited number of cases.

2. Monomethyl hydrazine poisoning occurs after eating toxic *Gyromitra* species. Death occurs in 15–40 percent of cases. Symptoms occur six to twenty-four hours after ingestion and consist of nausea, vomiting, abdominal pain, diarrhea, muscle cramps, loss of coordination, convulsions, and coma. There is no certain antidote.

3. Muscarine poisoning occurs thirty minutes to two hours after ingestion of *Clitocybe dealbata, C. cerussata, C. illudens,* and certain *Inocybe* species. Symptoms include sweating, salivation, lacrimation, blurred vision, abdominal cramps, watery diarrhea, hypotension, and bradycardia. A physician may use atropine to treat this intoxication.

4. Ibotenic acid and muscimol poisoning occurs thirty minutes to two hours after ingestion of certain *Amanita* species (*A. pantherina, A. muscaria*) and symptoms include dizziness, incoordination, ataxia, muscular jerking, hyperkinetic activity, stupor, and hallucinations. High fever and even death can occur with children. A physician may use physostigmine to treat this intoxication.

5. Psilocybin and psilocin intoxication occurs thirty minutes to one hour after ingestion of toxic *Psilocybe* and *Gymnopilus* species. Chief manifestations are hallucinations and alterations in mood and sleep. Fatalities are rare.

6. Coprine poisoning is similar to the desired effect of a drug called antabuse, which is used to treat alcoholism. The drug and coprine interfere with the normal metabolism of alcohol and result in flushing, paresthesias (burning or pricking sensations), metallic taste, tachycardia (rapid heart beat), hypotension (abnormally low blood pressure), nausea, vomiting, and sweating. This intoxication is avoided by not drinking alcohol after ingesting *Coprinus atramentarius* and *Clitocybe cavipes.* Coprine stays in the body for several days after ingestion

of these species, and ingestion of alcohol during this time could result in the syndrome of intoxication. A physician may use intravenous glucose or propranalol to treat this type of intoxication.

7. Nonspecific self-limited gastrointestinal upset occurs thirty minutes to two hours after ingestion of many different genera and species. It is usually treated with charcoal absorption, hydration, and mineral replacement and resolves in hours to days.

The information requested in the North American Mycological Association Poisoning Form provides valuable assistance to the physician managing a case of mushroom intoxication. It is recommended that this form be filled out and presented to the attending physician should a mushroom intoxication occur.

A Parable of Poisoning

One Thanksgiving weekend, two members of the Texas Mycological Society and another married couple went to Bastrop State Park for a camping weekend. The weather had been dry, and they didn't find many mushrooms, but one afternoon, while hiking, they came across a clump of golden yellow mushrooms. "Oh, look," cried one of the women, "here are some chanterelles! Let's pick them for dinner!"

The couple was certain these were chanterelles, so they didn't take a spore print, or consult the field guides they had brought along, or even compare their specimen to the photos in the book. They cooked and ate the mushrooms and found them to be quite tasty.

About an hour after dinner, without warning, the husband had a sudden, violent vomiting attack, and shortly after that the other man had the same experience. A flash of insight hit the woman who had found the "chanterelles" and *now* she consulted her mushroom book; reading the comments under the chanterelle description, she found a warning that *Omphalotus olearius* (the "jack-o'-lantern") is a poisonous mushroom that looks similar. As she was looking at the picture of the offender, the other woman became violently ill, too, so they all got in the car and drove to the nearest emergency room, thirteen miles away at Smithville. We shall spare the gentle reader the details of that ride, in which the driver also became suddenly and violently nauseous.

The victims called the TMS president, who confirmed that jack-o'-lanterns were the most likely culprit and reassured them that the mushroom the couples ate was a "sickener," not a killer. Within six hours of the memorable meal, the vomiting ceased, and all the victims were fine the next morning. They went hiking again and found more of the same mushrooms. Later that day, they made another trip to the emergency room—this time, to show the doctor what they had eaten and to share a laugh about their foolish experience.

MORAL: Mushroom books don't prevent poisonings. Only people can do that. Neither this book nor any other will help you if you don't use it!

References

Bivins, H. G., R. Knopp, R. Lammers, D. B. McMicken, O. Wolowodiuk. "Case Conference: Mushroom Ingestion." *Ann. Emerg. Med.* 14 (November 1985): 1099–1103.

Bresinsky, Andreas, and Dr. Helmut Besl. *A Colour Atlas of Poisonous Fungi.* Boca Raton, Fla.: CRC Press, 1989.

Cochran, Kenneth W. "Mushroom Poisoning Case Registry, North American Mycological Association, 1987–1988 Progress Report, Cases Reported 1 July 1987 to 30 June 1988." Annual Report of the Toxicology Committee to the North American Mycological Association Board of Trustees, August 1988.

Mack, R. B. "Toxic Encounters: Un Fleur du Mal. Gyromitrin Poisoning." *NCMJ* 47, no. 11 (November 1986): 535–536.

Rold, J. F. "Mushroom Poisoning: A Few Words of Caution for Those Adventurous Mycophagists." *Indiana Medicine* (March 1986): 246–248.

Rumack, B. H., and E. Salzman. *Mushroom Poisoning Diagnosis and Treatment.* West Palm Beach, Fla.: CRC Press, 1978.

FIGURE 3. NAMA Poison Form

North American Mycological Association Mushroom Poisoning Report Form

This is only a reporting form. For emergency treatment, contact your physician or the nearest poison center or hospital emergency room.

Please answer all the questions on this form by checking the appropriate box or by writing in the information requested, using a separate form for each person. Please check the "don't know" box if you do not know the answer.

I. Name of person filling out this form: ______________________

Address: ______________________

____

Telephone: ( ) ______________________

This form is about:

myself ☐ patient ☐ student ☐ club member ☐ other ☐

II. About the incident: Don't Know

A. Was mushroom eaten **Raw** ☐ or **Cooked** ☐ ☐

B. How much mushroom was eaten? ______________________ ☐

C. Was mushroom eaten: by a child ☐, accidentally ☐,

for food ☐, intentionally for recreation ☐

III.

A. What were symptoms of poisoning? Check all symptoms which occurred:

☐ Nausea	☐ Salivation	☐ Intestinal Cramps	☐ Flushing
☐ Vomiting	☐ Chills	☐ Muscle Spasm	☐ Drowsiness
☐ Diarrhea	☐ Rash	☐ Hallucination	☐ Dizziness
☐ Sweating	☐ Weakness	☐ Disorientation	

Don't Know

Were there other symptoms? Yes ☐ No ☐ ☐

What were the other symptoms? ______________________

____

Please duplicate if additional copies are needed, or request forms from Mr. Trestrail at the address on the other side or by telephone to (616) 774-7851 or (313) 971-2552.

B. Did person ever eat this mushroom before? Yes ☐ No ☐ ☐

C. Were the effects the same? Same ☐ Different ☐ ☐

D. Was treatment given? Yes ☐ No ☐ ☐

What was the treatment?

____ ☐

What were the results of treatment?

____ ☐

Case or chart number (if available) ________________ (Important for follow-up)

Patient's age ________________ Patient's sex ________________

Patient's name (optional) ________________________________

IV. About the mushroom:

A. Name the species: ________________________________ ☐

B. Who identified the species? ________________________ ☐

Herbarium specimen number (if available) ______________ ☐

C. Were any special mushroom tests done? Yes ☐ No ☐ ☐

List the tests and results: ____________________________

____

V. Other comments about the case or the mushroom, or attach a separate note:

____

____

____

____

____

____

Please send completed form to:

John H. Trestrail, III, R.Ph.
Blodgett Regional Poison Center
1840 Wealth, S.E.
Grand Rapids, MI 49506-2968

4. Cooking and Eating Wild Mushrooms

The main reason many people are interested in wild mushrooms is because they want to eat them. We encourage you to taste the mushrooms you find, but we simply must stress the danger in doing so indiscriminately or incautiously. Throughout this book we have included in the Comments section of each species' description any cautions you should exercise and have noted those mushrooms that are safest for an amateur to try—that is, those that you are most unlikely to confuse with toxic or poisonous species.

Our ten favorite abundant edible wild mushrooms are the following:

1. Boletes: *Boletus affinis, B. pseudoseparans,* or *B. pinophilus*
2. *Lentinus lepideus* or *L. tigrinus*
3. *Morchella esculenta*
4. *Macrolepiota procera*
5. *Agaricus campestris*
6. *Pleurotus ostreatus*
7. *Auricularia auricula*
8. *Lactarius volemus* (or *L. corrugis*)
9. *Hericium* spp.
10. *Cantharellus cibarius*

These, or other edible mushrooms that you find in the wild, or cultivated mushrooms, can be used in the recipes in this chapter (after confirming your identification). In some cases, we have made recommendations for the type of mushroom to be used, but we encourage you to experiment with substituting one edible mushroom species for another, thereby changing the flavor and texture of the finished dish to produce a variety of combinations.

A Word of Caution

Other authors of mushroom field guides have offered the following guidelines for eating a "new" species, and we repeat those cautions here.

1. Always select only young, firm specimens for the table. Those that are old or "mushy" may harbor bacteria.

2. Always cook your mushrooms thoroughly. Many raw mushrooms contain chemicals that are toxic; cooking often volatilizes these chemicals and minimizes

the danger of illness. This is true of *Armillaria tabescens.* But, no amount of cooking will destroy the toxins in the deadly Amanitas! So, again, read the descriptions of the mushrooms thoroughly, and be certain of your identification. One good rule to follow is the old adage, "When in doubt, throw it out!"

3. When eating mushrooms for the first time, don't mix different species or collections. This is to minimize the dangers of "unknowns" getting in.

4. Don't overindulge! And go easy on rich substances like butter or sour cream. Rich food, and too much of it, can easily give a person a stomach upset. It's not fair to blame the mushrooms when ordinary gluttony is the culprit.

5. Save a piece for the poison center. This is an excellent rule and can help the attending physician at the emergency room to determine what you have ingested and what treatment is necessary. If you go to the emergency room, take the sample with you. If your mushroom turns out to be delicious and doesn't cause any problem, place the sample under a big oak or pine tree near your house. With luck, you'll find mushrooms there in the future.

6. Cook and eat your mushrooms as soon as you can. If you can't cook them the same day you pick them, dry or otherwise preserve them. If you don't cook and eat them within a few days, it's best to throw them out.

Picking Mushrooms for the Table

If you find good edible mushrooms while hunting, we recommend the following: Select several specimens of different ages and remove them completely from the soil or wood. Place them in a bag or piece of waxed paper, start a spore print, and plan to examine them and confirm your identification using a field guide such as this book before cooking and eating any. With the other specimens you find, "field trim" them (cut off the dirty spots and base with a sharp knife) and place the clean mushrooms in a separate bag. This will minimize getting dirt on clean parts and will make mushroom cleaning easy. Refrigerate the mushrooms if possible so that they arrive in your kitchen in their firmest, nicest condition.

Cleaning Mushrooms

We recommend washing wild mushrooms as little as possible to avoid making them soggy. (Wild mushrooms contain 70–90 percent water, so additional water can change their texture for the worse.) In many cases, simply brushing the dirt off the mushrooms (our favorite tool looks like an oversized toothbrush) or cutting it off with a sharp knife is all that is needed. If they are very dirty, as with mushrooms found growing in sand, rinse quickly under running water and place in a colander to drain. Always cut off any old, chewed, or bug-eaten spots. With boletes, you may (or may not) want to discard the slime layers and pores (young specimens with soft pores can be delicious; older ones are tough and woody). We also recommend discarding any parts of the mushroom that don't cut easily with a good knife as too tough to eat. If you have a lot of mushrooms, avoid bruising by spreading them out in one layer rather than piling them on top of each other.

VM

Recipes

BASIC MUSHROOM-TASTING RECIPE

Clean and slice (no thicker than 3/8 inch) the mushrooms you have. Melt enough unsalted butter or margarine to cover the bottom of a pan big enough to sauté the mushrooms in a layer no deeper than 1/2 inch.

Cultivated mushrooms and some wild ones frequently have so little water in them that the butter may brown. In that case, clarified butter or a mixture of ½ butter and ½ peanut oil may be used. There should be so little butter that you can turn the pan upside down without spilling it. Place the mushrooms in the pan and sauté, stirring frequently, until the mushrooms are well wilted. Cover the pan and steam the mushrooms for several minutes. Then, remove the cover and continue to cook until any liquid emitted from the mushrooms has boiled away. Serve the mushrooms plain or on bread or plain crackers for tasting. You can add salt and pepper if desired, but many "purists" want to taste only the mushroom to be able to compare it to others.

This Basic Mushroom-Tasting Recipe can also be used as a start for many dishes. You can add any combination of the following: sour cream, heavy cream or evaporated milk, wine, lemon juice, onions, garlic, thyme, parsley, or other spices to make a sauce to be served over chicken breasts, rice, or pasta.

VM

Pickled Mushrooms from Texas

(Hotter Than from Anywhere Else!)

INGREDIENTS

2 cups fresh *Agaricus* (wild or cultivated), *Pleurotus*, or other fresh firm mushrooms
1 cup vinegar
3 garlic cloves, crushed
2 fresh jalapeño peppers, split in half lengthwise*
2 tablespoons olive oil
1 teaspoon crushed red pepper
2 tablespoons sugar
Tabasco sauce (to taste)
salt (to taste)

PREPARATION

Clean the mushrooms and trim the stems as needed. Quarter the mushrooms if they are more than 1 inch in diameter. If small, leave them whole. Bring the vinegar to a boil, stir in the other ingredients, and add the mushrooms. Boil for 15–20 minutes, then pour into jars, filling the jars to the top with the marinade, and seal. These will keep several weeks in the refrigerator and should be prepared at least a week before serving.

*Prepared according to these directions, these pickled mushrooms will be mild, with only a little "afterburn." True hot-food lovers recommend the addition of an 8-ounce can of pickled jalapeños to the marinade.

Traditional Pickled Mushrooms

INGREDIENTS

- 3 cups vinegar
- ¼ cup oil
- 6 tablespoons sugar (or more, to taste)
- 2 tablespoons pickling spice
- 1 teaspoon mustard seed
- 1 teaspoon ground coriander
- ½ teaspoon ground cloves
- 3 quarts fresh *Agaricus,* or other firm mushrooms, cleaned and quartered or halved if they are large

PREPARATION

Combine all the ingredients except the mushrooms in a large pot and bring it to a boil. Add the cleaned mushrooms and boil for 20 minutes. These may be canned by pouring into sterilized jars, which are then carefully sealed, or they will keep for several weeks if they are simply refrigerated.

Hope Miller's Hot Mushroom Dip

INGREDIENTS

- 2 pounds fresh mushrooms (*Lentinus lepideus, L. tigrinus, Boletus* spp., *Hericium* spp., *Armillaria tabescens, Lactarius* spp., or other firm edible species)
- 6 tablespoons butter
- 1 tablespoon lemon juice
- 4 tablespoons chopped parsley
- 2 tablespoons minced onions
- ¾ to 1 cup sour cream
- 2 teaspoons bouillon granules (or 2 bouillon cubes)
- 1 tablespoon flour
- 1 tablespoon soft butter

PREPARATION

Chop the mushrooms quite fine. Place in pan with butter, add lemon juice, and simmer 10 minutes. Add the onions and sour cream. Season with salt and pepper to taste and add bouillon granules or cubes. Simmer 10 minutes more. Make a paste of flour and butter. Add to mixture and stir until thickened. Serve hot.

ALTERNATE METHOD

Replace the 1 tablespoon flour with ½ cup fine bread crumbs and thicken. Take 1 can of crescent rolls and pat down in a 9-inch square baking pan to make a crust. Spread the thickened mixture evenly over the crust and with a second can of crescent rolls make a top crust. Bake at 350° for 20–25 minutes until golden brown. Cut into squares and serve.

Printed by permission of Orson K. Miller, from *Mushrooms of North America* (New York: E. P. Dutton, 1981).

Quiche in a Mushroom

INGREDIENTS

2 to 3 dozen *Agaricus* (preferably the larger, brown-capped, cultivated ones)
1 cup shredded Jarlsberg cheese
2 eggs
1 cup evaporated milk or cream
2 tablespoons flour
white or black pepper to taste
paprika

PREPARATION

Select large button mushrooms, clean them, and remove the stems. Turn them cap-side up and microwave on high 2½ to 3 minutes, until the juice comes out. Drain the mushrooms cap-side up and let them cool enough to handle. Place the mushrooms cap-side down in a large baking dish and fill each cap with shredded cheese.

Mix the eggs, milk, flour, and pepper in a large measuring cup and carefully pour a small amount into each mushroom cap, trying not to let the liquid overflow (a little overflow won't hurt). Sprinkle paprika over the caps and bake at 350° for 25 minutes until the cheese is melted and the custard is firm.

Cool enough to handle, and serve! Allow at least three per person—they're delicious!

Mushroom Whole Wheat Bread

(Makes 2 loaves)

STEP ONE: PREPARE THE SPONGE

1 cup warm (98°) warm water
2 packages (2 tablespoons) active dry yeast
a few drops of honey or molasses
1 cup bromated white flour
1 cup whole wheat flour

Add the dry yeast and honey or molasses to the warm water. Mix them together with a fork or whisk and let stand 5–10 minutes until the water becomes cloudy and bubbles form on the surface. (Note: if bubbles do not form, the yeast is old or the water is too hot, and the bread will not rise.) When the mixture is frothy, stir in the 2 cups of flour. Cover with a towel and let rise until doubled in size (about an hour).

STEP TWO: PREPARE THE MUSHROOMS

½ cup melted butter
1 pound edible mushrooms, cleaned and coarsely chopped

Sauté the mushrooms in the butter and cook until any excess moisture that has exuded from the mushrooms is evaporated off. Let the cooked mushrooms cool down until they are at room temperature.

STEP THREE: PREPARE THE MIX

⅓ cup honey or molasses
1½ teaspoons salt

Combine these ingredients and add the cooled mushrooms. Add this to the risen sponge, and mix them together until the mushrooms are thoroughly distributed throughout the mix. *(continued)*

Add up to 4 cups whole wheat and white flour, ½ cup at a time, until the dough is thick enough to remove from the bowl. When all the flour has been added, turn the dough onto a floured surface or place in a heavy-duty mixer, and knead it until it has the texture of your earlobe (about 15 minutes by hand; 5 by machine).

STEP FOUR: RISING

When the dough is thoroughly but not excessively kneaded, roll it into a ball, grease a fresh bowl, and place the dough in the bowl. Cover with a towel and let rise until doubled again, approximately 1 hour. When the dough has risen, remove it from the bowl, punch it down, and knead it again for another 15 minutes. Shape it into two loaves and place each in a greased loaf pan. Cover again with a towel, and when the dough has risen over the top of the loaf pan, place in a preheated 375° oven and bake 35–45 minutes until the loaves are golden brown.

NOTE: Yeast rises at 98°. At temperatures more than 5° warmer than that, the yeast will die and the bread will not rise. At lower temperatures, it will rise more slowly, but will not be harmed.

The Easiest Wild Mushroom Pizza

On a day when you have found firm edible boletes, *Lentinus lepideus, Pleurotus,* or other mushrooms in good condition, but don't feel like doing much cooking, try this.

Step 1. Call your favorite pizza delivery service and order a pizza with all your favorite toppings (except mushrooms, of course).

Step 2. While waiting for the pizza, preheat your oven to 375° and clean, slice, and cook your mushrooms according to the Basic Mushroom-Tasting Recipe instructions.

Step 3. When the pizza arrives, spread your mushrooms on top and put the pizza in the oven for 5–7 minutes, just to remelt the cheese and let the mushroom flavor mingle with the pizza. Enjoy!

"Any Kind of (Edible) Mushroom" Soup

INGREDIENTS

- 1 pound firm fresh mushrooms of your choice, very thinly sliced (remove stems if tough), but if using dried mushrooms, rehydrate 2–3 ounces in warm water or white wine for ½ hour or more; then substitute hydration liquid for white wine, below
- 2 tablespoons unsalted butter
- 1 tablespoon olive oil
- 1 Texas sweet yellow onion, (preferably a 1015), finely chopped
- 1 clove garlic, finely chopped
- 1 scallion, finely chopped (optional)
- ¼ to ½ cup white wine
- 12 ounces (1 can) chicken broth (or homemade broth, if available)
- 1 tablespoon chopped fresh parsley (reserve about 1 teaspoon for garnish)
- ¼ teaspoon dried or 1 teaspoon fresh basil, chopped
- dash or more Tabasco, to taste
- 12 ounces (1 can) evaporated milk
- salt and pepper to taste

PREPARATION

Heat butter and olive oil in a large saucepan. Add onion, garlic, and scallion and simmer a few minutes until clear, stirring frequently. Add the mushrooms and white wine and cook for 10 minutes until the mushrooms lose their firmness and the alcohol and about half the liquid evaporates from the pan. Add the chicken broth, parsley, basil, Tabasco, and pepper and simmer, covered, for 10–15 minutes. Purée about half the contents of the pan in a food processor or blender and return to the pan. Reduce heat so that it is not boiling and add the evaporated milk. Heat slowly, but without boiling, until steaming and delicious. Adjust with salt to taste. Serve in mugs and garnish with reserved parsley.

Chanterelle Enchiladas

INGREDIENTS FOR THE SAUCE

- 2 cups chanterelles (or other fresh mushrooms), cleaned and sliced
- 1 tablespoon corn, peanut, or olive oil
- 1 tablespoon butter or margarine
- 1 sweet yellow onion, finely chopped
- 2 tablespoons each, chopped red and green bell pepper or mild jalapeño pepper
- 1 clove garlic, minced
- 4 ounces cream cheese, cut into ½-inch cubes
- 1 cup cooked chicken pieces (canned or fresh)
- 8 corn tortillas, heated until soft in microwave oven (about 30 seconds)
- ½ cup grated Monterey Jack or Jarlsberg cheese
- ⅓ cup heavy cream

PREPARATION

Sauté the onion and peppers in the oil and butter until clear. Add the chanterelles and garlic; continue to sauté until the liquid has boiled off and the chanterelles are fairly crisp. Add the cream cheese and chicken. Stir until mixed thoroughly.

Place about ⅓ cup of the chicken mixture in the center of a tortilla and roll up. Place seam-side down in a casserole. Continue until all the tortillas have been filled. Spread any remaining chicken mixture over the top of the enchiladas. Sprinkle ½ cup of Monterey Jack or Jarlsberg cheese over the enchiladas and pour ⅓ cup of heavy cream over the top. If desired, sprinkle a little paprika on top for color. Bake at 350° for 30 minutes until the cream is absorbed and the cheese melted. Serves 4.

Chanterelle* Quiche

CRUST

1 cup flour
3 tablespoons cold butter
3 tablespoons buttermilk (approximate)

PREPARATION

Cut the cold butter and flour together in a bowl using two forks or in a food processor fitted with the steel blade until the butter-flour mixture is about the size of small peas. Then add the buttermilk, a little at a time, just until the mixture forms a workable ball. (Do not overwork.) Roll out the dough into one layer and line the bottom of a deep 9-inch pie pan.

QUICHE FILLING

1½ cups grated Jarlsberg or other Swiss-type cheese
2 cups chopped chanterelles (or other mushrooms) cooked with ½ cup onion in 2 tablespoons butter according to the Basic Mushroom-Tasting Recipe
custard made from 3 whole eggs, 1 cup milk, 2 tablespoons flour, ¼ teaspoon dry mustard

PREPARATION

Spread the grated cheese on the pie dough and cover with the mushroom mixture. Pour the custard over the cheese and mushrooms and sprinkle with paprika. Bake at 375° for 40–45 minutes, until the center is solid. Let cool for 10 minutes; cut and serve. Serves 8 as a side dish; 4 for dinner.

*Chanterelles are best in this quiche, but it is almost as good when made with any fresh edible mushrooms.

Deep-Fried Mushrooms

INGREDIENTS

For the batter:

- 1 egg
- 1 cup flour
- ½ cup milk
- ½ cup carbonated water
- dash salt
- Tabasco or pepper, to taste

- 1 pound commercial "button" mushrooms, or 1 pound *Pleurotus*
- oil for frying, at 350°

PREPARATION

Stir the batter ingredients together; dip the mushrooms in the batter to coat. Drop into the hot oil. Fry until golden; remove from oil and drain on paper towels or grocery sacks. Serve hot.

The Mushrooms

SUBDIVISION BASIDIOMYCOTINA
Class Hymenomycetes
Order Agaricales

Family Amanitaceae: The Amanitas

Every mushroom hunter must learn to recognize an *Amanita* because this commonly encountered genus contains some of the deadliest of all wild mushrooms. It also offers some edible species, but we do not recommend eating any Amanitas in Texas—edible and inedible or poisonous species are easily confused, which makes it dangerous. Also, in our opinion, none of the edible Texas Amanitas are especially choice. Certainly, none is delicious enough to warrant the risk.

On the positive side, the Amanitas have several distinct characteristics that are easy to learn and to recognize. Members of this genus have a combination of the following features:

1. General appearance: The species have tall, thin stalks and a stately appearance. Some are rather robust, often cream color to white, with distinctive, sometimes obnoxious odors; others have cap colors ranging from brown to yellow to brilliant red and are nearly odor free.

2. Gills: The gills of *Amanita* species are described as "free"; that is, they do not touch the stalk. To check your mushroom for free gills try one of these methods: "pop" the stalk out of the cap and examine it for fine lines or pieces of the gills adhering to it; or, slice the mushroom from top of cap to base of stalk right down the center. Look at the bisection where the cap meets the stalk, and again, check to see if the gills touch the stalk. Older caps that have fully opened are best for observing the free gills.

3. Ring: A ring, or annulus, is a piece of tissue called the *partial veil,* which extends between the gills and stalk in the embryonic mushroom. When the mushroom expands, it frequently remains as a ring or it may look much like a skirt on the stalk. The veil may also remain as pieces of tissue hanging from the edge of the cap.

4. Universal veil (if present): The *universal veil* is the covering material that surrounds the mushroom during its developmental stage. Remains of the universal veil can often be seen as a cup or *volva* at the base of the mature mushroom. The universal veil can be either *membranous,* remaining as a cuplike sac at the base

of the mushroom, or *friable,* breaking into patches or warts that may remain on the cap or be deposited along the stalk or at the base or some combination of these areas. Check the soil as you remove the mushroom for these remnants, since their presence and color is often important in mushroom identification.

5. Spore print: The spores of *Amanita* species are white to cream color in deposit. You should *always* take a spore print! If the spores of your mushroom are white or creamy, check for the other characteristics listed here *before* you eat it. The advanced collector can use an iodine solution called *Melzer's reagent* to determine whether the spores are amyloid by placing some of the spore powder on a glass slide with white paper under it and adding a drop of reagent. A clear blue color indicates a positive (amyloid) reaction; this characteristic is used to confirm the species' identification. Melzer's reagent can often be obtained through your local mycological society.

6. Ecology: The *Amanitas* are mycorrhizal; that is, the fungus forms a mutually beneficial association with the roots of trees, especially oak, hickory, and pine trees in Texas. They grow on the ground, usually single or several, although occasionally, large troops occur that sometimes appear to be in fairy rings during very wet seasons.

As you examine the photos in this section, look for these characteristics. Other genera of mushrooms may also have some of these characteristics, but, if you see even one of them in a mushroom you find, be doubly certain of your identification before you eat it; that is, be sure it is what you think it is and also that it *cannot* be a poisonous species. And *never* eat a Texas *Amanita* unless you are positive of its identification!

"Virosa" means poisonous, an appropriate name for this mushroom, which is one of several species of deadly poisonous white Amanitas, collectively called "destroying angels." These species are distinguished by their microscopic and chemical characteristics. A smaller but otherwise quite similar and equally deadly species is *Amanita bisporigera.*

Description: This mushroom has a smooth pure white cap and a persistent skirtlike ring above the middle of the stalk. A distinct membranous sac around the base is sometimes partially buried and revealed only when you dig it up carefully. It has free, narrow, white gills, closely spaced, and a white spore color. The odor is pleasant.

Comments: Poisonous. This mushroom doesn't stain a silver spoon, or turn rice pink, or conform to *any* of the "folk tales" that are supposed to distinguish poisonous from edible mushrooms. Yet it kills nonetheless! As little as five grams, cooked or raw, will cause extensive liver, kidney, and spinal cord damage to a child or an adult, leading (usually) to a painful death, though symptoms will be delayed for about six to twelve hours after eating. (No wonder this is a choice method for mystery writers!) Don't eat it, taste it, or experiment with it!

Season: Late spring to late fall.

Habit, habitat, and distribution: Single or in small groups, in soil, associated with and usually found under oaks; not present in sage brush, prairie, or desert areas.

Cap diameter: 5–16 cm (2–6″).

Stalk height: 7–20 cm (3–8″).

Stalk diameter: 8–20 mm (⅓–¾″).

OM

JL

Amanita polypyramis

Not edible

Polypyramis means "many pyramids" and describes the pyramid-shaped "warts" on this mushroom's cap. It often attains a very robust appearance and can be the largest mushroom in the Texas woods.

Description: The best recognition features are the very large size and overall white color, a strong chlorine odor, the pyramid-shaped white warts on the cap, and the presence of a veil either at the stalk or hanging from the cap edge. Even a button from these huge white mushrooms can weigh over a pound. Mature caps can be too large to span with your hand, and the stalk may exceed 35 mm or 1½ inches in diameter with an even larger base. When you carefully dig up this mushroom, you will notice that it lacks a rooting base. Remnants of the universal veil form the warts on the cap and also warts at the base of the stalk. The spore color is white.

Comments: Not edible; but with its strong bleachlike odor, who would want to eat it?

Season: Late fall and winter.

Habit, habitat, and distribution: Usually solitary, on ground in mixed woods, mycorrhizal with pines.

Cap diameter: 7½–21 cm (3–8″).

Stalk height: 8–20 cm (3–8″).

Stalk diameter: 10–35 mm (½–1½″).

VM

This *Amanita* was named for W. C. Coker, a botanist at the University of North Carolina during the early to mid–1900s. Dr. Coker published many books on southern fungi, including the Amanitas, the boletes, coral fungi, and the class Gasteromycetes, among others. His works are among the standard references on these groups.

Description: A tall, stately, pure white mushroom; the most notable feature is the presence of large pyramid-shaped warts clinging to the cap, stalk, and base. The cap is rounded and dry. Pieces of the veil are often found clinging to the edge of the cap. The gills are white to cream colored and free from the stalk. The stalk is usually slightly tapered toward the top, with a hanging, membranous, double veil that usually is persistent. Thick, white scaly patches are present on the stalk and at the base, where they may be white to brownish and are usually arranged in nearly concentric rings. The base is somewhat enlarged and is usually rooting. The spore print color is white.

Comments: This mushroom may be quite large and is easily recognized due to the white warts and concentric rings of warts at the base. The stalk is much more slender than *Amanita polypyramis,* which has a greatly enlarged base that may be several inches in diameter. It is not recommended for the table.

Season: Late summer and fall.

Habit, habitat, and distribution: Usually single, widely scattered on the ground under pine and oak, often brought out by the first cool fall rains.

Cap diameter: 7–14.5 cm (2¾–5¾").

Stalk height: 11–19.5 cm (4½–8").

Stalk diameter: 10–21 mm (⅜–⅞").

CO

Amanita abrupta

Not edible

This mushroom is named for the "abrupt" (not tapering) swollen base and is a striking white *Amanita* found in mixed woods.

Description: A pure white mushroom; the cap is covered with conical white warts. The cap edge often has partial veil remnants attached to it, and there is a prominent ring present on the stalk. The universal veil remains as small warts on the cap or over the abrupt bulb. The most notable feature is the "abruptly enlarged" base of the stalk. The gills are free and white, and the spore print color is white.

Comments: Not edible. As with all Amanitas, carefully dig up and remove the entire base. One can then see that the species has no saclike cup and could not be in the *A. virosa* group. In the photo, we have cleared away leaves that covered the base.

Season: Late summer and fall.

Habit, habitat and distribution: On ground in mixed woods; usually infrequent and solitary, but widely distributed throughout eastern North America.

Cap diameter: 4–10 cm (1½–4").

Stalk height: 6.5–12.5 cm (2½–5").

Stalk diameter: 5–15 mm (¼–¾").

VM

Not edible

This large white *Amanita* was named for Dr. Harry Thiers, a Texas mycologist who spotted it on a Texas A&M campus lawn when he was a student.

Description: The stalk and cap look as though someone had sprayed the mushroom with Christmas-tree flocking. The flecks will also be found on the ground and grass around it and will stick to your hands when you touch it. It has a straight stalk with a slightly swollen base and a distinct partial veil. The gills become creamy yellow in age. A distinct chlorine odor is present. The spore print color is a creamy white.

Comments: Not edible. This mushroom can be common on lawns in summer given good rains. It is the largest white *Amanita* we find in the summer. The universal veil consists of small sticky fibers over the cap and base of the stalk, which is not deep rooted.

Season: Summer.

Habit, habitat, and distribution: Singly or in small groups on lawns in warm, wet weather.

Cap diameter: 3–10 cm (1¼–4″).

Stalk height: 8–25 cm (3–10″).

Stalk diameter: 10–25 mm (⅓–1″).

VM

Amanita rhopalopus

Not edible/Caution!

This white *Amanita* has an enlarged, rooting, clublike base, as the name *rhopalopus,* from *rhopal-,* club, and *-opus,* shape, indicates.

Description: This is a white *Amanita* that smells highly of chlorine and has thick white to brownish patches like warts on the base and cap. These sticky warts will adhere to anything that touches them. The best characteristic to distinguish this from other large-based, chlorine-smelling white Amanitas with warts on the cap is the distinctive rooting base. Dig this one up carefully and deeply to avoid breaking it off. The brownish warts are the remains of the universal veil occurring on the cap and over the lower part of the stalk. The spore print color is a creamy white.

Comments: Edibility not reported, and it is not recommended for eating. As with all white Amanitas, consider it toxic. It is distinguished from *A. polypyramis* by the deeply rooted base and brownish warts, and it is usually of a smaller size and stature.

Season: Summer to winter.

Habit, habitat, and distribution: Usually single, in mixed woods.

Cap diameter: 5–18 cm (2–7″).

Stalk height: 6–20 cm (2½–8″).

Stalk diameter: 8–25 mm (⅓–1″).

VM

Amanita atkinsoniana

Not recommended/Caution!

This mushroom was named for G. F. Atkinson, a mycologist who worked in the eastern and southern states during the late 1800s.

Description: The cap is white, large, and covered with reddish brown to gray-brown conical warts. The cap is thick and does not form *striations* (short lines) along the edge. The stalk has a distinct ring along with rows of reddish brown scales or warts. These scales and the ones on the cap are remnants of the universal veil. The base is large and bulbous and may be pointed. The gills are cream white and may be stained reddish. The spore print color is white.

Comments: Edibility not reported, and like other white Amanitas, it is not recommended for eating. This is a common mushroom throughout the forested areas of Texas and has a distinctive chlorine odor, like many of the large-based, white Amanitas.

Season: Summer and fall.

Habit, habitat, and distribution: Usually solitary or in small groups in mixed woods.

Cap diameter: 6–13 cm (2–5″).

Stalk height: 6–21 cm (2–8½″).

Stalk diameter: 8–28 mm (⅓–1″).

DG

Amanita albocreata

Not recommended

Albo- is the Latin root meaning "white," and it's no surprise that this is a pale white mushroom.

Description: Small to medium-sized, slender mushrooms; the white to pale yellow cap is thin and nearly flat in age, with wartlike patches randomly distributed over the cap and pale yellow center. The cap is slimy when wet, with fine lines at the edges, and the fine warts that are remnants of the universal veil may wash or wear off. The gills are crowded and free to notched and white. The stalk is slim, tapering slightly toward the top, with minute wartlike or scaly remnants of the universal veil present instead of a distinct ring. The basal bulb is abrupt (enlarging at the base). The spore color is white.

Comments: Edibility of this mushroom is not known. It may be related to the *Amanita pantherina* complex and is presumed toxic. Look closely for the wartlike or scaly warts along the stalk to be certain that this is an *Amanita.*

Season: Summer and fall.

Habit, habitat, and distribution: Usually single to several, growing on the ground, often in grassy areas, in open coniferous and hardwood forests.

Cap diameter: 2.5–8 cm (1–3").

Stalk height: 8–20 cm (3–8").

Stalk diameter: 8–20 mm (⅓–¾").

JL

Onusta translates to "burdened or loaded down," a reference to the many crowded dark gray warts on the grayish brown cap.

Description: The white caps are rounded when young, opening to nearly flat in age, and are covered with universal veil remnants in the form of dark gray to brownish gray conical warts. The gills are white to creamy yellow, crowded, and free from the stalk. The stalk is white at the top, a darker gray at the base, and equal in diameter, with a delicate veil that often falls away. Grayish warts or scales, a remnant of the universal veil, are present along the stalk. The base is slightly enlarged at the soil level and deeply rooting, often extending several inches into the soil. The spore print color is white, and there is a strong chlorine odor.

Comments: This mushroom is often found in deep sandy soil during fairly dry conditions. Carefully dig the base out of the sand—the length of the base may double the visible height of the mushroom. As with all the chlorine-smelling Amanitas, it is considered toxic.

Season: Summer and fall.

Habit, habitat, and distribution: Single to several, usually found in sandy soil under birch trees near creeks and streams. Known throughout East Texas and the Coastal Plain.

Cap diameter: 2.5–10 cm (1–4").

Stalk height: 3.5–15 cm (1½–6").

Stalk diameter: 6–15 mm (¼–½").

AB

Amanita ceciliae

Not recommended/Caution!

This delicate *Amanita* was named for Cecilia Berkeley, the wife of the Rev. M. J. Berkeley (1803–1889), an early southern mycologist. In many older field guides, it is called *A. inaurata.*

Description: The cap color is quite variable, ranging from nearly white or gray to a deep tan, and is covered with white to gray warts or patches. These patches are the remnants of the universal veil. Short lines are present along the edge of the cap. Dig this one up carefully, and you will find neither a cup nor a notably enlarged base. The characteristic veil is reduced to ragged fragments close to the base, and the stalk is otherwise smooth. The spore print color is white.

Comments: Not recommended for eating. This is another highly variable species, appearing in conifers and mixed woods all year. We find it under pecan trees. It has several forms, ranging from a very slim, delicate mushroom to a much stouter, robust one.

Season: Most frequent spring through fall.

Habit, habitat, and distribution: Single, several, or occasionally in large troops in coniferous woods or hardwoods.

Cap diameter: 5–12 cm (2–5″).

Stalk height: 7–18 cm (3–7″).

Stalk diameter: 7–17 mm (1/4–3/4″).

VM

Amanita fulva

Edible/Caution!

This common mushroom is named for its color: *fulva* means "fox colored," or tawny.

Description: A slender mushroom with a tan to brown cap that has distinct lines along the edges and may be covered with white patchy warts on top. The stalk is a lighter tan color, and there is no partial veil and hence, no ring. The base is not enlarged and is encased in a distinct saclike white cup that sometimes has orange-brown stains. The color of the spore print is white.

Comments: Reported edible, but we do not recommend eating it! Dig the mushroom up completely to find the sac at the base for positive identification. Otherwise, it is very similar to *Amanita ceciliae.*

Season: Summer and fall.

Habit, habitat, and distribution: On soil, single to several in mixed woods or in coniferous woods.

Cap diameter: 4–10 cm (1½–4″).

Stalk height: 7–16 cm (3–6½″).

Stalk diameter: 5–10 mm (⅕–½″).

JL

Amanita cinereoconia

Edibility unknown/Caution!

This mushroom looks like it has been dusted with ashes, a characteristic reflected in its name: *cinereo-* means "like cinders" or "ash colored"; *-conia* refers to the cap.

Description: The universal veil of this mushroom breaks up as the mushroom expands to leave a silver-gray to brown powdery layer covering the cap, which is whitish to brownish gray. The stalk may also be covered with these remnants, and it is usually without a veil. The basal bulb is slightly enlarged and rooting, and a chlorine odor is present. The spore print color is white.

Comments: Edibility not reported, and it is not recommended for eating. We like this mushroom for the photographic challenge inherent with such a delicate, silvery capped specimen.

Season: Summer and fall.

Habit, habitat, and distribution: Usually single on the ground in mixed woods, but probably is associated with pines.

Cap diameter: 3–7.5 cm (1–3").

Stalk height: 4.5–12.5 cm (1½–5").

Stalk diameter: 4–13 mm (⅙–½").

DG

Pelioma means "bruise"—a reference to a blue-green discoloration on the cup and stalk base.

Description: The cap is gray to brown, with an olive tint, and the gills are often tinged grayish olive to brownish gray, sometimes with a slightly lavender tint. A veil is present on the stalk, along with scaly patches, and the base is enlarged and rooting. The cup at the base frequently shows a blue-green discoloration. There is a distinct chlorine odor. The spore print color is white.

Comments: Edibility not reported, and it is not recommended for eating. The blue-green stain is the best field characteristic. This mushroom is infrequently encountered, but the green staining makes it easy to identify when you find it.

Season: Summer and fall.

Habit, habitat, and distribution: Usually single, on ground, in mixed woods.

Cap diameter: 5–9 cm (2–3½").

Stalk height: 9–15 cm (3½–6").

Stalk diameter: 8–12 mm (⅓–½").

OM

Amanita mutabilis

Not reported/Caution!

Mutabilis means "changing"; here it indicates the color change, on handling, from white to pink.

Description: The cap is white to tan, smooth when dry and slightly sticky when wet, with a distinct, often skirtlike partial ring on the stalk and membranous saclike cup at the base. The flesh of the stalk and gills rapidly turns a rose pink when injured, and there is a distinct sweet odor. In this *Amanita,* the gills actually touch the stalk and leave a faint line on it. The spore print color is white.

Comments: Edibility not reported, and it is not recommended for eating. The mushroom occurs in sandy soil, and from half to two-thirds of the fruiting body will be below ground level. Therefore, you must dig carefully to reveal the saclike cup at the base. The odor is reported as oily to anise; to us, it simply smells sweet.

Season: Summer and fall.

Habit, habitat, and distribution: In sandy soil in mixed or pine woods.

Cap diameter: 6–11 cm (2½–4½").

Stalk height: 5–16 cm (2–6½").

Stalk diameter: 10–22 mm (½–1").

VM

This is an easy *Amanita* to learn to recognize—it is characterized by having a pink to pinkish beige, powdery cup layer. It was named for E. V. Komarek, the former director of Tall Timbers Research Station in Florida where it was first found.

Description: This small to medium-sized mushroom has a creamy white cap that is covered by powdery pink-tinted remnants of the universal veil. The gills are creamy white, distinctly free from the stalk, and crowded. The stalk is creamy white, tapering toward the top, with pinkish beige powdery scales at the top and a persistent, hanging pink veil. The base is somewhat enlarged, and patches of the powdery pink veil remain but are never in concentric rows. The spore print color is white.

Comments: This pretty pink *Amanita* is known from mixed coniferous and deciduous forests throughout the Gulf Coast. The chemical work that might determine whether it is edible or toxic has not been done; we simply recommend avoiding it for the table.

Season: Summer and fall.

Habit, habitat, and distribution: Single to several during hot, wet weather, fruiting in deciduous forests and mixed hardwood and coniferous forests throughout the Coastal Plain.

Cap diameter: 4–7.5 cm (1½–3″).
Stalk height: 6–11 cm (2½–4½″).
Stalk diameter: 5–14 mm (⅕–½″).

CO

Amanita daucipes

Not recommended/Caution!

This *Amanita* is easy to identify, with its large basal bulb and orange-pink color, which is reflected in the name *daucipes,* meaning "carrot foot."

Description: This is a large mushroom—it can reach 9 inches tall. Cap, stalk, and universal veil remnants are present as warts on the cap or fragments hanging from the cap edges, are all a pale pinkish orange. The base of the stalk is unusually large and orange tinted. The spore print color is white.

Comments: Edibility not recorded, and it is not recommended for eating. The "sweet" smell and orange-pink color distinguish this mushroom from all other species of *Amanita. A. daucipes* has been reported as larger than *A. polypyramis,* but in our experience it is consistently smaller in Texas.

Season: Summer and fall.

Habit, habitat, and distribution: Usually single or in small numbers, on ground in mixed woods.

Cap diameter: 6–30 cm (2–12″).

Stalk height: 8–21 cm (3–8″).

Stalk diameter: 8–30 mm (⅓–1¼″).

CO

Spissa means "thick, massive, or compact," an apt description of the large, thick cap of this mushroom.

Description: The thick cap is brownish to reddish brown, paler along the margins, with white to pale gray warts that are remnants of the universal veil and may wash off or wear off. The gills are free from the stalk, white to pale cream and close. The stalk is equal, tapering slightly at the base, white to cream in color and solid. A ring clings to the stalk in a mature mushroom (the cap of the one pictured has not yet opened). Remnants of the universal veil may also remain as powdery warts at the base of the stalk. The spore print color is white.

Comments: This mushroom is often found growing in dry, sandy soil during cool weather. It is closely related to other highly toxic mushrooms and should be considered dangerously poisonous!

Season: Late summer through winter.

Habit, habitat, and distribution: Usually single to numerous, occasionally found growing in fairy rings, in mixed coniferous and deciduous forests. Known throughout the eastern United States.

Cap diameter: 5–9 cm (2–3½").

Stalk height: 5.5–7.5 cm (2¼–3").

Stalk diameter: 7–18 mm (¼–⅔").

JL

Amanita rubescens

Edible/Caution!

Rubescens means "turning red," so named because of its tendency to bruise reddish, especially over the lower stalk. In Europe, this mushroom is called the "blusher."

Description: This is a white to tan mushroom with varying amounts of reddish to pinkish coloration of the cap, gills, stalk, base, and ring. The cap may be a bit deeper reddish brown, and the stalk base is also deeper in color. The flesh of the mushroom slowly bruises reddish when handled. The universal veil remnants consist of reddish gray patches over the cup and base of the stalk. The spore print color is white.

Comments: Edible, but be absolutely certain of your identification! We do not recommend it, especially for beginners. The red staining is the best identification characteristic for this mushroom.

Season: Spring, summer, and fall; most common in summer.

Habit, habitat, and distribution: Single to several in mixed woods; occasionally numerous.

Cap diameter: 5–13 cm (2–5").

Stalk height: 7–11 cm (3–4½").

Stalk diameter: 9–18 mm (⅓–⅔").

AB

The name means "the yellow one like *rubescens*" and refers to the similarity of this mushroom to *A. rubescens,* in its size and general appearance and in "blushing" red.
Description: This mushroom has a yellow to orange-yellow cap that is covered with yellowish warts. It has a ring on the stalk that generally persists as the specimen matures and a thin, membranous cup at the base. The stalk slowly bruises reddish where injured. The universal veil is deep yellow and occurs as warts on the cap or pieces surrounding the base. The spore print color is white.
Comments: Edibility unknown, and it is not recommended for eating, as it has been reported both edible and poisonous. We recommend leaving the final determination as one of nature's unsolved mysteries.
Season: Summer and fall.
Habit, habitat, and distribution: Occasionally numerous, on ground in mixed hardwood forests throughout East Texas timber belt, the Big Thicket, and the Coastal Plain.
Cap diameter: 4.5–10 cm (1½–4").
Stalk height: 7–14.5 cm (3–6").
Stalk diameter: 8–17 mm (⅓–⅔").

OM

Amanita brunnescens

Not edible/Toxic

The species name *brunnescens* means "turning brown," an apt description for the color change that occurs when parts of the white flesh of this mushroom are bruised or injured.

Description: This medium-sized mushroom has a brown to grayish brown cap, which is covered with white patches that are remnants of the universal veil, when young. The patches often wash or wear off, and in age the cap becomes nearly flat. The gills are white, free from the stalk, and crowded. The stalk is white, tapering slightly toward the top, and a membranous, persistent, white to gray ring is present. The base is the most notable feature, as it is abruptly enlarged and always has longitudinal clefts. The spore print color is white.

Comments: This *Amanita* is very common during wet fall seasons. It is often found fruiting in large numbers in mixed coniferous and deciduous forests. Toxicity is suspected, and it should not be eaten! The pale white variety, *A. brunnescens* var. *pallida,* may be found in the same habitats.

Season: Summer and fall.

Habit, habitat, and distribution: Single to numerous on the ground under conifers and mixed hardwoods.

Cap diameter: 3.5–10 cm (1½–4″).

Stalk height: 6.5–14.5 cm (2½–6″).

Stalk diameter: 8–21 mm (⅓–⅞″).

OM

Flavo- is from the Latin root meaning "yellow," and *-conia* refers to the conical warts on the cap; thus, this is an *Amanita* with a yellow universal veil that remains as warts on the cap or as ragged pieces around the base of the stalk.

Description: A small mushroom with an orange-yellow cap and yellow warts; it has a white stalk with a persistent yellowish ring. The gills are white, and the base is slightly enlarged.

Comments: Not edible, with small amounts of toxins. This is one of the most common Amanitas in Texas woods, usually the first *Amanita* to appear in summer, and is one of only a handful of mushrooms that have been recorded at every TMS Annual Mushroom Foray.

Season: Throughout the year, but most common in summer and fall.

Habit, habitat, and distribution: Single to several, occasionally numerous in mixed woods or under conifers.

Cap diameter: 3–9 cm (1–3½").
Stalk height: 5.5–11.5 cm (2–4½").
Stalk diameter: 7–14 mm (¼–½").

VM

Amanita citrina var. *lavendula*

Not edible

Citrina means "yellow, like citron" and indicates the lemon yellow cap of this common *Amanita; lavendula* (lavender) is the color of the cup.

Description: A stocky mushroom with a lemon yellow to brownish yellow cap, white stalk and distinct white veil, and a cup at the base. Remnants of the universal veil are always lavender and are seen as membranous patches on the cap and stalk and the cup at the base. The stalk may bruise lavender on handling. The gills have a chlorine odor. The spore print color is white.

Comments: Edibility unknown, and it is not recommended for eating. If one encounters an occasional universal veil that is yellowish white, it is *A. citrina* var. *citrina,* which is less frequent in Texas.

Season: Year round but most common in late fall and winter.

Habit, habitat, and distribution: On ground under pines, usually those species whose needles are clustered in groups of two or three; often found in large troops.

Cap diameter: 5–12 cm (2–5").

Stalk height: 6–13 cm (2–5").

Stalk diameter: 6–20 mm (¼–¾").

VM

According to legend, the mushroom was once denied to the common people and reserved for the Caesars.

Description: The cap color varies from bright red to orange, and the young mushroom emerging from the large, saclike, pure white membranous cup is very distinctive. In older specimens, the cap fades to yellowish orange and the gills and ring are distinctly yellow. Distinct lines called "striations" are present along the edge of the cap, and the stalk is orange-yellow. Look for the white cup, as it is often buried under leaf litter when the stalk is deep rooted. The spore print color is white.

Comments: Edible, but it is not recommended for eating due to the group's complexity and the number of variants that have not been tested. *Amanita arkansana,* a yellow-orange mushroom, is similar in all other respects.

Season: Late summer and fall.

Habit, habitat, and distribution: On the ground, usually in small troops, though occasionally numerous, in mixed woods.

Cap diameter: 5–12 cm (2–5").

Stalk height: 7–15 cm (2½–5").

Stalk diameter: 5–20 cm (¼–¾").

CO

Amanita muscaria

Poisonous

This is the species that is often pictured on kitchen canisters and children's toys. The name *muscaria* means "of the fly," and in folklore it is said to kill flies.

Description: The robust mushroom has bright red, rounded caps that do not fade in age. The meaty cap is covered with large, white, patchy warts that are remnants of the universal veil and may wear or wash off. The cap edges develop faint lines, or striations, in age. The gills and stalk are white, and a persistent membranous, white veil is present. The remnants of the universal veil are white and break into concentric rings around the base. The spore print color is white.

Comments: Not edible and reported toxic. It is common in the late fall and early winter under pines during wet seasons. The 2½ rings of universal veil remnants are white rather than yellow, distinguishing it from *A. muscaria* var. *flavivolvata.*

Season: Fall and winter.

Habit, habitat, and distribution: Mycorrhizal with pine in coniferous and mixed woods.

Cap diameter: 4–21 cm (1½–8").

Stalk height: 5–14 cm (2–6").

Stalk diameter: 7–22 mm (⅓–1").

JL

Amanita muscaria var. *flavivolvata*

Poisonous

Called the "fly mushroom" (*muscaria* means "of the fly"), this variety found in our Texas pine forests has distinct patchy warts on the cap that are yellow to pale orange.

Description: The caps are bright red when young, fading to dull orange in age. The cap edges develop faint lines called striations in age. The gills and stalk are white with a yellow veil. Universal veil remnants are yellow to orange (thus the variety name) and break into concentric rings around the base. The spore print color is white.

Comments: Not edible and reported toxic. This red-capped mushroom with yellow "polka dots" is closely related to the one commonly illustrated on postcards, children's toys, and kitchen canisters. The 2½ rings of universal veil tissue on the stalk are used to distinguish *A. muscaria* from *A. frostiana—muscaria* has 2½ to 3 rings.

Season: Fall and winter.

Habit, habitat, and distribution: Mycorrhizal with pine in coniferous and mixed woods.

Cap diameter: 4–21 cm (1½–8").

Stalk height: 5–14 cm (2–6").

Stalk diameter: 7–22 mm (⅓–1").

AB

Amanita frostiana

Not recommended/Caution!

This mushroom was named for C. C. Frost, a Vermont shoemaker who taught himself Latin in order to read mycology books of the day.

Description: Similar in appearance to *A. muscaria,* this orange-capped mushroom is distinguished by its slimy cap when moist, on which the yellow warts appear to "float." A yellowish veil is present on the white stalk, which lacks the 2½ rings of tissue typically found in *A. muscaria.* Warts that are remnants of the universal veil may also cling to the stalk as well as to the bulbous base. The gills are white, and it has a white spore print.

Comments: Edibility not reported, and it is not recommended for eating.

Season: Fall and winter.

Habit, habitat, and distribution: Mycorrhizal under pine, usually singly.

Cap diameter: 2–8 cm (¾–4″).

Stalk height: 5–6 cm (2–2½″).

Stalk diameter: 4–11 mm (⅙–½″).

VM

Family Lepiotaceae: The Lepiotas

The Lepiotaceae family (the Lepiotas) is a large and diverse group. At least two hundred species are found in the temperate and tropical regions, and no comprehensive monograph (description of all known species) has been done for the southern part of the United States. In the past, all members of this family were considered part of the genus *Lepiota,* but now several distinct genera are recognized on the basis of spore characteristics, including *Chlorophyllum, Leucocoprinus, Leucoagaricus,* and *Macrolepiota.* The diversity of the Lepiotas extends to their edibility as well as morphological features. Some are delicious edibles, some are toxic and cause gastrointestinal distress (vomiting and diarrhea), and some, including several of the smaller species, are believed to contain deadly amatoxins. We will illustrate and discuss only the larger and more common of the genera in this book.

Members of the family Lepiotaceae share several distinct characteristics that are easy to recognize by the following features:

1. General appearance: Many species have a stately appearance, and some are delicately "flowerlike" with yellow or reddish coloration. The larger species are often robust, frequently cream to white, with very noticeable scales or patches on the cap that do not wash off. On close inspection the scales are part of the outer skin of the cap (called the cuticle) and are not superficial as they are in *Amanita.* The smaller species are often very fragile, and some are brightly colored. The presence of scales or patches on the cap and, in some species, on the stalk, is one of the best distinguishing features.

2. Gills: The gills of Lepiotas are distinctly "free"; that is, they do not touch the stalk. If you slice a mature, fully opened *Lepiota* vertically from top of cap to base of stalk, you will see that the innermost end of the gills is well away from the stalk.

3. Ring: In an embryonic mushroom, the partial veil is a piece of tissue that extends between the gills and stalk. In Lepiotas, this tissue frequently remains as a ring, or annulus, on the stalk. The ring of many *Lepiota* species is fairly tough and membranous and likely to remain on the stalk in age. *Lepiota* species are separated from *Amanita* partly due to their lack of a cup.

4. Spore print: When you take a spore print, you will find the color of the spores of *Lepiota* species to be white

to cream color. The advanced collector can use Melzer's reagent to differentiate *Lepiota* from *Amanita* and other white-spored groups: spores of *Lepiota* will be yellowish or show a dextrinoid (red or reddish brown) reaction in Melzer's rather than the clear blue color (amyloid) reaction shown by the deadly but not all species of *Amanita.*

5. Ecology: The Lepiotas are saprophytic (breaking down dead material) rather than mycorrhizal (beneficially associated with the roots) and may be found in forested or grassy areas. Some are solitary, while others may occur in small groups. Occasionally, large troops can occur in arcs or "fairy rings" during very wet seasons.

As you look at the illustrations in this section and at your mushroom specimens, look carefully for these characteristics. Be doubly sure of your identification to avoid confusing the illustrated species with other toxic species or with an *Amanita.*

Procera means "lofty," an apt description of this tall, stately mushroom. It is occasionally referred to as the "parasol mushroom" because the extra long stalk and slightly conical cap resemble an umbrella.

Description: The cap and stalk of this mushroom are white and covered with fine brown scales. The cap is meaty, and the gills are white and thick. The stalk is unusually tall (6–9 inches [15–22 cm] is common), has a persistent membranous ring that is frequently moveable in age, is clothed with small brown scales, and is slightly bulbous at the base. The spore print color is white.

Comments: This is a delicious mushroom, one of our favorites. Be absolutely certain of your identification, as this is a highly variable species. Always check for the white spore print color and the brown scales on the stalk to be certain that you don't have *Chlorophyllum molybdites* (which has green spores, a smooth stalk, and is often found growing in "fairy rings"). We recommend that you get confirmation on your identification before you eat this the first time. In older works, this mushroom is often called *Lepiota procera.*

Season: From late May through November, most numerous in extended periods of wet weather.

Habit, habitat, and distribution: Scattered to numerous, and occasionally abundant in and at the edges of woods and along trails.

Cap diameter: 7–12 cm (3–5").
Stalk height: 12–25 cm (5–10").
Stalk diameter: 8–15 mm (⅓–⅔").

VM

Chlorophyllum molybdites

Toxic/Caution!

This mushroom is the one we are asked about most often: "What are those great white toadstools in my lawn?" The name refers to the green pigment of the spores, which looks like chlorophyll and turns the gills green. However, mushrooms do not possess chlorophyll.

Description: These are distinctive mushrooms—4 to 6 inches tall; with a cap that looks like a golf ball in youth and expands to 4 to 8 inches across at maturity, often growing in full or partial "fairy rings." The overall color is white, with reddish brown "scales" on the cap and a ring on the smooth stalk. The gills are white when young and gradually turn a dull gray-green from the maturing of the distinctly *green* spores. The base is slightly enlarged.

Comments: This is a classic warm-weather mushroom and will appear in lawns and grassy areas in great profusion after extended periods of summer rain. It is also one of the most commonly reported causes of poisoning, so *always* check for the *green spore print.* It is reported that the toxicity diminishes with thorough cooking—but we recommend not eating it. The toxins in this mushroom cause "gastric upset"; fatalities are not known, but hospitalization is not uncommon. You won't die from eating it, but as the old joke goes, "You'll wish you were dead." We also recommend against eating any mushroom that grows near or adjacent to heavily travelled city streets—mushrooms are known to adsorb and concentrate heavy metals (i.e., lead from gasoline fumes). If you do eat this mushroom, call the Poison Center, not us!

Season: Late spring through fall, but most numerous during wet summer months.

Habit, habitat, and distribution: Single to numerous on lawns and grassy areas. Oc-

(continued)

AB

Note light scales on cap.

(continued from preceding page)
curs in partial or complete fairy rings (arcs) when encountered in numbers.
Cap diameter: 8–15 cm (3–6″).
Stalk height: 8–15 cm (3–6″).
Stalk diameter: 8–18 mm (⅓–⅔″).

RIGHT: Left, scales washed off by rain; center, normal cap; right, white scales on cap.
BELOW: Mushrooms growing in arc or fairy ring.

CY

CY

VM

Note dark scales on cap.

Lepiota humei

Toxic/Caution!

This is "Hume's" *Lepiota,* named for H. H. Hume, who first collected it near Gainesville, Florida.

Description: The cap is white, with a brownish golden spot at the center and scales that match the cap's coloring. The gills are white, crowded, and free from the stalk. The stalk is white and smooth, with a distinct ring present, and its diameter is even above a slightly swollen bulb at the base. The flesh of the stalk shows a slow color change to deep pink, then brown, when bruised or cut. The spore print is white.

Comments: No reliable data exists on this mushroom's edibility. We therefore strongly recommend that you do not eat it! Allergic reactions are commonly reported from ingestion of *Lepiotas,* and this complex group is best left to the experts. *Lepiota humei* is much smaller than *Macrolepiota procera* and lacks the brown scales on the stalk.

Season: Appears from early summer through late fall in wet weather.

Habit, habitat, and distribution: Usually scattered, though occasionally abundant in lawns and grassy areas.

Cap diameter: 5–7.5 cm (2–3″).

Stalk height: 5–10 cm (2–4″).

Stalk diameter: 6–12 mm (¼–½″).

VM

This bright yellow mushroom is also called *Lepiota lutea* in older works, and *lutea* means "yellow," the color of this entire mushroom, which frequently appears in flowerpots and well-mulched beds.

Description: All parts of this mushroom are a bright yellow, except for tiny brown scales at the top of the cap. The cap is conical when young and opens to nearly flat with a raised center. The gills are buff, and the edges are dotted with minute scales or points. The stalk has a distinct ring and a swollen base, which is covered with yellow powder. The spores are white.

Comments: This is one mushroom we can identify with certainty over the phone. The caller usually says, "It's bright yellow and looks like it was dusted on top with nutmeg, and it's growing in my flowerpot." Don't eat it—it's toxic!

Season: Indoors, it can appear year round; outdoors, it is most abundant during the warm wet months of summer and fall.

Habit, habitat, and distribution: Usually single to several on well-mulched and well-watered soil.

Cap diameter: 2.5–6 cm (1–2½").

Stalk height: 3–10 cm (1–4").

Stalk diameter: 1.5–5 mm (1/10–¼").

(Also see frontispiece)

AB

Leucocoprinus cepaestipes

Not edible/Caution!

Cepa- means "onion," and *-stipe* means "stalk"; thus, it follows that this mushroom has an onion- or scallion-shaped stalk. In many older works the genus is listed as *Lepiota.*

Description: The cap is thin fleshed and white and covered with powdery white scales, which appear to line up along radial lines. The gills are white, crowded (many), and free from the stalk. The stalk is slender but bulbous and scallion-shaped at the base, and there is a distinct ring on the stalk. The spore print color is white.

Comments: This is a delicate, pure white species when young, darkening somewhat in age, often occurring in clusters, and it commonly appears on well-mulched soil. It should be considered toxic, as some people are sickened by eating it, so enjoy its delicate beauty and find other mushrooms to eat. This is a temperate to tropical species common in warm, wet months.

Season: Most common in summer and early fall.

Habit, habitat, and distribution: Usually in clusters of several specimens arising from a common base; appearing on rich soil and humus; frequently seen in flowerbeds and pots.

Cap diameter: 2.5–8 cm (1–3″).

Stalk height: 4–14 cm (1½–5″).

Stalk diameter: 3–6 mm (⅛–¼″).

VM

Not edible

Here's one mushroom name that doesn't require translating. Just try to pick one of these, and you'll agree that it is appropriately named.

Description: This mushroom has an almost transparent, thin-fleshed, yellow cap, which has distinct radial lines, or striations. The striations appear because the flesh of the cap is so thin that the gills actually pull the cap tissue downward, in an umbrellalike effect. The gills are white to yellow, and the spore print is white. The stalk is white, tall (6 inches [15 cm] or more), delicate, and slender, with a small bulb at the base and a distinct yellow ring.

Comments: An early morning mushroom, this one is so ephemeral that it is frequently gone by afternoon. Edibility not reported, and eating it is not recommended; you'd starve to death trying to collect enough to feed a mosquito!

Season: Summer and fall.

Habit, habitat, and distribution: Usually single to scattered in mixed woods; most common in high humidity, as dry weather dehydrates these delicate mushrooms into oblivion.

Cap diameter: 5–7.5 cm (2–3″).

Stalk height: 10–20 cm (4–8″).

Stalk diameter: 3–6 mm (1⁄8–1⁄4″).

VM

Lepiota americana

Edible/Caution!

The species' name of this mushroom shouldn't need translating. It is easily recognized due to its distinctive reddening on the stalk when handled.

Description: The cap is white, with a brown spot in the center that is ringed with concentric rows of reddish brown scaly patches. The white flesh of the cap stains red at first when injured, darkening to brown, and often reddens in age or on drying. The gills are white, free from the stalk, and very crowded. The stalk is white at first, darkening or reddening to a deep reddish brown. The stalk is swollen at or below the middle, tapers at the base, and the flesh stains yellow, changing to orange when cut. The spore print is white.

Comments: This species is edible and delicious, but there are toxic species in the *Lepiota* genus, so make sure you see the yellow- to orange-staining pattern in the stalk flesh and the reddening of the cap flesh.

Season: Summer and early fall.

Habit, habitat, and distribution: Found single to numerous, often on sawdust, mulch, or compost, as well as on rich soil and around stumps.

Cap diameter: 3–15 cm (1½–5″).

Stalk height: 7–14 cm (2¾–5¾″).

Stalk diameter: 5–20 mm (⅕–¾″).

AB

Family Hygrophoraceae: The Hygrophori

The name *Hygrophorus* means "water bearer" and reflects the very moist texture of these mushrooms, which may be brightly colored and very attractive. This is a cool-weather group as a whole, and only a few species are regularly found in most parts of Texas. The following features are likely to be noted:

1. General appearance: These are small to medium-sized mushrooms, mostly growing on the ground and not on leaf litter, sticks, or rotting wood. Colors of the caps include bright red, green, orange, and yellow, as well as white, gray, and even black. The higher water content often gives a translucency to the cap and stalk that is easily observed if you hold the mushroom up to the light.
2. Gills: The gills of *Hygrophorus* are thick and waxy, light in color, and attached directly to the stalk (the lower edge of the gill goes straight to the stalk). The "waxy feel" of the gills can be a difficult concept for beginners, but try this: pull out a piece of a gill and rub it between your thumb and first finger. Your fingers will feel as if you had rubbed a piece of candle wax.
3. Stalk: The stalks of *Hygrophorus* are smooth and fleshy, without any trace of a ring. However, a number of species do have a partial veil. (A partial veil is a membrane that covers the gills of an embryonic mushroom. When the mushroom expands, the partial veil breaks and can leave remnants on the stalk or on the edge of the cap.) The diameter is equal, and there is no swelling at the base. The stalk is always attached at the center of the cap and may be hollow.
4. Spore print: Members of the genus *Hygrophorus* have a white spore print.
5. Ecology: Most species occur as decomposers on humus while others are associated with trees or other plants. Some are specific to certain types of trees (in the South, notably pine species); others are more ubiquitous.

Many of the *Hygrophorus* species are edible, though most are on the bland, watery, and slimy side. A few are toxic, and, in our opinion, very few are really worth eating. They are, however, some of the most beautiful species to be found in the woods, and, with their bright colors, are easy to spot. Look for them mostly during cool, damp times, as in the winter months.

Hygrophorus coccineus

Edible/Good

The species' name, *coccineus,* means "red." These mushrooms are often called "waxy caps," and this species is sometimes referred to as the "red waxy cap," a very descriptive name.

Description: A truly beautiful mushroom with a smooth, bright red cap, distinctly rounded above yellow gills, and with a smooth, slender yellow to red stalk. The pigments in the cap often fade dramatically in wet weather to orange or straw color. The overall size averages 2 inches. It has widely spaced gills that have the typical "waxy" feel of *Hygrophorus.* Pinch off a piece of the gill and rub it between thumb and forefinger—it leaves a waxy residue similar to candle wax. The spore print color is white.

Comments: This mushroom is often prolific in late fall and winter on the same slopes where chanterelles appear in summer. It is edible and can be quite good, though it tends to be soggy. Cooking methods that tend to dry it out are the most desirable.

Season: Late fall through the winter.

Habit, habitat, and distribution: Several to numerous at the base of trees or on ground in mixed woods; often quite common in beech, magnolia, and loblolly pine habitats.

Cap diameter: 1.5–7 cm (½–3").

Stalk height: 3–7.5 cm (1¼–3").

Stalk diameter: 3–8 mm (¼–⅓").

JL

Edible

This *Hygrophorus* gets its name from its diminutive size.

Description: The small, bright red to orange-red cap is dry, with edges that curve under in youth. The cap shape is rounded rather than conical. The gills are directly attached to the stalk, or descend slightly down it, and are medium spaced. The stalk is thick and smooth and fades from bright red as the mushroom ages. The stalk may also be unexpectedly long, with as much as half its length hidden in the leaf litter on the forest floor. The spore print color is white.

Comments: The flavor is generally described as bland, and the small size makes this mushroom of little interest for eating.

Season: Winter and spring.

Habit, habitat, and distribution: Single to many on decayed material; this is one of only a few *Hygrophorus* species that sometimes occur on decayed wood.

Cap diameter: 1–4 cm (¼–1⅝″).

Stalk height: 2–5 cm (1–2″).

Stalk diameter: 2–5 mm (⅛–¼″).

AB

Hygrophorus cantharellus

Edible

This *Hygrophorus* superficially resembles the smaller species of chanterelles, and it was named *cantharellus* due to this likeness. The white spore print and sharp-edged gills without veins between them, however, put it in the genus *Hygrophorus*.
Description: The small, brightly colored cap and tall, slender stalk are a distinct deep red to orange red, fading in age. The cap is thin fleshed, with very widely spaced gills that extend down the stalk. The gills are yellow to orange, thick and sharp edged, and they leave a waxy residue when rubbed between your fingers. The stalk is smooth and unusually long compared to the diameter of the cap. The spores are white.
Comments: Although not poisonous, it is seldom numerous enough to collect for the table. Abundant fruitings are sometimes encountered on humus and well-decayed logs.

Season: Summer and fall.
Habit, habitat, and distribution: Single to many on decayed material; this is one of only a few *Hygrophorus* species that can occur on well-decayed wood.
Cap diameter: 1–3.5 cm (3/8–1 3/8").
Stalk height: 2.5–10 cm (1–4").
Stalk diameter: 1.5–5 mm (1/16–1/4").

AB

Hygrophorus conicus group

Not edible

The species' name for this mushroom means "cone shaped," referring to the cap. Both the common orange-red capped variety and the dark gray to black variety, described here, are known from Texas.

Description: The dark form described here has a gray to black, cone-shaped cap and a long stem that is usually somewhat lighter and often tinged yellow at the base. The gills are white to gray, and the spore print is white. These mushrooms are pale when young but change to gray or black so rapidly that they might seem to have always been dark in color.

Comments: This is a variable species, meaning that the color and form can be quite different from collection to collection. In this case, the variation ranges from the orange-red capped mushroom that is usually seen in other parts of the United States to this very dark gray version.

Season: Late summer and fall.

Habit, habitat, and distribution: Several to numerous, scattered on the ground, under oak, and in lawns.

Cap diameter: 2–7.5 cm (¾–3").

Stalk height: 7.5–10 cm (3–4").

Stalk diameter: 8–16 mm (⅓–⅔").

AB

VM

Family Russulaceae

Genus Russula: The *Russulas*

The name *Russula* is from the Latin word meaning "red," and it is not surprising that many species in this genus, including some of the most common ones, have red or pink caps. Some of the *Russula* species are quite delicious, and many are common during wet summers. Other species are toxic, causing vomiting and diarrhea, so it is important to observe the characteristics carefully. *Russula* species are easy to learn to recognize and share some or all of the following features:

1. General appearance: These mushrooms are generally short and stout, with brittle flesh and a cap diameter that is equal to or greater than the height of the stalk. In youth the cap is generally rounded, with the edges rolled under. As the mushroom ages, the perimeter of the cap expands and rises until the cap is nearly flat. Many *Russula* species have caps that are brightly colored: red, pink, purple, and even green are common, as are white, yellow, brown, and gray species. Unlike *Lactarius,* the outer "skin" of the cap, called the cuticle, can be peeled away from the cap flesh beneath. The stalks are short and even, sometimes bruising gray, red, or black, and they snap cleanly when broken, like chalk. Unlike the closely related genus *Lactarius,* no latex is present.
2. Gills: The gills of *Russula* are evenly spaced and medium distant from each other. In some species, all the gills are entire (each gill extends all the way from the stalk to the cap edge); in others, short gills alternate with long ones. The gills are notched or directly attached to the stalk and are usually white when young, though they may become buff to orange in age as the spores mature.
3. Spore print: *Russula* is a genus with white, yellowish, buff-colored, or orange spores. Spore print color is important to determine the species.
4. Ecology: *Russula* species occur on the ground and may associate with a wide range of conifer and hardwood hosts. There are many species in the United States, and one species or another can be found at any time of year. Only a few easily identified species are illustrated here. There is no overall guide to the genus for North America.

Russulas occur in woods, on lawns with trees, in brush, and in pastures with trees. It's a dry day when you come back from a mushroom hunt saying, "We didn't even find any Russulas!" The largest number of species occur in the summer and early fall.

Not edible/Toxic

The name *emetica* (from "emetic," to induce vomiting) has been applied across the United States to a large group of red-capped, peppery mushrooms. The Texas version is more likely to be *Russula emetica* var. *silvestris,* which means "the variety of the emetica group that is found in (mixed) woods." The true *R. emetica* var. *emetica* is found in sphagnum under boreal forest conifers, but a number of look-alike red Russulas will be encountered by the avid mushroom hunter.

Description: This mushroom is easy to spot due to its red cap, which will often be seen poking up out of leaf litter. The bright red color may fade in age. The gills may be attached or notched and are white, as is the stalk. The spore print color is white to creamy.

Comments: The odor is mild, but the taste is strongly peppery and bitter. As these are members of the *emetica* ("inducing vomiting") group, they are not edible.

Season: Summer and fall.

Habit, habitat, and distribution: Single to numerous on ground in mixed woods; often common in hot, humid weather.

Cap diameter: 2–7 cm (¾–3").

Stalk height: 2.5–5 cm (1–2").

Stalk diameter: 10–20 mm (⅓–¾").

JL

Russula rosacea

Not edible

The "rosy" *Russula,* with its rosy pink cap and pink-tinged stalk, is a very pretty mushroom.

Description: The cap of this mushroom is deep rose pink to red, often fading to pale pink in age. The gills are creamy white to pale yellow, attached or slightly running down the stalk, and close together. The stalk is smooth and dry, usually pink, or with perhaps a blush of red. The spore print color is pale yellow.

Comments: Considered inedible (though not poisonous) and to be avoided, due to the slightly bitter taste.

Season: Summer and fall.

Habit, habitat, and distribution: Single to numerous under conifers and in mixed woods.

Cap diameter: 2.5–7.5 cm (1–3″).

Stalk height: 3.5–7.5 cm (1½–3″).

Stalk diameter: 10–25 cm (⅓–1″).

VM

Edible

Mariae means "Mary's." Charles Peck described this reddish purple–capped *Russula* and named it for its discoverer, Mary Elizabeth Banning (1832–1901), one of the few women mycologists of the day. Peck credited over a dozen species as having been found and described by Ms. Banning.

Description: The cap of this mushroom is broadly rounded, becoming flat in age. The color is a dark crimson or purplish, with a deeper colored center. Often the cap has a velvety or "powdered" appearance. The flesh is white and slightly pink under the outer layer (cut through the cap, and the flesh just under the red "skin" will be pink). The gills are white, close, and become yellow in age. Some gills are forked at the stalk. The stalk is usually white at top and bottom and the color of the cap in the middle; rarely entirely white. The spore print color is creamy yellow. The odor and taste of the mushroom are mild to slightly acrid.

Comments: Although edible, this mushroom is not very tasty and is hardly worth the bother. It is a common summer mushroom in the hardwood and mixed forests of East and Coastal Texas.

Season: Summer.

Habit, habitat, and distribution: Single to numerous under hardwoods, especially oaks. In August, it can be one of the most numerous mushrooms in the woods.

Cap diameter: 2–7 cm (¾–3″).

Stalk height: 2.5–7.5 cm (1–3″).

Stalk diameter: 10–25 mm (⅓–1″).

JL

Russula flavida

Edible

The Latin root *flav-* is often seen in mushroom names and is generally an indication of yellow color, as in this case, a yellow *Russula.*

Description: The most notable characteristic of this *Russula* is the bright yellow color of the cap and stalk. The cap has a deep gold sunburst in the center, lightening toward the edge. The gills, which are white when young, darkening to yellow as the spores mature, may be forked and are fairly close or crowded. The stalk is solid, yellow at the base, lightening to white toward the top. The spore print color is yellow.

Comments: Considered edible, the taste and odor are described as "not distinctive." If the cut flesh stains gray or ashy gray, you have another species, perhaps *Russula decolorans* or possibly *Russula flava,* which are found under exotic birches.

Season: Summer and fall.

Habit, habitat, and distribution: Single to numerous under oaks during hot, moist weather.

Cap diameter: 4–10 cm (1½–4″).

Stalk height: 3–5 cm (1¼–2″).

Stalk diameter: 10–20 mm (⅓–¾″).

OM

This *Russula* takes its name from the variations in cap color that it can show. As the name indicates, it is a variable species.
Description: The cap of this mushroom is smooth and dry (though it can be slimy when moist), with cap pigmentation ranging from pinkish purple, dull purple, olive, yellow, green to blue-green, white, or tan. The stalk is white and thick. The best characteristic for recognition is the consistent greenish tinge to the cap and the presence of distinctly forked, white to slightly brownish gills. The spore print color is white.
Comments: Look for the forked gills to distinguish this mushroom from other *Russulas,* and the longer, nonbruising stalk to distinguish it from members of the *compacta* group. It is edible and considered good when young.

Season: Late summer and fall.
Habit, habitat, and distribution: Single to numerous under mixed woods.
Cap diameter: 5–10 cm (2–4″).
Stalk height: 5–10 cm (2–4″).
Stalk diameter: 15–40 mm (½–1½″).

DG

Russula compacta

Not edible

Translating the name of this mushroom should be easy—it's the "compact" *Russula,* short and stocky, wider than it is tall, and fairly dense.

Description: When young, the caps are tan to pale rusty brown, but they darken in age to deep tan or dark cinnamon and spread to 4 inches (10 cm) or more over a 2-inch (5-cm) tall, white to tan stalk. The best characteristics for identification are the gills, which are white in youth, often forking near the stalk, and staining brown in age, as well as the cap and stalk, which stain ochre or brown when broken or bruised. The spore print is white.

Comments: A distinct fishy aroma is often noted, especially in older specimens. One author describes it as "better stomped than chomped," and a closely related species from Japan has been reported toxic. We recommend avoiding it for the table.

Season: Summer and fall.

Habit, habitat, and distribution: Single to numerous in hardwoods and mixed woods.

Cap diameter: 5–15 cm (2–6″).

Stalk height: 4–10 cm (1½–4″).

Stalk diameter: 10–30 mm (⅓–1¼″).

VM

This *Russula* has only recently been described and identified. It is a stocky species with orange gills and spores—thus the name *ochri-* (orange), *-compacta* (compact).

Description: This white to tan-capped mushroom has a short, thick stalk and spreading cap. The cap can span 5 inches (12.5 cm) when mature, yet the mushroom still stands less than 3 inches (7.5 cm) tall. The species is distinct among *Russulas* for its deep orange spore print. A second good characteristic is the gills, which often split or "fork" halfway from the stalk to the cap.

Comments: In the photo, notice the deep orange area on a mushroom cap—these are spores from another cap above it. This mushroom, previously known only from Virginia, is an excellent example of the unusual species to be found throughout our mycologically rich state, if only people will start looking for them!

Season: Summer.

Habit, habitat, and distribution: Several to many under hardwoods and in mixed woods.

Cap diameter: 5–12 cm (2–5").

Stalk height: 4–7.5 cm (1½–3").

Stalk diameter: 12–25 mm (½–1").

VM

Note forked gills.

VM

Russula aeruginea
Edible/Choice

The green cap of this mushroom is very distinctive, and logically enough, *aeruginea* is Latin for "green."

Description: When young and in wet weather, the cap is greenish gray, smooth surfaced and shiny, as if wet or sticky, with tiny lines along the edge of the cap. At maturity, the cap is smooth and uncracked. The gills are white and attached directly to the stalk. The stalk is short and composed of brittle tissue that shears off and comes apart cleanly when broken. The spore print color is white to yellowish.

Comments: Edible and delicious, and a common summer mushroom in hardwood forests. It is distinguished from *R. virescens* by being smaller and smooth capped rather than quilted.

Season: Summer and fall.

Habit, habitat, and distribution: Single to numerous under oaks, often found alongside *Lactarius volemus* and *L. corrugis.*

Cap diameter: 3–9 cm (1¼–3¾").

Stalk height: 4–8 cm (1½–3").

Stalk diameter: 10–20 mm (⅓–¾").

VM

You can't help but notice the green color of the cap of this mushroom, and it's no surprise that *virescens* translates to "colored green."

Description: When young, this mushroom closely resembles *R. aeruginea,* but as the cap expands to maturity, the surface breaks up into minute cracks or "quilted" pieces. The gills are white and attached directly to the stalk. Like most *Russulas,* this is a short mushroom with a white, brittle stalk composed of tissue that breaks like Styrofoam plastic foam or chalk, rather than tearing into long fibers when broken. The spore print color is white to yellowish.

Comments: Edible and delicious and a common summer mushroom in hardwood forests. The "quilted" cap distinguishes this mushroom from the smooth-capped *R. aeruginea.* This mushroom is considered one of the best in Europe and Asia as well as in North America.

Season: Summer and fall.

Habit, habitat, and distribution: Single to numerous under oaks, often fruiting at the same time as *Lactarius volemus* and *L. corrugis.*

Cap diameter: 5–13 cm (2–5").

Stalk height: 3–9 cm (1¼–3½").

Stalk diameter: 10–30 mm (⅓–1¼").

DL

Russula ballouii

Not recommended

This *Russula* was named for the late nineteenth-century mycologist W. H. Ballou. He lived and collected mushrooms in New Jersey.

Description: The small caps are reddish brown to brick red, breaking up into small scales against a dull yellow background as the mushroom ages. Tiny lines called striations appear along the cap edge in age. The gills are white to pale yellow, and each gill runs all the way from the margin to the stalk with no forking. The stalk is covered with fine fibers, is colored like the cap, and the colored layer also breaks up into small scales. The spore print color is white.

Comments: The best field characters for this small red *Russula* are the scalelike patches on the cap and stalk and the tiny fibers on the stalk. Edibility has not been reported, and it is not recommended for eating.

Season: Fall.

Habit, habitat, and distribution: Single to several, not common, under hardwoods.

Cap diameter: 2.5–5 cm (1–2″).

Stalk height: 2.5–4 cm (1–1½″).

Stalk diameter: 4–12 mm (⅙–½″).

OM

Genus Lactarius: The *Lactarii*

Members of the genus *Lactarius* (from the Latin word for milk) have a unique characteristic: when the flesh or gills of a fresh young mushroom are cut, nicked, or broken, a milklike latex is observed. The latex may be white, white changing to yellow, orange, red, or blue. Several Lactarii are quite delicious, and many are common during wet summers. Other species are toxic, so it is important to observe the characteristics carefully. *Lactarius* species are easy to learn to recognize and share some or all of the following features:

1. General appearance: The species are generally short, stout, and sturdy, with a cap diameter that is equal to or greater than the height of the stalk. Even in youth, the cap is generally almost flat, with the edges rolled under. As the mushroom ages, the perimeter of the cap expands and rises, leaving the center slightly depressed. Many *Lactarius* species have concentric zones of color in the cap, usually brown, orange, or tan; one species is indigo blue. The outer layer of the cap cannot be peeled back (see *Russula* descriptions). The stalks are short, even, and snap cleanly when broken, like chalk.

2. Gills: The gills of *Lactarius* are evenly spaced, with each gill extending all the way from the stalk to the cap edge, and attached to the stalk. Latex may be seen by cutting or nicking the gills of a young or fresh specimen and observing to see if droplets of liquid form along the cut edges. Cut older specimens in half and look along the zone of gill attachment to the cap. The latex may be clear and watery, milky, or variously colored. In humid climates, the latex can be abundant; in drier times, it may be discerned only by looking for dried globules along injured areas.

If the latex stains yellow or lilac, the mushroom is not edible, as this group of *Lactarius* often causes stomach upsets. If the latex turns some other color, or does not change color, the next step is to smell and taste a small piece of the cap. Touch your tongue to the "milk," or chew a small piece of the cap; then spit it out. You must decide if the taste is mild, peppery, or acrid. In the case of the latter two, you should avoid eating them or even tasting a large piece!

3. Spore print: *Lactarius* is a genus with white, yellowish, or buff-colored spores. It is always important to determine the color of spores.

4. Ecology: *Lactarius* species occur on the ground and are mycorrhizal, and most are associated with a specific host. Knowing the mushroom-host relationship can help you determine where to look for a particular species. More than two hundred species occur in the United States, and a large number of them are native to the eastern United States. Some edible species can be found at any time of the year, with the largest number occurring in summer or fall. Some of the more common species are treated here. L. R. Hesler and A. H. Smith's *North American Species of Lactarius* is available for the more ambitious student.

Lactarius indigo var. *diminutiva* (see opposite page) VM

Lactarius indigo

Edible/Good

The "blue" *Lactarius* really *is* as blue as it looks in the photo! Common throughout the Gulf Coast, it is abundant and edible.

Description: The cap, gills, and stalk of this mushroom are all colored blue. The cap has concentric zones of blue hues, and when cut or bruised, fresh specimens will exude a blue milk. The gills are the best place to check for this blue exudate, though older specimens will often have dried out too much to show the reaction. The spore print color is white.

Comments: This is one mushroom that is normally found in floodplain areas that have recently been under water. Look closely for it, as it is often partly buried under leaves. Two distinct varieties occur frequently throughout the Coastal Plain: one averages 3 inches (7.5 cm) in diameter; the other is smaller, usually about 1 inch (2.5 cm) in diameter, and is called *L. indigo* var. *diminutiva.* Otherwise, the two varieties are very similar. It is a delicious edible.

Season: Summer and fall.

Habit, habitat, and distribution: Single to scattered; occasionally abundant under pines and mixed woods; if you find one, look closely in the same area for more.

Cap diameter: 2.5–10 cm (1–4").

Stalk height: 2.5–6 cm (1–3").

Stalk diameter: 8–12 mm (⅓–½").

VM Closeup of gills showing blue lactation.

AB

Lactarius paradoxus
Edible

The "paradoxical" *Lactarius,* it has mixed purple and blue gills, yet stains green.
Description: The cap has concentric silvery to gray-blue zones on top, and the cap edges may be purple. Turn it over and notice that the gills are purplish blue. The latex is a dark reddish brown milk that stains green. All parts of the flesh will show bright green stains on bruising. The stalk is short and thick. The spore print color is buff to yellow.
Comments: This mushroom is found under live oaks and in lawns. Look closely for it, as it may be so short that it doesn't rise above leaves or grass. One must often cut the fungus in two and observe the latex where gills and cap meet because the latex content is so minimal that it is hard to get a distinct exudate by cutting the gills or bruising it. It is edible, and many consider it quite tasty.

Season: Fall and winter.
Habit, habitat, and distribution: Single to several under red oak and live oak woods, pines or palmetto palms, or in mixed woods and lawns.
Cap diameter: 5–8 cm (2–3″).
Stalk height: 2.5–3 cm (1–1¼″).
Stalk diameter: 10–15 mm (⅜–⅝″).

VM

Edible/Good

This species of *Lactarius* gets its name from the wavy surface of the reddish brown caps, which looks almost corrugated.

Description: *L. corrugis* is a robust species with a dry, reddish brown to rusty brown, wrinkled cap and white to pale brown gills that are attached directly to the stalk. The latex that exudes from the gills when cut or nicked is white, often copious, and stains the gills brown. The spore print color is white.

Comments: These are among the most delicious of the *Lactarius* (along with *L. volemus*). The brown staining by the white latex is distinctive. If the mushroom is very fresh, we suggest baking rather than frying it because the latex can get sticky.

Season: Summer and early fall.

Habit, habitat, and distribution: Solitary to numerous in mixed woods; widely distributed throughout the Coastal Plain and East Texas areas.

Cap diameter: 5–12.5 cm (2–5″).

Stalk height: 5–10 cm (2–4″).

Stalk diameter: 10–20 mm (⅜–¾″).

JL

Lactarius volemus

Edible/Choice

Volemus means "flowing enough to fill the hand" and refers to the copious quantities of latex that exude from this mushroom when it is cut or broken.

Description: This mushroom has a smooth, orange-brown cap that may be slightly velvety but lacks zones of color. The gills are white to cream colored, and the stalk is thick, orange-brown, and velvety. On handling, the mushroom develops a slightly "fishy" odor. The most distinctive feature for identification is the presence of a white latex that stains the flesh brown. The spore print color is white.

Comments: Don't let the odor fool you—these mushrooms are delicious! *Lactarius volemus* and *L. corrugis* are good choices for a beginner to eat provided you are careful to observe the intense brown stains resulting from the cut surfaces, which ooze a white latex at first.

Season: Summer and early fall.

Habit, habitat, and distribution: Single to numerous in mixed woods in warm, humid weather.

Cap diameter: 5–13 cm (2–5").

Stalk height: 5–10 cm (2–4").

Stalk diameter: 10–20 mm (⅜–¾").

OM

Xanthydrorheus translates roughly to "yellow flowing," which describes the clear, watery latex that immediately changes to yellow. This latex will be apparent when the gills of young, fresh mushrooms are cut or nicked.

Description: This is a small mushroom with a somewhat rough, dingy yellowish olive cap that may have a knob-shaped bump in the center. The cap is flat when young, becoming slightly depressed in the center in age. The gills are creamy yellow, fairly thick and distant, and attached directly to the stalk or running shortly down it. The flesh of the cap and stalk are white. The stalk is solid when young, becoming hollow at the base in age. There is no odor, and the taste of the latex is mild. The best feature for identification is the clear latex that immediately turns yellow. The spore print color is white.

Comments: We can find no record of the edibility of this mushroom. The small size and latex color change from white to yellow tends to remove it from the list of edibility candidates. *L. subtomentosus* resembles it physically, but is larger and has a bitter-tasting latex.

Season: Summer and early fall.

Habit, habitat, and distribution: Single to numerous in mixed oak woods in warm, humid weather.

Cap diameter: 0.9–2.5 cm (⅓–1″).

Stalk height: 1.1–2.2 cm (½–9⁄10″).

Stalk diameter: 2–4 mm (1⁄12–⅙″).

AB

Lactarius yazooensis

Not edible

This species of *Lactarius* takes its name from the place where it was first collected, the Yazoo River in Mississippi.

Description: *L. yazooensis* is a medium to large species with a concentrically zoned cap that is depressed at the center and has distinctly inrolled edges, even when fully mature. The concentric zones are alternating yellow and orange-tan. The cap is hairless, sticky in wet weather, and appears shiny and smooth in dry weather. The gills are close and even, white when young, deepening on drying to a dark orange shade, and are attached directly to the short, stubby stalk. The latex that exudes from the gills when cut or nicked is white, and there is no staining reaction. The latex is very bitter and peppery, and during wet weather may be quite profuse. The spore print color is white.

Comments: This is an easy species to recognize, with its inrolled edges, concentric zones of pale orange and white, and the very bitter latex. We do not recommend it for the table, due to the extreme bitterness, which is quite noticeable even after drying.

Season: Summer and early fall.

Habit, habitat, and distribution: Several to many, scattered on the ground under oak. Previously described as known only from Mississippi, but now confirmed throughout the Coastal Plain and East Texas areas.

Cap diameter: 5–12.5 cm (2–5″).

Stalk height: 5–7.5 cm (2–3″).

Stalk diameter: 10–20 mm (3⁄8–3⁄4″).

VM

Toxic

Piperatus is from the Latin for "peppery," and "*glaucescens*" reflects a shade of silvery blue-green. This peppery *Lactarius* has a white latex that dries to a greenish color.

Description: *L. piperatus* var. *glaucescens* is a medium to large species with a smooth, white cap that opens out to become vaselike, with a depressed center. The cap darkens to a dull tan in age. The gills are very close to crowded and even, white to pale cream colored, and attached to and running down the short, thick white stalk. The latex that exudes from the gills when cut or nicked is white when fresh, but on drying, turns to a greenish shade. The latex is very bitter and peppery, and during wet weather may be quite profuse. The spore print color is white.

Comments: This is a very common white, peppery mushroom throughout the forested areas of the Coastal Plain and East Texas. The very bitter latex and unzoned white cap and close gills are the best identification characteristics. This mushroom has been reported to be toxic, and it is certainly too bitter and acrid tasting for eating.

Season: Summer and early fall.

Habit, habitat, and distribution: Several to many, scattered on the ground under oak, common during wet summer months and widely distributed.

Cap diameter: 5–12.5 cm (2–5").

Stalk height: 5–7.5 cm (2–3").

Stalk diameter: 10–20 mm (3/8–3/4").

AB

Lactarius aquifluus

Not recommended

Aquifluus derives from the Latin roots for "water" and "fluid"; not surprisingly, this *Lactarius* secretes a clear, watery latex.

Description: *L. aquifluus* is a small to medium species with a smooth, reddish tan cap and stalk. At maturity, the cap can be flat, depressed in the center, or with an upraised knob, but it almost always retains slightly inrolled edges at the margin. Clear, watery spots are often visible on the cap, especially in humid weather. The flesh of the cap and stalk are a pale tan to reddish brown color. The gills are very close and even, white to pale pinkish tan in age, and directly attached to the stalk or running slightly down it. The latex that exudes from the gills when cut or nicked is clear and watery. The odor is fragrant and sweet, often described as "like brown sugar," and is quite noticeable, even when the mushrooms are dry. The spore print color is buff.

Comments: This mushroom is common in peat bogs of the boreal forests in the northern United States but is also frequently found among mosses in southern woods. The best identification characteristics are the watery latex and watery spots on the cap. This mushroom is not recommended for eating, since it is closely related to other toxic species, but rarely is this mushroom found in enough quantity to be a temptation.

Season: Summer and early fall.

Habit, habitat, and distribution: Several to many, scattered on the ground under oak, common during wet summer months and widely distributed.

Cap diameter: 5–12.5 cm (2–5″).

Stalk height: 5–7.5 cm (2–3″).

Stalk diameter: 10–20 mm (3/8–3/4″).

AB

Lactarius allardii

Not edible

This species, one of the largest of the Lactarii, is named for A. H. Allard, who was an assistant to W. H. Coker, an early American mycologist.

Description: The cap color is quite variable, ranging from light to dark cinnamon brown or light brick red in an adult specimen. The young caps and those covered by leaves or other debris are white, and adult caps may be mottled with several colored areas. The cap is smooth, not zoned, depressed in the center, and the margin is inrolled. The gills are white, crowded, often forked, and attached to the stalk. The stalk is short, white when young and becoming mottled like the cap in age. The best characteristic for identification is the latex, which is white, changing to greenish in about an hour, then to olive, and finally to brownish. The flesh and gills stain a pinkish lavender on bruising. The spore print is white. The taste is quite acrid and bitter.

Comments: This *Lactarius* and all the other acrid, bitter-tasting species are not recommended for the table.

Season: Summer and early fall.

Habit, habitat, and distribution: Single, occasionally several, on the ground under pine and oak. Known from throughout the South and as far north as Michigan.

Cap diameter: 6–15 cm (1¾–6″).

Stalk height: 2–4 cm (¾–1½″).

Stalk diameter: 10–13 mm (⅓–½″).

AB

Lactarius maculatipes

Not recommended

Maculatipes means "spotted foot," referring to the brown spots that are found at the base of the white stalk.

Description: Nearly pure white when young, this mushroom develops a broad cap with depressed center and concentric rings of white, honey yellow, and maize yellow shades. The gills are a pinkish flesh color, often forked near the stalk, and close. The latex is milk white, slowly turning pale yellow as it dries, and bitter to the taste. The stalk is equal, covered with the brown spots for which it was named, becoming hollow in age and tapered at the base. The spore print color is yellowish white.

Comments: Like all acrid, bitter Lactarii, this species is not recommended for the table. It is a common summer species, found under oak, often in large numbers.

Season: Summer into fall.

Habit, habitat, and distribution: Single to numerous, on ground under oak, often in mixed deciduous woods, known from Texas to Florida and north as far as Michigan.

Cap diameter: 5–10 cm (2–4″).

Stalk height: 3–8 cm (1¼–3¼″).

Stalk diameter: 10–23 mm (⅓–1″).

VM

The species' name of this peppery *Lactarius* means "next to" or "near," a reference to its similarity to other species in the genus.

Description: The cap is slightly powdery and depressed at the center, with concentric zones of brownish red and white. The margin of the cap opens fully and in age is uplifted and fluted. The gills are attached to and running down the stalk, white when young, becoming tan in age. The stalk is a pale yellow, becoming a pale olive green when bruised. The latex is white, scanty, does not change color, and tastes quite peppery. The spore print color is pale yellow.

Comments: The best diagnostic characters are the stocky stature and relatively small size, the zoned cap, and the development of olive-tinted stains when injured. Like the other peppery Lactarii, it is not recommended for the table.

Season: Late fall and winter.

Habit, habitat, and distribution: Several to many, on sandy soil under oaks.

Cap diameter: 2.5–6 cm (1–2½").

Stalk height: 1.3–2 cm (½–¾").

Stalk diameter: 8–10 mm (⅓–⅜").

AB

Lactarius salmoneus

Not recommended

This is a very distinctive *Lactarius,* with bright salmon pink to orange gills, for which it gets its species' name.

Description: The caps are small, white, nearly plane or slightly depressed at the center, bruising a reddish color. Turn it over and you'll see the bright salmon orange gills, which, when nicked, will exude a bright salmon-colored latex that tastes mild. The stalk is slender and a salmon orange color. The spore print is creamy white.

Comments: Presumably, this species is edible, but it is too small to make good eating. It is often found during the summer months in floodplain areas.

Season: Summer and fall.

Habit, habitat, and distribution: Single to several, often in wet, swampy areas in floodplains recently under water.

Cap diameter: 2.5–3.8 cm (1–1½").

Stalk height: 2–2.5 cm (¾–1").

Stalk diameter: 3–6 mm (⅛–¼").

AB

The species' name *hygrophoroides* means "like a *Hygrophorus,*" indicating that this *Lactarius* species superficially resembles members of the genus *Hygrophorus* in having a brightly colored cap, widely spaced gills, and a slender stalk.

Description: The cap is an orange cinnamon to reddish brown color and is small in size. The gills are attached to the stalk, white at first, turning cream to buff, and are unusually broad and well separated for a *Lactarius.* The latex is white, copious, and does not stain or change color. The stalk is slender, the same color as the cap or a bit lighter, and is equal in diameter. The spore print color is white.

Comments: This is a delicious edible and can often be collected in sufficient quantity for the table. The medium stature and distant gills that contain unchanging, plentiful white latex are the best field characters.

Season: Summer and early fall.

Habit, habitat, and distribution: Several to many on the ground in mixed conifer and hardwood forests, often fruiting in great quantity during a hot, wet summer.

Cap diameter: 3–10 cm (1¼–4").

Stalk height: 3–5 cm (1¼–2").

Stalk diameter: 5–15 mm (¼–½").

AB

Lactarius croceus

Not edible

Croceus means "like a crocus" or "saffron colored," and as you might expect, the mushroom is bright yellow-orange. This southern species was first collected and described in North Carolina.

Description: The cap is saffron yellow to bright orange, broadly rounded with a depressed center, slimy when young, usually without alternating bands of color. The gills are attached to the stalk, white, becoming honey yellow to cream colored, moderately broad, with some forking. The stalk is slender, equal in diameter, and becomes hollow in age. The latex is white and turns bright yellow when exposed to air, staining the gills and flesh. The latex is highly acrid and peppery. The spore print color is a pale yellow.

Comments: As a rule, the *Lactarius* species that stain yellow and taste acrid should not be eaten. This species is no exception. The best field characters are the combination of the bright orange-yellow cap and stalk, yellow stains, and acrid taste.

Season: Summer and early fall.

Habit, habitat, and distribution: Scattered to numerous on soil in deciduous woods.

Cap diameter: 5–10 cm (2–4").

Stalk height: 3–6 cm (1¼–2½").

Stalk diameter: 10–20 mm (⅓–¾").

AB

Not edible

Chrysorheus means "exuding a gold liquid," an apt reference to the yellow latex that exudes from the gills of this species when cut or nicked.

Description: The cap is a pale yellowish or pale pinkish-orange, with a deeply depressed center in age. The gills are attached to the stalk, with many forks near the stalk, and they are a pale yellow to orange color. The latex is white and copious, quickly changing to yellow. The stalk is equal in diameter, stuffed in youth, becoming hollow in age. The spore print color is pale yellow, and the latex is quite peppery.

Comments: This peppery species commonly under oaks has been reported toxic. In dry weather it is often confused with *L. vinaceorufescens*, which is typically pinkish tan without spots or ridges and often develops purplish red stains in age and most often under pines. However, in both species the white latex will change to yellow in seconds once exposed to the air.

Season: Late summer to early winter.

Habit, habitat, and distribution: Single to several on ground in hardwood and mixed conifer and hardwood forests.

Cap diameter: 3–7 cm (1½–2¾″).

Stalk height: 3–4 cm (1¼–1½″).

Stalk diameter: 10–15 mm (⅖–⅗″).

OM

Family Tricholomataceae: The Tricholomas

The Tricholomataceae family is the largest, the most diverse, and, for beginning mycologists, the most difficult family of white-spored mushrooms to learn to identify. Over one thousand species have been distinguished in more than seventy-five genera.

There is no easy definition that can be used to recognize members of this family. Rather, many authors suggest placing mushrooms in this family by *eliminating* them from the five other major pale-spored mushroom genera, as follows:

Members of the Tricholomataceae can be distinguished from members of the genus *Amanita* because they lack a cup, and from the Lepiotas because those that have a veil do not have free gills. They do not exude a latex like the Lactarii do, nor do they have the brittle tissue composition of the Russulas. And lastly, they lack the waxy gills of the *Hygrophorus* species.

In this book for beginners, we are going to deviate from scientific classification schemes and separate this large family into three "divisions" (a nontaxonomic term) based on size and growth habit. We refer to the first division as "shelving mushrooms"—those that grow on wood and often have a short, lateral stalk or lack a stalk so that these mushrooms appear like "shelves." The second division is the "larger" species—those that are fleshy, growing on the ground, and have gills that run down the stalk. The third division is the "smaller" species—thin fleshed, often fragile and slim stalked, usually growing on the ground. One genus may have representatives in several or all of these divisions.

As you compare your specimen to the descriptions and photos included in this book, remember that we are including only the most common and easily distinguished species. Don't let yourself get frustrated if you have trouble identifying your mushrooms, especially in this section. A field guide such as this has space limitations and cannot include all the known species, so if you have trouble identifying a mushroom, it is not necessarily due to your lack of skills. Learning to place your specimen in the correct group, to say, "It's a member of the Tricholomataceae family," is an accomplishment of no small merit. After all, mushroom identification is a *lifetime* adventure—that's the challenge of it!

The Shelving Tricholomas

This "division" (an artificial grouping based on similar growth habit rather than on structural likenesses) consists of a large number of the members of the Tricholomataceae family that grow on wood and form gilled fruiting bodies that have noncentral or nonexistent stalks and expand in layers, much like shelves.

1. General appearance: These species have large, fleshy caps with stalks that are either off-center, growing out of the side of the cap, or entirely absent. Rows of these caps appear to emerge directly from limbs, trees, or buried wood, and they frequently overlap in wide layers. *Pleurotus* is a common example, found across Texas, frequently on live or dead willow or other trees. During rainy times of the year, large clusters of smooth, white, fleshy caps emerge directly from the wood, so numerous that it is not uncommon to collect many pounds from a single fruiting.

2. Gills: The gills of these shelving mushrooms are usually distinct and thin edged. The gills are often white or light colored and are frequently attached to and running down the stalk in those species where stalks are present.

3. Spore print: The spores of these species include many pale hues, including white, light pinkish, lilac, pale yellow, and light tan. As with all fungi, it is always important to take a spore print by placing a young cap, gill-side down, on white paper for six to twelve hours or until enough spores have been deposited to determine their color.

4. Ecology: These mushrooms are found on living or dead wood and play an important role in primary decay. They are also of economic importance because of their tendency to carry out this decay process in wood and trees that humans do not wish to see damaged.

In this group, the best edible species is *Pleurotus ostreatus,* the "oyster mushroom" (so called because the white caps look much like oyster shells).

Pleurotus ostreatus

Edible/Choice

The genus name means "side cap" and refers to the stalk being off-center; *ostreatus* means "like an oyster" and refers to the cap shape. This is a delicious edible that is easy to learn to recognize and that is found in all parts of Texas on pine, oak, and willow.

Description: The large and meaty caps are smooth and colored white to gray. The gills are also white and medium distant. The gills of older specimens show a yellow coloration and lose their firmness. The stalks are often nearly nonexistent, as the caps emerge in rows or layers directly from living or dead trees. The spores have a lilac or lilac-gray color in deep deposit.

Comments: We have seen instances where thirty or more pounds can be collected from a single log. Look on trees, stumps, and logs along river bottoms, following good rains. A note to the mycophagist: Trim away any parts that are old, tough, or discolored, and eat only young, firm specimens. Small black beetles are often found hiding between the gills, but a brisk "shake" of the cap will usually dislodge them.

Season: Can be found at any time of year, but most common in cooler months of spring, fall, and winter.

Habit, habitat, and distribution: On dead or often on decayed parts of living trees, especially willow and cottonwood.

Cap diameter: 5–15 cm (2–6").

Stalk height: 0–2 cm (less than an inch).

Stalk diameter: 0–5 mm (less than ¼").

JL

This species is named *dryinus,* meaning "oak," because it is found on oak trees, but this variety occurs on other types of trees also—the ones pictured here are on beech.
Description: The caps are white and are covered with fine gray-brown scales. The caps are thick and fleshy, and the edges of the cap are rolled under in youth. The gills are white and descend down the stalk. The stalk is thick, and a veil is present in young specimens; the veil disintegrates to a thin line or ring zone on the stalk in age. The spore print color is white.
Comments: The best diagnostic features are the faint veil and the scales on the cap. The photo illustrates specimens with unusually long stalks. Edibility not known.
Season: Summer and fall.
Habit, habitat, and distribution: Single to several arising on dead (or occasionally, living) hardwoods; occasionally common on beech in parts of East Texas.
Cap diameter: 4–15 cm (1⅔–6″).
Stalk height: 7.5–15 cm (3–6″).
Stalk diameter: 15–40 mm (⅗–1½″).

VM

Panus rudis

Not edible

Panus, which means "tumor" (so named for the appearance of the young rounded caps that appear to form like expanding blobs on the tree's surface), is a tropical genus that has several members found throughout the Coastal Plain and South and East Texas. The species' name, *rudis,* means "reddish," and these nearly stalkless mushrooms with tiny stiff hairs on the cap look like hairy red "ears."

Description: The caps are a dull pinkish brown to reddish brown and are covered with tiny hairs. When young, the edges of the cap are inrolled. Underneath, the gills are white and fairly close together. The stalks are very short or almost nonexistent. Many caps frequently appear in overlapping rows from dead limbs or trees. The flesh is tough and stringy when broken or pulled apart. The spore print color is white.

Comments: This species is commonly found on recently downed hardwood (in later stages of decay, other species take over). Not edible; it is tough and bitter.

Season: Present at all times of the year, but most prevalent in the hot summer months.

Habit, habitat, and distribution: Several to many on freshly downed hardwoods; a tropical species that is known from southern, southeastern, and eastern parts of Texas.

Cap diameter: 1–5 cm (1/3–2").

Stalk height: 0–1.25 cm (up to 1/2").

Stalk diameter: 0–6 mm (up to 1/4").

DG

Anthracophyllum lateritium

Not edible

This is a tropical species known from South America; the species' name means "brick colored."

Description: This is a small shelflike fungus that usually forms in large numbers on downed logs; the caps are smooth and a dull brown color. The gills are the most notable feature—they are a deep red color and ridgelike. There is no stalk, and the caps are like hemispheres growing directly out of the wood. The spore print color is white.

Comments: Edibility has not been reported, and therefore, it is not recommended to be eaten. This tropical species is only known in the United States from the Gulf Coast area. Be sure to check the spore print because small species of *Crepidotus* appear similar but have a brown spore print.

Season: Spring and summer.

Habit, habitat, and distribution: Several to numerous, occasionally in large masses, in rows on decaying wood.

Cap diameter: 0.6–2.5 cm (¼–1").

VM

Phyllotopsis nidulans

Not edible

This mushroom got its scientific name because it looks like small "nests" (*nidulans* means "nesting"). The most notable features, however, are the distinct orange color and foul odor, most pronounced in age.

Description: The caps of these mushrooms are deep orange, covered with fine hairs, and the gills are a lighter orange shade. Rows of these caps are fused together and often overlap. There may be a very short stalk or none at all, as the caps often emerge directly from the substrate—usually a downed log. The spore print color is a pale pink to apricot pink.

Comments: This orange, fuzzy mushroom is easy to spot, and to confirm your identification, smell the gills of a cap. Specimens growing on hardwoods have a very obnoxious odor (those on pine are much milder). The odor has been described as "of rotting cabbage." Consider this one inedible—it is reported to taste as bad as it smells.

Season: Fall and winter.

Habit, habitat, and distribution: Several to many, in overlapping rows, on downed wood, especially conifers; common in winter.

Cap diameter: 1–5 cm (⅓–2").

Stalk height: 0–1.25 cm (up to ½").

Stalk diameter: 0–6 mm (up to ¼").

DL

The Larger Tricholomas

Among the large and diverse Tricholomataceae family, an artificial "division" can be distinguished of large, fleshy species with central stalks and with or without veils that grow on the ground or on wood. Some species grow in clusters from a single base; others occur in groups from individual bases; all have distinct gills and pale-colored spores.

1. General appearance: This is a complex and difficult group precisely because the species often typify "mushrooms." The fruiting bodies are often large, soft, and fleshy. Some species are covered with velvety "hairs"; others are smooth fleshed. The stalks are generally even, emerging from the ground or from wood that is either buried or above the surface. The stalks are usually smooth, with or without a ring.

2. Gills: The gills are white or pale colored, and attachment to the stalk may be either direct, with a small free "notch" at the bottom of the gill, or running down the stalk. Attachment can be difficult to determine, and in looking for this characteristic use specimens in which the cap has fully expanded. The lower edge of most species is smooth, but in one genus (*Lentinus*), the gills have edges that are serrated or "saw toothed."

3. Spore print: The spore print colors found in the species described here include white, pinkish, and cream. A spore print should always be taken by placing the mushroom cap, gill-side down, on white paper for six to twelve hours or until a deposit of spores can be seen on the paper. This is especially important if you want to eat the mushrooms. Several edible and good species found in this family can be confused with toxic species that look similar but have darker colored spores.

4. Ecology: Most species in this artificial grouping are decayers of dead wood, including standing trees and buried wood. Several species have importance economically because they are parasites of oaks or pine trees, including several species of *Armillaria.*

Several edible and good species are listed in this section, but there are also toxic species, so please be especially sure of your identification and carefully compare the descriptions and characteristics shown here with your specimen. Only a few of several hundred species that you might find are illustrated, so remember the first rule of mycophagy: "When in doubt, throw it out!"

Armillaria tabescens

Edible/Good

The species' name *tabescens* means "decomposing," an apt description for this common edible appearing in the fall throughout Texas as autumn rains drench the state.

Description: The golden brown caps of this mushroom form dense clusters with inrolled edges. Tiny hairs cover the caps, and the gills run down the stalk. The stalks are smooth, and there is no ring. Often many mushrooms emerge from a common base around the roots of living or dead trees. The spore print color is white and can often be seen on the tops of caps that are below others.

Comments: These mushrooms are edible, but be sure to gather them young and fresh and cook them *thoroughly.* Stomach upsets can occur from insufficient cooking, and the mushrooms should be fresh and firm. The clusters fade into "gloopy" brownish black piles, as their name implies, but you certainly don't want to use that characteristic to confirm your identification before consuming. In our experience, *Armillaria tabescens* is far more common than *A. mellea* in Texas.

Season: Fall; expect these when the first drenching fall rains come.

Habit, habitat, and distribution: Clustered in groups of several to many. These are parasites of oak and fruit at the base of living or dead trees. When these are out in our Houston neighborhoods, they seem to be on every tree stump. We have also seen great masses fruiting on the roots of large trees that have been uprooted by tornadoes and hurricanes. The parasitic activities of this mushroom weaken the roots and probably contribute to the trees' destruction by heavy winds.

Cap diameter: 3–10 cm broad (1¼–4").

Stalk height: 5–15 cm (2–6").

Stalk diameter: 6–20 mm (¼–¾").

VM

Mellea means honey, and this is the "honey mushroom," a delicious edible, though also a tree killer. Look at the base of the cluster at night for fox-fire—the luminescent mycelium.

Description: This mushroom fruits in clusters of mushrooms with honey-colored caps that are covered with tiny hairlike fibers. The edges of the caps are inrolled when young and expand in age. The stalks of the mushrooms are long, even, and smooth, with a ring present. Many mushrooms frequently arise from a common base on living roots and dead stumps. The spore print color is white.

Comments: Cook *thoroughly*! Stomach upsets can occur from insufficient cooking, and the mushrooms should be gathered while fresh and firm. Be certain of your identification, and compare your specimens carefully both to *Armillaria tabescens,* without the ring, and to the orange, toxic *Omphalotus olearius,* which has a similar clustered growth habit and can occur at the same time of year. Look for the ring, and confirm the white spore print to avoid errors.

Season: Fall.

Habit, habitat, and distribution: Several to numerous in clusters from the roots of living and dead hardwoods.

Cap diameter: 3–10 cm broad (1¼–4″).

Stalk height: 5–15 cm (2–6″).

Stalk diameter: 6–20 mm (¼–¾″).

JL

Hohenbuehelia geogenia

Edible/Fair

The species' name means "of the earth" and refers to the growth habit on the ground.

Description: About the size and shape of shoehorns, these mushrooms have hazel brown to yellow brown caps and white gills. They emerge, often in clusters, from highly mulched ground (we find them on wood chips) or dead wood. They are flexible and break only when doubled over. The stalk is distinct and white and usually off-center. The tissue inside the cap turns deep blue in Melzer's reagent. The spore print color is white, but the spore powder turns blue in Melzer's reagent.

Comments: Other than cap color, microscopic features differentiate this species from the common and smaller *H. petaloides.* Both species are common on jogging trails in damp weather and is considered edible, though not choice. We have not tried them.

Season: Summer and fall.

Habit, habitat, and distribution: Several to many on buried wood or mulch. Widely distributed.

Cap diameter: 2–7 cm (¾–3″).

Stalk height: 1–4 cm (⅓–1½″).

Stalk diameter: 6–25 mm (¼–1″).

JL

This mushroom is commonly hunted in Europe, where it is called the "wood blewit," but in this case, the scientific name (meaning "nude") better describes the color and texture of this mushroom. In some older books the genus name may be listed as *Lepista.*

Description: When fresh, the smooth cap is a pale shade of violet or bluish gray; in age the cap is usually tan. The cap is convex when young, with the edges rolled under. The gills are close together, notched at their attachment to the stalk, and are usually light to very dark lavender when young (fading in age). The stalk is smooth and is also a light lavender color. The mushroom has a swollen base, with no trace of fibers along the stalk. The lavender color will be quite noticeable if you slice the mushroom in half lengthwise. The spore print color is a dull pinkish.

Comments: Always check the spore print color! Other genera of rusty-spored mushrooms have some lavender to purple members, such as *Cortinarius alboviolaceus. Clitocybe nuda* is an excellent edible, with delightful flavor and solid texture. Notice especially the short, stocky stature of this mushroom—its overall appearance is one of the best identification characteristics. These mushrooms are decomposers of straw, litter, and grass, and one mycelium patch may fruit several times in a season. They can be inoculated into mulch piles by placing the caps on the mulch and allowing them to cast spores into it.

Season: All year, but especially prevalent during cool, damp weather.

Habit, habitat, and distribution: Single to numerous on decaying leaves, grass, mulch, and so forth. Widely distributed and common during cool, damp weather.

Cap diameter: 4–10 cm (1½–3").

Stalk height: 2.5–7 cm (1–3").

Stalk diameter: 10–25 mm (⅓–1").

VM

Clitocybe gibba
Edible/Good

The genus name *Clitocybe* translates to "sloping head," indicative of the "funnel" shape of many of its members. This common species is often called "common funnel cap" and is typical of members of the genus.

Description: This species has the very smooth flesh typical of the genus, which is often described as resembling fine pigskin leather. The cap and stalk are a light yellow tan, and the gills extend some distance down the stalk. At maturity, the cap develops a deep depression that resembles a laboratory funnel, which is probably the best characteristic to distinguish it from others of the same genus. The base is equal, not bulbous, solid not hollow, and the spore print is white.

Comments: Edible and good, this is a common decomposer of pine litter and is often found among stands of pine. It can be found in quantity during wet summers, though the mushroom is generally solitary to scattered.

Season: Summer and fall.

Habit, habitat, and distribution: Single to numerous, scattered on ground under pines.

Cap diameter: 3–8 cm (1¼–3″).

Stalk height: 3–8 cm (1¼–3″).

Stalk diameter: 4–10 mm (⅙–⅓″).

AB

This species was named in Europe where it is often found fruiting on olive trees (*olearius* means "of the olive"). It is one of several species that are commonly called "jack-o'-lanterns" because the mushrooms are luminescent—they glow in the dark. However, it may take five or six minutes in total darkness to have one's eyes adjust to the low level of luminescence. In many older books this species is called *Clitocybe illudens* or *Omphalotus illudens.*

Description: These are large orange-brown mushrooms (the color is much like an old pumpkin) with orange gills running halfway down the stalk. The gills are sharp edged with no veins between them. They frequently occur in groups of three or four emerging from a single base on dead wood, and the clusters are easy to spot. The spore print color is white, and the odor is definitely musty.

Comments: Fresh specimens (and even fairly dried-out caps that have been rehydrated for several hours by wrapping wet paper towels around the stalks) will emit an eery greenish light from the gills for hours after being picked. They are not edible, causing violent stomach upset (refer to the chapter on mushroom toxins for a description of a toxic reaction to this mushroom). They grow on decaying wood, but the wood is often well decomposed and buried under litter, making this important characteristic difficult to distinguish. They are easily mistaken for the edible *Cantharellus cibarius,* and should be compared closely to the description for that mushroom.

Season: Fall and winter.

Habit, habitat, and distribution: Usually several mushrooms are found in a cluster, on downed hardwood; often found in floodplain areas.

Cap diameter: 4–16 cm (1½–6″).

Stalk height: 4–20 cm (1½–8″).

Stalk diameter: 10–40 mm (⅜–1½″).

VM

Panus crinitis
Not edible

This is a tropical species that takes its name, *crinitis,* from the long, fibrous hairs that cover the cap.

Description: These small (1 to 3 inches [2.5–7.5 cm] across) brown mushrooms usually appear in a cluster on wood. They have a distinctly depressed center and tough, hairy, fibrous fruiting bodies, which are difficult to cut or tear and are frequently seen in warm, wet weather. The gills descend along the stalks, which are very thin but tough. The spore print color is white.

Comments: Reported edible, and it is eaten in Central American countries, but we find it too tough and hairy to eat. It is a common sight on downed hardwoods throughout the Coastal Plain, Big Thicket, and East Texas areas. Due to its tough, leathery texture, it often dries out and remains on the logs where it fruited for months.

Season: Can be seen at any time of year, but fresh fruitings usually occur during the wet months of summer or fall.

Habit, habitat, and distribution: Scattered to numerous on downed wood, each mushroom arising from its own base but often covering an area several feet long along the trunk of a downed tree.

Cap diameter: 2.5–7.5 cm (1–3″).

Stalk height: 2–4 cm (¾–1½″).

Stalk diameter: 2–4 mm (1/12–1/6″).

DG

Not edible

This is a tropical species that was discovered in North Carolina and named by Miles Joseph Berkeley and Moses Ashley Curtis, two prominent British amateur mycologists, in 1868. In the United States, it is found only in the South, and East Texas probably marks its westernmost boundary.

Description: This mushroom is easiest to identify when found young, as pictured here. At this stage, the cap is small and tightly inrolled, and the entire mushroom is a deep purple color. As it ages, the color fades to cinnamon brown, and the cap spreads to an inch or more in diameter. At all stages, the minute hairs on all surfaces give it a velvetlike appearance. The mushrooms arise from a hard knot of fungus tissue called a *sclerotium* and can be found in the same places year after year. The spore print color is white.

Comments: Part of what makes mushroom identifying in Texas so challenging is the overlapping ranges of southern, tropical, and desert mushrooms with northern species. Adding to the challenge is the emerging new information provided by mycologists, which has resulted in this mushroom being moved from *Lentinus* to *Panus* where it now belongs.

Season: Spring and summer.

Habit, habitat, and distribution: Several, scattered; on wood, often buried.

Cap diameter: 0.6–2.5 cm (¼–1″).

Stalk height: 5–10 cm (2–4″).

Stalk diameter: 6–12 mm (¼–½″).

VM

Lentinus lepideus
Edible/Choice

The genus *Lentinus* (which means "pliant") contains several thick-fleshed species with the distinctive characteristic that the gills have serrated or "saw-toothed" edges. The species' name *lepideus* means "scaly" and refers to the scales along the cap and stalk.

Description: This species appears on pine or hardwoods in clusters of three to five large white, thick-fleshed mushrooms covered with yellow, brown, or reddish brown scales on the cap and stalk. When young, a ring may be present, though it disappears quite early. The gills are white, crowded, and distinctly serrated along the lower edge. The spore print color is white.

Comments: This species is variable in the amount and color of the scales on the cap and stalk. It is sometimes found on telephone poles and other creosoted wood. A similar species, *Lentinus tigrinus* (the species' name is from the root for "tiger," because its scales often resemble stripes, especially at the base of the stalk), is found on hardwoods in fall and winter. They can be distinguished by examining the spores under the microscope. Both species are among the best edibles in the region, though you shouldn't eat any found growing on creosoted wood because the mushrooms can pick up toxic chemicals from the treated wood. This meaty mushroom should be considered for commercial value as a crop in Texas in the future. The commercial "shiitake" (pronounced "she-ta-key") is a related species, *Lentinus edodes,* found in similar habitats in Asia.

Season: Spring and summer, immediately after rains.

Habit, habitat, and distribution: Several in clusters on downed pine, occasionally on hardwood, often recurring through the hot summer until the first hard freeze.

Cap diameter: 4–15 cm (1½–6").

Stalk height: 5–8 cm (2–3").

Stalk diameter: 12–40 mm (½–1½").

AB

Edibility unknown

Detonsus means "sheared off," perhaps referring to the caps, which often have an off-center stalk so that it looks as if half the cap is missing. This small mushroom fruits on living or dead hardwoods and is a common tropical species.

Description: The caps of this mushroom are thin fleshed and tan. These mushrooms may be seen fruiting along the sides of dead trees that are still standing. This growth habit and the white, saw-toothed gills, which stain red when bruised, are the best identification characteristics. The gills are very close together and direct or running slightly down the thick stalk, which is the same color as the cap, and they are usually attached at the edge. The base of the stalk may be slightly enlarged, and the spore print color is white.

Comments: Edibility of this mushroom has not been reported. It has a slightly "radishy" odor. Little is known about this tropical species.

Season: Summer.

Habit, habitat, and distribution: Scattered to numerous along the trunk and branches of dead, or occasionally living, trees. Found in the tropics, extending north along the Coastal Plain and into East Texas.

Cap diameter: 2.5–5 cm (1–2").

Stalk height: 2.5–4 cm (1–1½").

Stalk diameter: 6–9 mm (¼–⅜").

VM

Oudemansiella radicata
Edible

The genus name for this mushroom honors C. A. J. A. Oudemans, a Dutch botanist and physician. The species' name *radicata* means "having a root." The "root" is actually the elongated base of the stalk.

Description: The caps are bell shaped when young, opening to flat at maturity. They are viscid, brown, sometimes white, wrinkled with a darker spot in the center, with thin, watery flesh. The gills are white, distant, sometimes with brown edges, and attached directly to the stalk. The stalk is quite long (often three to five times longer than the cap diameter) and quite straight and erect above ground. There is no ring, and when the stalk is carefully removed from the ground, a "rooting" base up to 4 or 5 inches (10–12.5 cm) long will be found. The spore print is white.

Comments: Formerly *Collybia radicata,* this is a common mushroom throughout East Texas and the Coastal Plain. It is edible, but not choice.

Season: Summer and fall.

Habit, habitat, and distribution: Usually single to several, scattered, on or near hardwood stumps and buried wood.

Cap diameter: 2.5–7.5 cm (1–3″).

Stalk height: 7.5–15 cm (3–6″).

Stalk diameter: 6–8 mm (¼–⅓″).

VM

The Smaller Tricholomas

Among the species found in the large and diverse family called the Tricholomataceae is a group of mushrooms that are quite small in stature. Here, we have artificially grouped those species that are small in stature (less than 4 inches [10 cm] tall), and which have slender, often fragile stalks. This group contains some members that are technically edible, but most are too small to be worth trying to collect for the table.

1. General appearance: The species described here include many of the tiny, delicate species that are found growing on decaying leaves and small twigs. The caps are generally thin fleshed, and the stalks are often slender and fragile. A few of these species will be found only in the early morning, as they dry out in the warm sunshine and disappear by midday, and if you try to collect them, they may wither before you can get them home.

2. Gills: The gills of mushrooms in this artificial division are frequently thin and distant (quite far apart). In most species the gills are white and often running down the stalk or attached directly to it.

3. Spore print: The spore print of these mushrooms is white, yellowish, or other light colors. Often, a spore print is difficult to obtain, as the cap tends to dry out before the spores can be released. When taking a spore print from thin-fleshed mushrooms, we recommend covering the cap with an inverted paper cup to prevent excess drying.

4. Ecology: Generally, the most important ecological role of these mushrooms is in the decay of dead grass, mulch, and forest litter. Some, however, are mycorrhizal species.

These mushrooms are among the first to emerge after a soaking rain, often coming up very quickly, or they fruit as the wood dries out. We are often asked about the edibility of these species, and many are edible, but most are too tiny and thin fleshed for the table. And if you consider normal shrinkage from water loss during cooking, we say, "Why bother?" We enjoy these delicate species for their flowerlike beauty and for the challenge of knowing the species and photographing them.

Xeromphalina campanella

Nonpoisonous

The species' name *campanella* means "bell shaped," referring to the shape of the cap of these tiny mushrooms. *Xeromphalina* is a combination of the Latin roots for "dry" and "navel or umbilicus," which refer to the smooth, nonsticky caps that are indented at the center.

Description: The most noticeable feature of these small, tan to orange mushrooms is their tendency to fruit in great groups, often several hundred or more, on downed conifers. The caps are bell shaped in youth. As the mushrooms mature, the outer part of the cap expands and rises, leaving the center depressed, much like a navel. The distant, thick gills run down the stalk, and the cap flesh becomes quite thin, yellowish, and almost translucent. The stalks are thin but tough and fibrous, curve up from the substrate, and are yellow at the top and brown at the base, with a distinct pad of thick, cottony, yellow-orange fibers at the base and no ring.

Comments: These tiny mushrooms are too small to be of value for eating, but no species in this genus is known to be toxic. A closely related species, *Xeromphalina kauffmanii*, occurs on hardwood stumps and logs. It has straight stalks but is also present in dense clusters.

Season: Any wet time of year.

Habit, habitat, and distribution: Several to quite numerous on downed conifers; to be expected in any deep woods where downed logs are soaked and are slow to dry out. Known from the Texas Coastal Plain and from the East Texas forested areas.

Cap diameter: 0.3–2.5 cm (1⁄8–1″).

Stalk height: 1–5 cm (2⁄5–2″).

Stalk diameter: 0.5–3 mm (up to 1⁄8″).

AB

Laccaria laccata
Nonpoisonous

The names *Laccaria* and *laccata* both derive from the Latin "paint" (from the same root as our "lacquer"), and many members of this genus are brightly colored in pinks, reds, and violets. This one, however, is a fairly drab pinkish brown.
Description: The cap of this mushroom is about the size of a nickel, smooth, dry, and colored pinkish brown. The center is usually depressed in mature specimens, and the edges of the cap may be wavy. The gills are thick, distant, and usually a light pink color. The most notable feature is the long, slender, tough and fibrous stalk, colored like the cap. (This is one mushroom you can grab and yank out of the ground—the entire stalk will easily pull free.) The base of the stalk may have a mass of white, cottony fibers clinging to it. The color of the spore print is pale lilac.
Comments: This mushroom is so common that it has been referred to as a "mycological weed." One of the first mushrooms to appear after rains, it often remains in place for several weeks and is said to be edible, but not very tasty. All species of *Laccaria* are mycorrhizal with forest trees. Similar species include *Laccaria amethystina,* which has a violet coloring overall, and *L. bicolor,* which has cottony thick purple fibers at the stalk base. The gills are waxy like those of *Hygrophorus,* but the pale lilac spore print and spines on the spores distinguish it from *Hygrophorus.*
Season: All year.
Habit, habitat, and distribution: Scattered to numerous on sandy soil, often among the first spring mushrooms and also among the last winter ones. Extremely common throughout the United States.
Cap diameter: 1–4 cm (⅓–1½").
Stalk height: 2–10 cm (¾–4").
Stalk diameter: 4–8 mm (⅙–⅓").

VM

Laccaria amethystina
Nonpoisonous

The species' name *amethystina* reflects the pale lavender color of this mushroom, which reminded W. A. Murrill, the mycologist who first described it, of amethysts.
Description: This is a small mushroom, with the cap, stalk, and gills all a delicate shade of lavender. The cap is thin fleshed, with widely spaced, uneven gills. The center of the cap is often depressed in mature specimens. The most notable features are the overall violet color and small stature. The color of the spore print is pale lilac.
Comments: This small mushroom is often found on sandy soil under or near live oaks. It is a mycorrhizal species. The gills are waxy like those of *Hygrophorus,* but the pale lilac spore print and round spores distinguish it from *Hygrophorus.*

Season: All year.
Habit, habitat, and distribution: Scattered to numerous on sandy soil, often among the first spring mushrooms and also among the last winter ones.
Cap diameter: 0.5–2 cm (1⁄5–3⁄4″).
Stalk height: 2–7.5 cm (1–3″).
Stalk diameter: 4–8 mm (1⁄6–1⁄3″).

VM

This tiny purple mushroom has a very appropriate name: it comes from the combination of *iantha* for violet and *cephala* for head.

Description: The violet color of the cap of this delicate mushroom makes it hard to ignore. The cap is very thin fleshed, with fine lines along the cap edges. The gills are white and widely spaced. The stalk, white and lavender to gray, is slightly enlarged toward the base. The spore print color is white.

Comments: Too tiny to be of value for eating and generally tasteless, these translucent lilac mushrooms are a delight for the eyes. Oddly enough, there is a slight "gunpowder" odor to them. Other species of *Collybia* such as *Collybia dryophila* and *C. subsulphurea* are similar in stature but have brown caps and white gills in the former and close yellowish gills in the latter species. They are common on decaying leaves during cool wet spring weather.

Season: Summer.

Habit, habitat, and distribution: Scattered to numerous under pines, often fruiting in large troops. In our experience they are often in low spots that are occasionally under water.

Cap diameter: 2.5–5 cm (1–2").

Stalk height: 2.5–7.5 cm (1–3").

Stalk diameter: 3–6 mm (1/8–1/3").

VM

Strobilurus conigenoides
Not edible

The genus name *Strobilurus* means "like one that arises with a cone" and indicates this tiny mushroom's growth medium—magnolia cones. It is often listed as a *Collybia* in older guides.

Description: The caps are about ½ inch (1.25 cm) across, light tan to yellow, slightly darker in the center. The gills are white, distinctly but not widely separated, and attached directly to the very slender, almost translucent white stalks. In warm wet weather, several to many small tan mushrooms with slender, hairlike stalks will be found growing on decaying magnolia cones. The spore print color is white.

Comments: This is one of several species that are found only on magnolia cones, and it is indicative of the selectivity some mushrooms demonstrate for a substrate. It can be found anywhere that magnolia cones are allowed to decay. The caps are too small to be considered for edibility.

Season: Summer and fall.

Habit, habitat, and distribution: Several to many, growing on decaying magnolia cones; usually with separate bases, but often in quantity. We have also found it growing on sweet-gum balls.

Cap diameter: 0.5–1.5 cm (¼–½").

Stalk height: 2–5 cm (¾–2").

Stalk diameter: 1–1.5 mm (less than 1/10").

VM

Not edible

This small mushroom gets its name from the Latin root *visc-*, meaning "slippery or viscous." The genus *Mycena* is typified by very small mushrooms, often so thin as to be translucent, with white spores.

Description: This fragile mushroom has a gray, conic cap that has a tinge of yellow. In age, the cap looks quite pale and ashlike. The gills are somewhat distant and pale white. The stalk is thin, pliant, and pale yellow, with patches of white, cottony fibers appearing like fine threads at the base. The odor is strongly disagreeable, and the spore print color is white.

Comments: This small mushroom and others of the same genus are not found in sufficient quantity for the table. They are often difficult to identify because there are more than two hundred species known from the United States. It is good to recognize the genus, but it may be folly to try to make a specific determination. For the advanced amateur, the standard reference is Alexander Smith's *North American Species of Mycena.*

Season: Late fall and winter.

Habit, habitat, and distribution: Single to several on pine duff and at the base of pine trees.

Cap diameter: 1–3 cm (⅓–1¼").

Stalk height: 5–9 cm (2–3½").

Stalk diameter: 2–3 mm (up to ⅛").

JL

Mycena inclinata

Not recommended

This, the "inclined" *Mycena,* is common on pine stumps throughout eastern North America. The fibers along the lower half of the stalk and the clustered habit are the best identification characteristics.

Description: The thin-fleshed caps are pale brown to gray, conical in youth, opening to broadly bell shaped. The gills are close and white, attached to the stalk, but readily pulling away. The stalk is equal, tubular, and hollow, covered along the lower half with tiny fibrous spots. The spore print color is white.

Comments: Too small to be considered for the table, this delicate mushroom often fruits in large groups on downed pine. Since there are more than two hundred species of *Mycena* known from the United States, this genus is often difficult to pin down to species accurately—and usually, the thin-fleshed specimens dry out and disappear before you can confirm your identification.

Season: Spring and fall.

Habit, habitat, and distribution: Densely gregarious on decaying hardwood and conifer logs and stumps during spring and fall.

Cap diameter: 1–3 cm (⅓–1¼").

Stalk height: 5–10 cm (2–4").

Stalk diameter: 1.5–3 mm (up to ⅛").

VM

Not recommended

The species' name *albuscorticis* is from the Latin roots for "white" and "leather," combining to form an appropriate name for this tough, white mushroom.

Description: The cap is white, thin fleshed, and nearly translucent. The gills are attached to the stalk, thick and moderately well separated. The stalk is central or off-center to the cap, somewhat thicker at the base, solid and shiny white above, blackish at the base. The spore print color is white.

Comments: This species, too small to be of value for the table, is often found on blackberry stalks and twigs and stalks of other shrubs. It has also been called *Marasmius candidus* and *M. magnisporus;* it may be one of a complex of closely related species.

Season: Summer and fall.

Habit, habitat, and distribution: Single to several, often found in rows on berry bushes and other decaying litter.

Cap diameter: 1–3 cm (1/3–1 1/4").

Stalk height: 1–2 cm (1/3–2/3").

Stalk diameter: 1–1.5 mm (up to 1/12").

JL

Family Pluteaceae: *Pluteus* and *Volvariella*

There are two mushroom families that have spores that are pink to salmon, flesh colored or rose in deposit. The Pluteaceae family is the most commonly seen in Texas and contains two major genera: *Volvariella* and *Pluteus.*

1. General appearance: Members of this family are medium sized with smooth central stalks. They are usually found growing on wood or other decaying plant material. *Pluteus* species are always on wood and lack a cup, and *Volvariella* species may be on hay bales, straw, corncobs, or wood, and have a distinct cup called a *volva.*

2. Gills: All species in this family have free gills, that is, the gills do not come all the way to the stalk but leave a distinct gap. This feature is best seen in mature specimens, when the cap is fully expanded. The gap between the ends of the gills and the stalk will be revealed. The gills are white and crowded in young specimens, but deepen to a dull rose color as the spores mature.

3. Cup (volva): Members of the genus *Volvariella* have a distinct cup, a saclike piece of tissue left in place at the base of the mushroom when the mushroom expands to full height. *Pluteus* species lack this cup.

4. Spore print: The primary distinguishing factor between members of this family and others is the pale pink, flesh pink, or rose pink color of the spores in deposit. Always determine the color of the spores. There are many stories of people who thought they had a *Volvariella* species and did not check the spore print color. *Amanita* species have white spores, and many have a cup. Failing to distinguish accurately between these two mushroom types can be a costly or even a deadly mistake.

5. Ecology: The mushrooms in this family are decayers of plant material. *Pluteus* is a common genus, often found on downed limbs, logs, and dead stumps. *Volvariella* is somewhat less common but occurs on wood and on mulch, grass, wheat, or rice straw. In parts of Asia, *Volvariella volvacea,* the "paddy-straw mushroom," is raised commercially and is a common part of many oriental dishes. *Amanita* is often mistaken for *Volvariella* and illustrates the necessity for making a spore print. *Amanita* species do not grow on wood.

The best way to avoid a case of poisoning through "mistaken identity" is through careful study of the characteristics shown in the photos in this section and by comparing your find with other species mentioned in the text as similar, especially the genus *Amanita.*

Edible

Cervinus means "pertaining to a deer," probably referring to the drab brown color of the cap. This mushroom is a common one, found growing singly or in small clusters on dead and downed wood.

Description: The cap of this mushroom is smooth and rounded, tan with a darker spot in the center. On close inspection, the darker spot is found to consist of tiny dark hairs. The cap is fleshy with white "meat." The gills are white and crowded when young but quickly deepen to pink from the maturing spores and are obviously free in mature caps. The stalk is white, smooth, and ringless, and the mushroom will usually be found emerging directly from decaying wood. The spore print color is salmon to pink. To confirm your identification, break the cap and smell it—a "radishlike" aroma will be quite evident.

Comments: Edible, though still radishy; we call this "the mushroom that tastes like nothing." Common and ubiquitous, it plays an important role in the breakdown of dead wood. There are a number of other species of *Pluteus* including *P. admirabilis* with a yellow cap, *P. granulatus* with very fine fibers on the cap, *P. pellitus* with a white cap, *P. petasatus* with a white cap and brown center, and the tiny *P. nanus.*

Season: Year round in temperatures above freezing; decaying rapidly in warm weather.

Habit, habitat, and distribution: Single to several, arising from freshly downed wood. Occasionally very prolific.

Cap diameter: 5–14 cm (2–6″).

Stalk height: 5–12 cm (2–5″).

Stalk diameter: 6–15 mm (¼–½″).

VM

Volvariella bombycina

Edible

Volvariella is the diminutive of *Volvaria,* meaning "having a volva," which is the saclike cup at the base of the mushroom. *Bombycina* means "silky" and describes the smooth fibers on the cap.

Description: The cap is egg shaped when young, bell shaped in maturity, and is covered with tiny silky fibers. The gills are free and close together, changing color from white to pink as the spores mature. The stalk is smooth and white, with no ring present, and may be slightly enlarged at the base. The universal veil remains as a thick, deep cup that is dull yellowish brown and persistent. The spore print color is salmon to pink.

Comments: Edible, with the following precaution: look for the growth habit on dead wood and the pinkish spore color and for the absence of a veil. These characteristics should distinguish it from an *Amanita;* if you can't tell, don't eat it! The cultivated *Volvariella volvacea,* often called the "paddy-straw mushroom" and used in oriental food, is closely related to this species, as is *V. speciosa,* which has a smooth white stalk and a white to brown, smooth cap. It is often abundant on mulch and straw and on dead plant remains in cultivated fields including corncobs and rice hulls.

Season: Late summer and fall.

Habit, habitat, and distribution: Single to several, growing on dead hardwoods, especially on oak stumps. Occasionally common.

Cap diameter: 5–12.5 cm (2–5″).

Stalk height: 6–10 cm (2½–4″).

Stalk diameter: 10–20 mm (⅓–¾″).

VM

Family Entolomataceae: The Entolomas

There are two families of mushrooms that have spores that are some shade of pink in deposit. The Entolomataceae is the largest family and also is the most difficult for beginners learning to distinguish individual species. The name Entolomataceae means "having an inrolled edge." The only genus that is well represented in Texas is *Entoloma,* which is the largest genus in the family. More than two hundred species have been recorded in the southeastern United States. They range from tiny to quite large, and the genus contains a number of species that are toxic and dangerous.

1. General appearance: These are usually medium- to large-sized mushrooms that grow on the ground rather than on wood, buried wood, or mulch. The cap of some species is rounded in youth, opening to flat in age. In some species, the caps are conical or with a depressed or upraised center. The stalks are thick and smooth, composed of long fiberlike cells that often give the stalk a "twisted" appearance.

2. Gills: The gills in most species are attached to the stalk, often with a notch at the lower edge, or running down the stalk. To observe this feature, take a mature (wide-open) specimen and slice it vertically through the cap and stalk. Where the gills meet the stalk, you should see that the upper portion is attached, while the lower part may have pulled away. The color of the gills is often white or light gray when young but deepens to flesh colored or deep rose pink as the spores mature.

3. Spore print: The color of the spores in deposit is some shade of pink, though it may range from salmon to a deep rose color. Always check for the spore print color!

4. Ecology: These mushrooms range from fleshy mycorrhizal species to those that are small, delicate, and grow in decomposing grass or needle litter. Many of the species actually fruit during wet rainy periods when most mushrooms are not visible.

Caution! Many members of the Entolomataceae are poisonous or toxic and contain chemicals that cause severe gastrointestinal upset. Only *E. abortivum* is distinctive enough for beginners to eat, and in our experience it tends to be bitter. We recommend against eating any members of this group.

Remember, too, as you compare specimens that you find to the photos in this section, that we are illustrating only a few fairly common species. With more than two hundred species known from the southeastern part of the United States, that leaves a great deal of room for confusion. Mycologists have recognized several genera, including *Entoloma, Nolanea, Leptonia,* and *Pouzarella,* to mention four of them. They are distinguished on technical characteristics both macroscopic and microscopic. Many knowledgeable amateur (and professional) mycologists are quite content to be able to recognize members of this group as "it's an *Entoloma*"; learning to identify individual species in this group is one of the challenges that makes mushroom hunting a lifetime endeavor.

Entoloma abortivum

Edible/Fair

The species' name *abortivum* refers to the occurrence of "aborted" forms—those that do not emerge as normal mushrooms. Frequently, both normal and aborted forms appear on well-rotted wood together.

Description: The "normal" form of this mushroom is medium to large, with a dry, tan to gray cap, slightly darker in the center. The gills run down the stalk, are white to gray when young and deepen to pink from the maturing spores. The stalk is ringless, smooth, with an off-white band at the apex just beneath the gills. The color of the spore print is salmon pink. The "aborted" form looks like a white to gray or tan ball, which, if cut in half, has a pinkish marbled appearance. Often the aborted form occurs in clumps or groups of five or more specimens, united from a single base, often looking much like a smooth cauliflower.

Comments: The aborted form is a result of infection of the developing fruiting body by the cottony fibers (rhizomorphs) of *Armillaria mellea.* We cooked and ate the aborted form on the recommendation of a mycologist from the northern United States who claimed they were delicious, but we found them to be bitter, and most were left on the plate (a rare occurrence!). In fairness, many mushrooms develop a bitterness in age, and our specimens may have been a little old. Gather the normal forms for eating *only* if the aborted form appears alongside to avoid accidentally getting any closely related but toxic *Entoloma* species.

Season: Late summer to winter.

Habit, habitat, and distribution: Several to numerous on well-rotted hardwood limbs and small logs under hardwoods or in mixed woods; sometimes only the aborted form appears; other times both occur together.

Normal form:

Cap diameter: 5–12 cm (2–5″).

Stalk height: 7.5–12 cm (3–5″).

Stalk diameter: 6–12 mm (¼–½″).

Aborted form:

Diameter: 2.5–12 cm (1–4½″).

Height: 2.5–10 cm (1–4″).

JL

Entoloma strictius

Caution! / Poisonous

The species' name *strictius* means "upright" and refers to the tall, straight stalk. (This refers to the lengthy stalk relative to the cap diameter; the stalk still appears twisted, like many others in the genus *Entoloma.*)

Description: The caps are conical, gray-brown to tan, and have a nipplelike "knob" at the top. The gills are white when young, attached or nearly free from the stalk, and the color deepens to pink as the spores mature. The stalk is long and silky, with twisted, longitudinal lines, usually white to gray. The base often has white threads of mycelium, the vegetative part of the fungus, clinging to it. The spore print color is salmon pink.

Season: Spring through summer and fall.

Habit, habitat, and distribution: Several to numerous on the ground, often on rotting logs or decaying material.

Cap diameter: 2.5–5 cm (1–2″).

Stalk height: 5–10 cm (2–4″).

Stalk diameter: 1.5–5 mm (1/16–1/4″).

DL

The species' name *vernum* means "spring," which refers to its appearance in very early spring. This can be the first mushroom to be found after the winter frost and can even appear in South Texas between cold snaps.

Description: The caps are gray-brown to brown or almost black, conical in youth, and with a distinct nipple-shaped "knob" in the center when mature. The cap is smooth, appears almost waxy, and is deeply striate at the margin in age. The gills are gray when young, attached or nearly free from the stalk, and the color deepens to a deep rose brown as the spores mature. The stalk is long, with twisted, longitudinal fibers, usually deep gray brown. The base may have white threads of mycelium, the vegetative part of the fungus, clinging to it. The spore print color is salmon pink.

Comments: This early spring mushroom is not edible. It is often found alongside cypress baygalls in moist areas of the Big Thicket in eastern Texas. It is well known throughout eastern North America, from New York and Canada to Tennessee.

Season: Late winter to early spring.

Habit, habitat, and distribution: Several to numerous on the ground, often on rotting logs or decaying material.

Cap diameter: 2.5–7.5 cm (1–3″).

Stalk height: 5–12.5 cm (2–5″).

Stalk diameter: 1.5–5 mm (1⁄16–1⁄4″).

VM

Family Bolbitiaceae: The Conocybes

The name Bolbitiaceae comes from the Greek for "cow dung," describing a favorite substrate for this family of small mushrooms with rusty brown to dark brown spores. Three genera are found in this family: *Agrocybe, Bolbitius,* and *Conocybe.* Only *Conocybe* will be treated in this guide, as it is a common genus of lawn and wood mulch fungi.

1. General appearance: These are generally small mushrooms; the *Conocybe* genus is quite small, with long slender stalks and cone-shaped caps (*Conocybe* means "cone head").

2. Gills: This is a family that features attached or notched (partially attached) gills—that is, those that grow up to and touch the stalk or have the upper part of the gill attached and the lower part free, so that a "notch" is apparent when the mushroom is sliced in half longitudinally.

3. Spore print: The spores of this family are in the rusty brown, cigar brown, dark brown, or earth brown range. The spores are *not* chocolate brown or purple brown, as in the Agaricaceae or the Strophariaceae.

4. Ecology: These are decayers of wood—most are found on wood mulch or rich soil or grassy areas.

This is a family that should be avoided if you are experimenting with eating mushrooms that you find. The small size of most species will discourage you, and many species contain toxins. The family contains many very similar-looking species that must be differentiated using microscopic characteristics, and the prevalence of toxic members of this and other closely related groups simply makes this a very dangerous group for the beginner to consider for the table.

Lactea means "milky white," and *Conocybe* means "cone head," thus providing an apt description of this common lawn mushroom.
Description: The caps are very fragile, creamy yellow, and conical. The gills are nearly free, white to tan when young, darkening to cinnamon brown as the spores mature. The stalk is long and slender, with a small bulb at the base, and quite fragile. The spore print is reddish brown.
Comments: Popping up on a dewy morning and gone by midday, this mushroom can spring up in numbers from a few to a hundred. The tiny cream-colored caps with gold centers rise above the grass. The gills are colored brown from the spores, and the ringless white stalks are fibrous and fragile (note the broken one in the picture), with a distinct bulb at the base. Toddlers in the "grazing" stage are frequently found clutching pieces of this mushroom, much to the consternation of their mothers, though it has proven not to be violently toxic in small quantities. However, it is not recommended for eating due to its small size and toxic close relatives.
Season: Generally a summer mushroom, but it can be found during any warm, wet period.
Habit, habitat, and distribution: Prolific on lawns and rich, organic soils.
Cap diameter: 1–2.5 cm (3/8–1").
Stalk height: 4–10 cm (1½–4").
Stalk diameter: 1.5 mm (1/16").

VM

Conocybe tenera

Not recommended/Caution!

Tenera means "tender, delicate," a good description of this slender species that is quite common in lawns and gardens.

Description: The cap is conical, expanding in age, but still with a "dunce-cap," cone-shaped point, brown to cinnamon brown or yellow brown. The gills may be attached, free, or notched at the contact point with the stalk and are pale cream when young, becoming rusty brown as the spores mature. The stalk is slender, equal or with a slightly enlarged base, smooth or slightly mealy, colored like the cap or paler. The spore print color is rusty brown to cinnamon brown.

Comments: Do not eat this species—a closely related one, *C. filiaris,* is poisonous! This is a common species on lawns and on mulch. The specimen shown here was growing in a botanical garden. *C. lactea* has a much paler cap.

Season: Spring through fall.

Habit, habitat, and distribution: Several to numerous, often gregarious on rich soil, mulch, dung, and humus; sometimes in forest litter.

Cap diameter: 1–2.5 cm (⅜–1").

Stalk height: 4–9 cm (1½–3¾").

Stalk diameter: 1–4 mm (up to ⅙").

VM

Family Cortinariaceae: The Cortinarii

The name Cortinariaceae comes from the Latin *cortina,* which means "curtain" or "veil" and refers to the structure of the universal veil, which is made up of thin fibers. The Cortinariaceae is a large family of rusty brown to brown-spored mushrooms, which range from mycorrhizal terrestrial mushrooms to decomposers of moss and wood. Many genera in this family are characterized by having the cobwebby universal veil for which the family is named. A note of caution: this family contains around a thousand species, many of which are toxic to deadly, and they are responsible for almost as many deaths as Amanitas, so never eat "little brown mushrooms"! Study the photos and descriptions thoroughly in this section, and make careful comparisons to your specimens.

1. General appearance: This is a very diverse family. Members can be very tiny, medium, or quite large. Cap and stalk colors vary from orange to brown to purple and red. About the only color that is seldom seen is white. Most occur singly, but some types fruit in clusters arising from a common base. Many are mycorrhizal (growing around and into the roots of plants) and are found on the ground; others are decayers of moss and wood. These colorful mushrooms are often seen in fall and winter.

2. Gills: The gills of most species are directly attached to the stalk. The color of the young gills is often white, yellow, green, or blue, but it changes to some shade of brown as the spores mature. Usually, but not always, one can determine the color of the spores from looking at the gills or rusty brown fibers on the stalk on a mature specimen. At least it is obvious that one has a dark-spored mushroom.

3. Universal veil: Genera in this family typically lack an obvious cup at the base, but the universal veil may leave remnants that are seen as a "cobwebby," rusty brown veil. In embryonic stages, the veil fibers cover the "button"; as it expands, they often stretch from the base of the mushroom to the cap edges, much like a sheer curtain. By the time the cap is fully expanded, little remains of these fine fibers except as noted above.

4. Spore print: The spore prints of members of this family are usually some shade of brown, including rusty brown, orange, "cigar brown," yellow brown, or dull brown. The color of the spores should not be chocolate

brown to purple brown, which underscores the need to obtain a spore print. Often, on close inspection of the ground beneath these mushrooms, or on leaves or twigs, or on the caps of lower mushrooms, sufficient spores will be seen in deposit to make a determination of their color.

5. Ecology: Many of the genera in this family form mycorrhizal relationships with oak or pines; others derive their nutrients from dead materials such as wood or moss. They are widely distributed and most prevalent in fall and winter.

This is a large and diverse family, containing only a few edible members and many toxic and poisonous ones. Exercise great caution with any brown-spored mushroom found on the ground in wooded areas or on decaying wood. As with other families, only a few of the most common and easily recognized species are illustrated here.

Spectabilis means notable or visible; and when this mushroom is fruiting, the large golden clusters are quite noticeable. In Japan this species is called the "big laughing mushroom" because of its hallucinogenic properties—when eaten, a person tends to burst into laughter and experience other typical symptoms of hallucinogenic mushroom ingestion (see *Psilocybe cubensis* description).

Description: This large orange-yellow mushroom (stalk, cap, gills, and flesh are all this color) often fruits in clusters on stumps or buried wood. The caps are a bright orange, convex (rounded) when young, and opening to nearly plane (flat) in age. The gills are the same bright orange color and are attached or running slightly down the stalk. The stalk is thick and meaty, the distinct partial veil visible at first, often disappearing as the mushroom expands. The spore print color is a bright rusty orange.

Comments: This mushroom has an extremely bitter taste and is similar to other toxic *Gymnopilus* species, such as *G. aeruginosus*, which is also hallucinogenic. It is occasionally common on wood in large clusters in low areas where flooding has occurred in late fall.

Season: Fall to winter.

Habit, habitat, and distribution: Occasionally single, more often in clusters of several to many arising from a single base from buried or decaying wood. It is encountered most often in floodplain areas where it can occasionally be prolific.

Cap diameter: 5–20 cm (2–8").

Stalk height: 5–15 cm (2–6").

Stalk diameter: 12–50 mm (½–2").

JL

Cortinarius marylandensis

Toxic/Caution!

Marylandensis honors the state of Maryland, where this variant *Cortinarius* was first collected.

Description: These mushrooms are usually small, with a cap not much larger than a half dollar. All parts are a deep rust red color. The cap is smooth and thin fleshed, and the gills are close and directly attached to the stalk. The stalk is long and slender. The spore print is a deep rusty brown.

Comments: This is another of the common but inedible species of *Cortinarius* that is often found in floodplain areas after heavy rains. In the dye pot, it yields beautiful deep shades of pink and rose.

Season: Summer, fall, and winter.

Habit, habitat, and distribution: Scattered to numerous under beech and pine species. It is often found in bottom lands and floodplains that have recently been under water.

Cap diameter: 2.5–5 cm (1–2″).
Stalk height: 3–7.5 cm (1¼–3″).
Stalk diameter: 3–5 mm (⅛–¼″).

DS

RIGHT: Fungi-dyed wool.

VM

Not edible

The species' name for this mushroom, *cinnamomeus,* means "cinnamon colored" and indicates the brown shade of the cap of mushrooms in this group. It is among the latest of the winter mushrooms to fruit and is often hidden under pine needles.

Description: There are several closely related species that share the following characteristics: The caps are brown and fairly drab. Some are cone shaped; others are rounded. The gills are bright yellow when young and darken in age as the spores mature. But the most notable characteristic is the yellow to yellow-brown stalk, which fades to tan at the base. Any remnants of the veil are minute, only visible as rusty brown threads, colored from the spores that adhere to them.

Comments: Edibility unknown, and eating it is *not recommended*! This group of *Cortinarius* species contains several closely related species differing by subtle macroscopic and microscopic features. Little brown mushrooms are to be avoided, except for the dye pot, where they yield burgundy to red hues.

Season: Winter.

Habit, habitat, and distribution: Single to several, widely scattered, and mycorrhizal with pines and other conifers.

Cap diameter: 1.5–6 cm (½–2½″).

Stalk height: 2.5–10 cm (1–4″).

Stalk diameter: 3–10 mm (⅛–⅜″).

VM

Cortinarius semisanguineus

Not edible

Sanguineus means "blood colored," referring, in this case, to the color of the gills; the *semi-* prefix is attached to distinguish this species from *C. sanguineus,* which is red all over.

Description: The cap of this mushroom is medium sized and a drab tan color. In maturity, the cap's center rises like a nipple. The gills are a deep ruby red and are attached directly to the stalk. The stalk has a partial veil that is cobwebby. This veil is most visible in age, when the rusty brown spores have caught on it. The stalk is smooth and may be slightly enlarged at the base. The spore print color is rusty brown.

Comments: This species is inedible and should not be experimented with—other closely related species are known to be toxic. It is a favorite for those who dye wool with mushrooms. In the dye pot, it yields deep pink to rose color. It is a late-winter species, occasionally found as late as February during a warm, wet winter.

Season: Winter.

Habit, habitat, and distribution: Scattered to numerous under pine species with which it is mycorrhizal. Common in the East Texas pine forests where it is often found very late in the season, sometimes even after freezing weather has occurred.

Cap diameter: 2.5–6 cm (1–2½").

Stalk height: 3–7.5 cm (1¼–3").

Stalk diameter: 3–5 mm (⅛–¼").

JL

Cortinarius alboviolaceous

Not edible

Alboviolaceous means "the white violet one" and draws attention to the pale violet color and white universal veil sheath on the stalk of this mushroom. (Most purple species of *Cortinarius* are much deeper in color.)

Description: The cap is bell shaped when young, opening out to nearly flat at maturity, and is a pale silvery violet color. The gills are directly attached or notched and are pale violet in youth, deepening to a dark cinnamon brown as the spores mature. The stalk is usually enlarged and club shaped, like a "foot," which is the best identification characteristic. The stalk is unusually long, and the universal veil remains as a distinct white sheath that extends halfway up the stalk. Part of the universal veil also remains at the center of the stalk, which is usually easy to spot because of the rusty brown spores that have stuck to it.

Comments: Recent chemical work has revealed that nearly all *Cortinarius* species contain some toxic chemicals. Consider this one inedible, and be careful not to confuse it with *Clitocybe nuda.* To be sure of your identification, *always* take a spore print! *Clitocybe nuda* will be pale pink spored; this mushroom has dark rusty brown spores, and the gills of older specimens become rusty brown.

Season: Winter.

Habit, habitat, and distribution: Single to scattered under oak and beech during wet winter months.

Cap diameter: 3–8 cm (1¼–3¼").

Stalk height: 4–12 cm (1½–5").

Stalk diameter: 5–10 mm (⅕–½").

VM

Cortinarius iodes

Not edible

Iodes means "violet," which is an appropriate name for this purple-capped mushroom.

Description: This mushroom's cap is bell shaped when young and opens to nearly flat in maturity. The cap color is purple, though it may fade to tan in age. The gills are directly attached or notched and are violet in youth, deepening to a dark cinnamon brown as the spores mature. The stalk is enlarged and club shaped, like a "foot." The universal veil frequently disappears or remains only as a faint zone of tiny fibers on the stalk. Often the veil is visible only because of the brown spores that stick to it. The spore print is rusty brown.

Comments: Like all *Cortinarius* species, this species should be assumed to contain some amounts of toxic chemicals. Consider this one inedible. Compare this with the edible *Clitocybe nuda,* which has a pale pink spore print and pale gills that remain lavender in age.

Season: Fall and winter.

Habit, habitat, and distribution: Single to scattered under oak and beech during wet winter months.

Cap diameter: 3–12 cm (1¼–5").

Stalk height: 4–12 cm (1½–5").

Stalk diameter: 10–25 mm (⅓–1").

AB

This is a new species of *Cortinarius,* at present known only from East Texas. It is named for David Lewis, a TMS member who found it in the Lance Rosier Unit of the Big Thicket National Preserve.
Description: This medium-sized mushroom has a bright yellow cap, brown gills, and a bright yellow stalk. Tiny fibers from the cobwebby veil, called a *cortina,* remain like a ring around the stalk and are usually visible only because the brown spores catch on them.
Comments: This mushroom has a bright yellow cap that is very close to the color of chanterelles, from which it can be distinguished by its brown spores and distinct gills. It is often found in the same woods and at the same times of year. This mushroom illustrates the diversity of mushrooms in Texas and is just one of many species that we know and recognize that have not been described and named in mycological literature.
Season: Late spring through fall.
Habit, habitat, and distribution: Usually scattered to several along the roots of pine (thus often in arcs) found along slightly upraised ridges.
Cap diameter: 2.5–7.5 cm (1–3″).
Stalk height: 5–10 cm (2–4″).
Stalk diameter: 8–12 mm (¼–½″).

VM

Galerina autumnalis
Deadly/Caution!

Galerina is a genus of small, brown-spored mushrooms that have conic to convex caps and brittle stalks. The genus name means "helmet," a rough description of the cap shape. *Autumnalis* is from the same root as our "autumn," but this species can be found at almost any time of the year.

Description: These are small mushrooms with brown caps. The caps are typically thin and smooth, with fine lines visible along the edges. The gills are brown to rusty brown and are usually partially or fully attached to the stalk. The stalk is thin and fragile and is often hollow. Young specimens will have a cobwebby veil (cortina) or a small membranous ring on the stalk, but it is smooth and not scaly below. The spore print color is a deep rusty brown.

Comments: Some *Galerina* species (including this one) are *deadly* poisonous, leading to the rule: "Never eat little brown mushrooms!" These species should definitely be avoided. We have found large fruitings of this mushroom on lawns on the Rice University campus in early summer.

Season: All year.

Habit, habitat, and distribution: Single to several on wood, ground, or in moss or grass.

Cap diameter: 1–4 cm (⅓–1½").

Stalk height: 2–10 cm (¾–4").

Stalk diameter: 3–6 mm (⅛–¼").

AB

Family Stropharariaceae: The Stropharias

A family of common mushrooms, always found growing on dead plant parts and deriving nourishment from the degradation of dead materials. Spore prints range from purple-brown or purple-black to brown in *Pholiota*. Most of the hallucinogenic (mind-altering) species are in this group, but few good edibles are included. The species fall into two size categories—those that are quite small, and some that are medium sized. They generally have some combination of the following characteristics:

1. General appearance: The species that are small and fragile often have brightly colored caps, but, in our experience, in Texas the larger species are far more common. These may be single or in clusters, have rounded caps when young that open to nearly flat, and firm, thick stalks that often have a ring. The gills become purple-brown as the spores mature.
2. Gills: The gills of most species in this group are directly attached or notched and are not free or running down the stalk. The color of the gills is generally white to pale tan in youth, becoming purple-brown as the spores mature.
3. Ring: The partial veil (a piece of tissue that extends between the gills and stalk in the embryonic mushroom) may remain as the mushroom expands, forming a ring, or annulus, on the stalk that looks much like a skirt, or pieces may hang from the edge of the cap. In *Naematoloma* only a narrow zone of fibers remains on the mature specimens.
4. Spore print: The spore print of members of this group is some dark shade of purple or brown, usually purple-brown or purple-black, but at times it can be so dark that it almost looks black. Always take a spore print! Do this by placing a section of the cap gill-side down on white paper for several hours, until a deposit of spores is present on the paper.
5. Ecology: These mushrooms are important decomposers of plant material or certain other substances, such as the dung of animals. *Psilocybe* species, for instance, are often found on cattle dung, which they decompose.

Few species in this family are of interest to the mushroom eater. However, *Stropharia rugosoannulata,* which fruits on mulch beds and is raised commercially in Europe, is an important exception. Several species are toxic, and some toxic species in the genus *Psilocybe* have hallucinogenic properties. It is important to note that those mushrooms that contain hallucinogenic chemicals are toxic—death due to allergic reaction to these mushrooms has been reported a number of times. The brown-spored genus *Pholiota* is not discussed in this book, as members of this genus are not often encountered in Texas. It is important to be able to recognize the characteristics of this family to determine the genera and their species.

So, continue the habits you have formed as you study this book—read the descriptions closely and identify the important characteristics in the photos as you compare the mushrooms you find to our descriptions.

Fasciculare means "bundled" and refers to this mushroom's characteristic growth habit, which is to appear in profuse clusters. The greenish yellow (sulfur) color gives them a name by which they are occasionally known, "sulfur tufts."

Description: This is a very common, low growing mushroom, found in great clusters on decaying wood, especially along exposed roots. The caps vary in color from greenish yellow to tan, rounded at first, then opening up to become wide and flat. The gills are also greenish yellow to olive and attached directly to the stalk, becoming dingy purple in age. The stalk is long, slender, and curved, yellow to tan, often showing zones of tiny fibers that are the remains of the universal veil, and purple-brown color zones from spore deposits. The spore print color is purple-brown to purple-gray.

Comments: This is one of the most commonly found mushrooms in wooded areas in summer and fall. Unfortunately, this mushroom is toxic, causing severe stomach upset. It is rarely reported in poisoning cases because the intense bitter taste discourages anyone who might try to eat it! *Naematoloma sublateritium* is somewhat larger, has a brick red cap and gills that are yellowish in youth, becoming purple-brown in age. *N. capnoides* is orange with gray gills and, like *N. fasciculare,* is found in clusters on wood.

Season: Summer and fall.

Habit, habitat, and distribution: Usually numerous, in clusters called fascicles, or *tufts,* on wood, often on buried wood, and often extending for several meters along tree roots.

Cap diameter: 2–5 cm (¾–2").

Stalk height: 5–12 cm (2–5").

Stalk diameter: 3–10 mm (⅛–⅓").

AB

Psilocybe cubensis

Toxic/Hallucinogenic

This is the "magic mushroom," so-called because of its hallucinogenic properties. It was named *cubensis* because it was first described from Cuba. It is common in pastures across the state following periods of cool, rainy weather.

Description: The Texas version of this mushroom is variable in size and can be quite large—the cap is often 3 to 5 inches (7.5–12.5 cm) across and colored light brown with a golden "sunburst" in the center. It is commonly found fruiting on fresh cow patties. The stalk is thick and white with a prominent white veil. The veil is frequently colored dark purple by the falling spores. The gills are buff when young, becoming deep purple in age. The flesh of the cap and stalk rapidly bruises blue (within fifteen seconds). The spore print color is a deep purple-brown.

Comments: This is the mushroom of choice for those who wish to alter their consciousness—three caps consumed by an adult usually produce hallucinations in less than an hour; the "trip" lasts three to four hours or more (see chapter on mushroom toxins). But this does not mean it is harmless: the mushroom has been the cause of death in a number of cases. Allergic reaction is fairly common and can be fatal; combination of this mushroom with other drugs and/or alcohol can be toxic; and actions undertaken while on the "trip" (jumping out of windows or from moving cars) are not uncommon. Children are particularly at risk, and it can be life threatening to them. It is also illegal to possess this mushroom since it contains a controlled substance. Always check for the spore print (purple) and the staining reaction (if it doesn't stain blue, it's not *Psilocybe cubensis*!). This mushroom has been reported from all parts of Texas where cattle graze, usually due to newspaper reports of arrests of would-be "trippers" or through the Poison Control Center when bad reactions occur.

Season: Spring and fall.

Habit, habitat, and distribution: Single to several arising from fresh cow dung patties; occasionally quite numerous.

Cap diameter: 2.5–12 cm (1–5").

Stalk height: 5–15 cm (2–6").

Stalk diameter: 6–12 mm (¼–½").

VM

The species' name of this mushroom means "little crown," probably referring to the shape of the young caps. This is an early spring species.

Description: The cap is smooth and tan to cream colored, often somewhat slimy in wet weather. (This characteristic can be misleading, however, as the cap often dries in the warm sunshine.) The gills are a light purple-brown when young and change to a deep purple as the spores mature. The stalk is short and white and has a prominent superior ring that may fall away in age. The spore color is a dark purple-brown.

Comments: This is a ubiquitous mushroom of lawns and roadsides and has a general appearance quite similar to *Agaricus campestris.* However, the gills are never pink, the spores are purple-brown rather than chocolate brown, and the cap lacks the hairlike fibers or close scales of the *Agaricus.* The mushroom is considered inedible and toxic and is a cause of severe gastric upset in cases of mistaken identity.

Season: Spring and early summer.

Habit, habitat, and distribution: Single to numerous, scattered on lawns, watered areas, and on grass. Often seen on golf courses and on manicured lawns in the spring.

Cap diameter: 2.5–7.5 cm (1–3″).

Stalk height: 2.5–10 cm (1–4″).

Stalk diameter: 3–12 mm (1/8–1/2″).

VM

Family Agaricaceae: The Agaricus

This family of chocolate brown–spored mushrooms contains the "common grocery store mushroom," *Agaricus bisporus,* as well as many other delicious edibles and a few that can produce violent vomiting and diarrhea (but, fortunately, none that will kill you!). So, if you want to enjoy some of the most flavorful and meaty mushrooms available in woods, lawns, and pastures, learn to recognize the distinctive features listed here to avoid the toxic species, and be very careful in making your identification.

1. General appearance: The species have short, thick stalks and thick, fleshy caps. An important feature to look for is the presence of tiny hairlike fibers or scales on the cap, usually at the center. Most caps are white, tan, reddish, or brown in color. The stalk is usually shorter than the cap is wide, frequently giving the mushroom a stocky appearance. The stalk may be slightly enlarged or bulbous at the base.

2. Gills: The gills of *Agaricus* species are a pale pink to white when young and change to a deep chocolate brown as the spores mature, often in just a few hours. The gills are free from the stalk (they end well away from the stalk, so that the stalk appears attached to the cap). If the stalk is gently twisted it will come free in a "ball-and-socket" fashion. If you "pop" the stalk out of the cap, it becomes detached smoothly, with no pieces of gills adhering to the sides. This is easiest to see in a mature specimen, one in which the cap has fully expanded.

3. Ring: The ring, or annulus, is usually quite distinct. In young specimens, it is often seen clearly stretching as the cap pulls away from the stalk. The type of veil formed can be quite variable: some have a very noticeable, skirtlike ring, others have only a scaly area, and others have an "intermediate" ring, a short one that may stand straight out from the stalk. Some species have a double veil.

4. Spore print: Most *Agaricus* species will have chocolate brown spores, though a few have spores that are purple brown. You can determine this even in "store-bought" produce, and you must always check the spore print on all wild mushrooms you plan to eat.

5. Staining reactions: One may encounter either staining reactions or pigmented flesh in the genus. Some species bruise very light yellow on the cap and the surface of the stalk. Other species have flesh that turns

yellow when bruised or yellow gradually becoming orange to orange-red. *Agaricus silvaticus* bruises deep red. However, *A. xanthodermus* has a butter yellow pigmented stalk base and is a toxic species.

6. Odors: Check for odors by crushing a small piece of the cap, stalk, and bottom of the stalk, then holding it to your nose. Aromas you may encounter include "musty" or "mushroomy," almond, anise (all good signs for the would-be eater), or "phenolic" (a chemical odor like creosote or phenol). The phenolic ones, which often show yellow staining, are to be avoided!

7. Ecology: *Agaricus* species are saprophytic and break down dead material including leaves and herbaceous material such as dead grass. Thus, they potentially can fruit at any time of year, but most are found when the weather is cool and moist—fall and spring.

The best edible groups are those that don't stain or have a dull brownish stain when bruised and a delicious mushroomy or almond odor. The "big brown mushrooms" sold loose at gourmet grocery stores are an example of this group and are delicious! The chemical-smelling (phenolic) ones, which show strong or fleeting yellow stains, can cause extreme stomach upset and are to be left strictly alone! The yellow-staining ones with a sweet smell and persistent yellow staining that does not fade to brown or wine color are edible. Those that show no color reactions and have only a faint, musty odor, like the common "grocery store mushroom," are okay to eat but not notably flavorful.

We recommend that you study this section closely and be sure of your identification before sampling your find. But, do splurge and buy some "browns" next time you see them at your favorite grocer's—they are simply delicious, and the texture is wonderfully meaty. We far prefer them over the white ones that have as little flavor as the cardboard cartons they are packaged in!

Agaricus campestris

Edible/Good

Campestris means "of the fields"; this common meadow mushroom is an inhabitant of fields, pastures, and grassy, manicured lawns. Many people call them "pink bottoms" because of the delicate pink gills in young specimens.

Description: This wild mushroom is closely related to the commercially cultivated mushrooms. The cap is smooth and white, thick and meaty, with very few fibers, mostly at the center. The gills are pink in youth and darken to a deep chocolate brown as the spores mature. The stalk is smooth and white, with remains of the universal veil forming a thin ring, and with a nonbulbous base. It has a mushroomy odor (i.e., not almond or anise, and especially not phenolic or chemical), and does not change color when bruised or rubbed. The spore print color is chocolate brown.

Comments: The specimens pictured were found along the greens of a golf course and are edible and delicious! Look for them in cool, wet weather (especially three days after a good rain) on grassy areas: lawns, golf courses, parks, baseball fields, or pastures. They thrive in grass fertilized by home owners and lawn-care specialists. The spores mature rapidly, and the gill color changes from pink to brown in just a few hours. The young ones, with light pink gills, are the firmest and most delicious!

Season: Spring and fall.

Habit, habitat, and distribution: Single to numerous, in grass, where they often form arcs or complete "fairy rings" (mass fruitings in which the fruiting bodies come up in circular patches; in former times, it was believed that these circles of mushrooms came up where fairies danced).

Cap diameter: 4–11 cm (1½–4⅓").

Stalk height: 2–6 cm (¾–1½").

Stalk diameter: 10–25 mm (⅓–1").

VM

This *Agaricus* species has smaller spores than most others in the genus and pink coloring. This species is called the "almond mushroom" because of its almond odor; it is often described as smelling like cherry pits. The best identification points are this characteristic and the species' association with coastal grasses.

Description: The caps of this mushroom are dry and silky. Tiny pinkish fibers cover the caps when young and darken to brownish in age. The gills are pink when young, darkening in a few hours to dark chocolate brown as the spores mature. Important characteristics to confirm your identification are the minimal ring, lack of a bulbous base, and almond odor. A color change to yellow or orange occurs on the stalk due to handling or bruising.

Comments: These specimens were found in grass under live oak along the Texas Coastal Plain and are edible. They are fairly thin fleshed, and the spores mature so quickly that refrigeration is needed to keep them fresh enough to eat. These are found in warm, wet weather. Caution! If it's warm enough for this species, the grass you find it in is likely to be *full* of chiggers. (We can testify to that!) So collect it carefully. The young ones, with light pink gills, are the firmest and most delicious.

Season: Summer and fall; in warm, wet weather.

Habit, habitat, and distribution: Single to several in grass, under live oak; widely distributed throughout South Texas and the Coastal Plain.

Cap diameter: 2.5–7.5 cm (1–3″).

Stalk height: 2–6 cm (¾–2⅓″).

Stalk diameter: 3–12 mm (⅛–½″).

VM

Family Coprinaceae *The Coprini*

The Coprinaceae family takes its name from the Latin *copr-*, a combining form meaning "dung," which is a common habitat for a large number of genera that, to the amateur mycologist, are dismayingly similar in stature and form.

In this section, we shall cover three genera that are common across the state, springing up on well-watered lawns and on mulch almost everywhere. These mushrooms are often small in size, have tan, brown, or cinnamon-colored caps, and are usually thin stalked and dark spored. Among the genera we will treat here are *Panaeolus, Conocybe,* and smaller members of the genus *Coprinus* (the larger species of *Coprinus* will be covered in the following section as they have some distinct characteristics that set them apart).

Even to a taxonomist, or an amateur mycologist with experience in making microscopic determinations, these mushrooms can be difficult to distinguish. And this is not a good group for an inexperienced mushroom hunter to work with or try for edibility—some mushrooms in this group contain toxic chemicals, and many have not been tested for edibility at all.

The major characteristics of the *Panaeolus* and *Conocybe* genera are as follows:

1. General appearance: These mushrooms are small in stature. The caps are usually less than 1½ inches (4 cm) across and often are much smaller. The stalks are even in diameter, usually smooth, but in some genera a ring or zone of fine fibers is present on the stalk. The overall proportion of height to width is about 1 : 1, with the stalk usually quite slim and often much paler than the cap.

2. Gills: The gills may be either directly attached to the stalk or notched so that the upper part of the gill is attached to the stalk and the lower portion is free. However, in this group, the gills are *not* free. Most species in this group have fairly widely spaced gills, and several genera have alternating long and short gills so that only about half of the gills reach all the way from the outer cap edge to the stalk. The color of young gills is light cream to tan, darkening to some shade of brown or black as the spores mature, often with an intermediate stage that is referred to as "mottled."

3. Ring: A ring or zone of fibers, which are remnants of the partial veil, may be present in some species. However, lack of such a ring should not be used as a

primary characteristic for species' determination—it is often so fragile that it disappears rapidly.

4. Spore print: The spore print color of the mushrooms in this artificial group is some shade of brown or black. *Always* take a spore print, and if the color of the spores is dark, be extra cautious about eating your specimens! There are several common species that are potentially very dangerous in this group.

5. Ecology: Most of the mushrooms in this group derive their nutrition from decaying matter, often grass, dung, or other humus. Thus, they are often among the first mushrooms to come up after a rain and may appear at any time of year. These general characteristics apply very well to members of the genus *Panaeolus*. Members of the genus *Coprinus* have some additional, very distinctive characteristics and will be discussed separately.

Carefully compare the characteristics of specimens you find to the photos and descriptions in this book. Only the most common and easily identified species are treated in this work, and due to the similarity of harmless and toxic species, we recommend avoiding these mushrooms altogether for ingestion.

Panaeolus phalaenarum

Edible/Caution!

In America, this mushroom was previously known as *Panaeolus solidipes*, which means "solid foot" and refers to the slight enlargement at the base of the stalk. This mushroom is a common inhabiter of dung.

Description: The cap is yellow to buff and bell shaped. Remnants of the partial veil are often seen as little pieces that look almost like "fringe" around the cap edge. The cap tissue often dries out and breaks up into scales as it ages. The gills are attached or notched at their attachment to the stalk and will darken from gray through a mottled appearance to black as the spores mature. The stalk is smooth and the same color as the cap, sometimes appearing slightly twisted. The stalk is equal or slightly enlarged at the base. The spore print color is black.

Comments: This is a common, non-hallucinogenic mushroom that is often found on horse dung, straw, and manure. It is said to be edible, though we haven't tried it! We recommend against eating it, especially for beginners—the small size, likeness to other toxic species, and habit on dung are discouraging anyway. The "fringe" along the cap edge is a characteristic common to many members of the genus *Panaeolus* and varies from minimal to almost "shaggy." This species is found all over the state, especially on cow dung, whenever the weather is cool and damp.

Season: Spring and summer.

Habit, habitat, and distribution: Single to several, on dung or well-mulched soil. Usually visible in early morning and often drying out by early afternoon.

Cap diameter: 1.3–5 cm (½–2″).

Stalk height: 7.5–10 cm (3–4″).

Stalk diameter: 5–15 mm (¼–½″).

AB

Panaeolus subbalteatus
Toxic/Hallucinogenic

The name of this mushroom means "somewhat belted," an apt description of the dark band around the edge of the cap (clearly visible in younger specimens).

Description: These are small mushrooms with a medium brown to reddish brown, bell-shaped cap when moist. As the cap dries out, the color lightens to some shade of tan to cinnamon. In this species, any "fringe" on the cap edge is minimal and visible only in young specimens. The gills are attached to the stalk in youth, pulling away as the cap opens, and darkening from gray to black as the spores mature. The stalk is smooth, light tan, and hollow, but is not fragile. The color of the spore print is black.

Comments: This is a common mushroom on well-manured lawns and gardens, especially if spent compost from a mushroom farm has been used in the garden. The specimens shown here turned up growing in a highly composted bed among the lettuce leaves, where we posed them for the photo—guess where we get our compost mulch! This is a mildly hallucinogenic species that can be quite variable, even poisonous—thus, we don't recommend it. It can be quite dangerous to toddlers at the "grazing" age.

Season: Spring and summer.

Habit, habitat, and distribution: Single to several on well-manured or mulched gardens; widespread.

Cap diameter: 2–6 cm (¾–2½").

Stalk height: 4–10 cm (1½–4").

Stalk diameter: 3–6 mm (⅛–¼").

VM

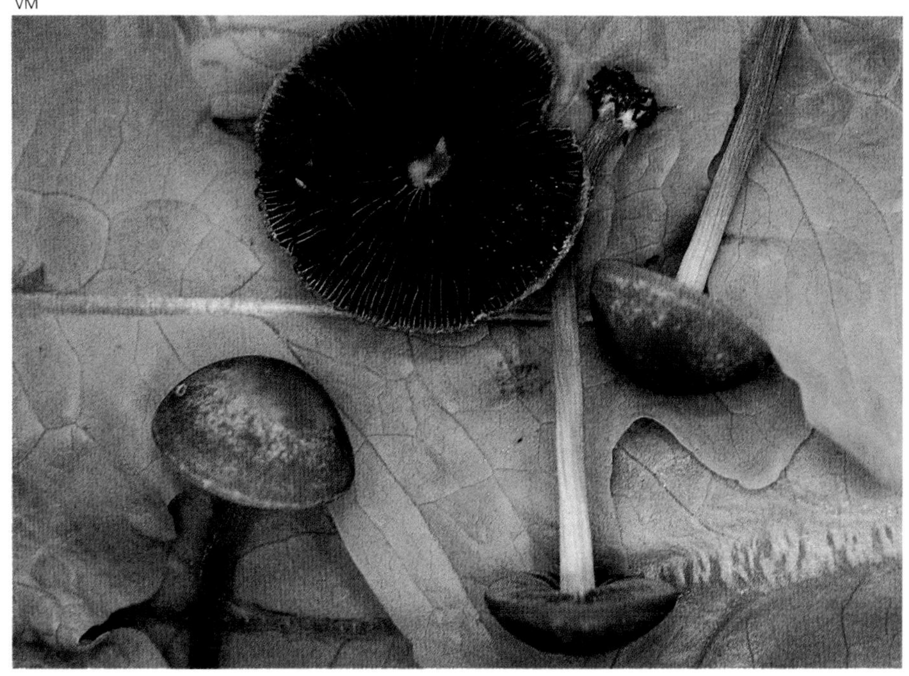

Panaeolus campanulatus

Toxic/Hallucinogenic

This mushroom takes its name from the bell-shaped ("campanulate") cap that never opens fully.

Description: The caps are gray-brown, tinted olive, and never open fully. The top is rounded and often has toothlike remnants of the partial veil clinging all around the edge. The gills are gray when young, often pulling away from the stalk as the mushroom loses moisture, becoming black in age. This mature color is somewhat uneven, causing a mottled appearance to the gill edges at midmaturity. The stalks are white, usually quite long and thin (often four or more times longer than the width of the cap), and a pale and disappearing ring may occur, frequently visible only due to the accumulation of black spores at the site. The spore print color of this mushroom is black.

Comments: This mushroom has been described as either toxic or "mildly hallucinogenic" when eaten raw, but usually there is no effect. We do not recommend it for culinary or recreational purposes. Found throughout the state, wherever cattle are pastured, it is one of the first mushrooms to come up after a rain.

Season: Fall, winter, and spring.

Habit, habitat, and distribution: Single to several on dung, especially "cow piles," at times prolific.

Cap diameter: 1–4 cm (⅓–1½").

Stalk height: 6–15 cm (2½–6").

Stalk diameter: 1–3 mm (up to ⅛").

JL

Genus Coprinus

Coprinus is a genus with several distinct characteristics that make it fairly easy to distinguish. It is of importance to the person who wants to eat wild mushrooms because it contains good edibles, some inedible species, and one that is toxic in combination with alcoholic beverages.

1. General appearance: The genus *Coprinus* is an easy one to learn to spot: when young, the caps are "bullet shaped," rarely open fully, and are often covered with delicate white fibers. Many species mature to look like a half-open umbrella, with the edges often curled up or recurved. These edges will be black, taking their color from the maturing spores.

Deliquescence is a common characteristic of members of the genus *Coprinus*—it means "digesting to liquid" and refers to a phenomenon in which the mushroom secretes enzymes that digest the gills. In many cases, the gills "dissolve" into a black, inky liquid leaving only tatters of the outer layer of the cap; hence the common name, "inky caps." You have to be an "early bird" to gather *Coprinus:* many species fruit, release their spores, and digest themselves away between sunrise and noon!

2. Gills: The gills of *Coprinus* are white or pale gray in youth but darken to black as the spores mature. They are attached to the stalk, and in the bullet-shaped "buttons," they extend from top to bottom, parallel to the stalk.

3. Ring: Many *Coprinus* species have a persistent, membranous ring on the stalk that is the remnant of the universal veil. In some species, the ring detaches from the stalk and may be found circling the base of the stalk.

4. Spore print: A spore print will reveal black or deep blackish brown spores. However, in many species, a spore print is likely to reveal a black, gooey liquid that is the result of deliquescence of the gill.

5. Ecology: The name *Coprinus* means "living on dung" and indicates this mushroom's role in the ecology, that of decayer of dead material. The species are also found on decaying wood, straw, and grass.

Coprinus comatus is the best edible in the genus and the largest. Other smaller species are also edible; and one species, *C. atramentarius,* produces a toxic reaction in some people when consumed with alcoholic beverages. (This reaction can occur even if the alcohol is ingested the day after eating the mushrooms!)

Coprinus comatus

Edible/Good

This mushroom is common enough to have a common name, "shaggy mane," indicating the "shaggy" scales on the bullet-shaped cap. The scientific name, *comatus,* means "hair," also referring to these scales.

Description: This mushroom is easy to learn to recognize. Its cap is white and distinctly cylindrical or "bullet shaped" when young. The center is a pale tan to deep brown. As the mushroom ages and the spores mature, the cap opens like an umbrella. The gills are white when young, deepening to black, and free from the stalk. Deliquescence ("self-digestion") occurs from the edges toward the center. As the edges deliquesce, they often roll up. The stalk is white, fairly thick, and hollow or stuffed at maturity, equal in diameter, and is often left standing with black, inky liquid dripping down the stalk. A ring is present in youth but often comes loose and falls to the base of the stalk. The spore print color is black.

JL

Comments: This mushroom is generally found in cold rainy winter months. It is a good edible but should be eaten as young as possible, before the deliquescence, or self-digestion, begins. Go out looking for this one early in the morning; it digests itself rapidly, but to prevent deliquescence, cover it in water. The Texas version of this mushroom is usually smaller than its counterparts from other areas; it is usually less than 6 inches tall. *Coprinus comatus* fruits from buried wood, unlike many species of *Coprinus.* We have seldom seen more than half a dozen or so specimens at one time, but in some areas of the United States it occurs in large numbers. We expect that in the cooler areas of the state, it may fruit more prolifically.

Season: Cool, wet weather, usually winter.

Habit, habitat, and distribution: Single to scattered, on rich, usually hard-packed soil, or in grass. It grows from buried wood or dead roots.

Cap diameter: 4–10 cm (1½–4").
Stalk height: 5–12.5 cm (2–5").
Stalk diameter: 10–20 mm (⅓–¾").

This small *Coprinus* species is often found on dung or compost piles; the name *sterquilinus* means "growing on dung." It closely resembles *C. comatus* but is smaller in size.

Description: The cap of this mushroom is tan, with white, abundant, delicate hairy scales. The gills are gray in youth, deepening to black, with rapid deliquescence. The stalk is white with an inferior ring, which is often moveable or missing in age. The stalk is often hollow or stuffed in age. The spore print color is black.

Comments: This mushroom can be found at any time of the year when it is consistently damp for seven to ten days. It is edible, *but* be careful to note the key features described above. It could be confused with toxic species that grow on dung.

Season: Year round (given mild weather).

Habit, habitat, and distribution: Fruiting in clusters of several to many, on decayed wood, compost, grass, or straw. It is to be expected throughout the state.

Cap diameter: 1.2–3.5 cm (½–1½″).

Stalk height: 5–7.5 cm (2–3″).

Stalk diameter: 4–8 mm (⅙–⅓″).

VM

Coprinus laniger

Inedible

This species was named *laniger,* which means "wooly," because the vegetative fungus body (mycelium) from which it arises forms a yellow to orange mat called an ozonium, which looks as though it fruited on an old blanket!

Description: The most noticeable thing about this mushroom is the wooly "mat," bright orange-yellow, from which the mushrooms arise. The caps are tan, smooth, with tawny wartlike scales over the surface and deep lines around the edges. The gills darken from gray to black as the spores mature and deliquescence occurs. The stalk is white and smooth. There is no ring, and the spore print color is black.

Comments: This is a small "household" mushroom that frequently appears when wood (especially wood used in construction, or landscape timbers) becomes wet. It has been known to occur on household framing and even in basements. *C. variegatus* is a closely related species fruiting on wood, with a white universal veil in patches over the maturing cap.

Season: Year round, but most common in summer.

Habit, habitat, and distribution: Fruiting in clusters on decayed wood in service, logs, limbs, and stumps, often recurring several times through the season.

Cap diameter: 2.5–5 cm (1–2″).

Stalk height: 2.5–5 cm (1–2″).

Stalk diameter: 6–8 mm (¼–⅓″).

VM

Edible

Plicatilis means "pleated" and refers to the deep lines along the cap edge—so many that the mushrooms resemble small party-favor umbrellas!

Description: These small mushrooms have a brown center that soon turns silvery gray, and radial lines form from the margin almost to the cap center. Thus, they look like silvery gray parasols on the ground. There is almost no substance to the cap. The gills are gray, free from the stalk, and attached to a collar. The gills darken as the spores mature, but this mushroom dries out and breaks up as it dries, so the mushrooms rarely last long enough for deliquescence to occur. The stalk is white and very fine, with a small enlargement at the base. The color of the spore print is black.

Comments: Troops of this mushroom may number into the hundreds, springing up overnight and gone by noon on a dry, sunny day. They are edible but not notable and are just too small for the table.

Season: Summer.

Habit, habitat, and distribution: Scattered to numerous, on lawns and other grassy areas, most common where cut grass dries out and decays. This mushroom is to be expected throughout the state when moisture is sufficient.

Cap diameter: 1.2–4 cm (½–1½").

Stalk height: 1.2–5 cm (½–2").

Stalk diameter: 1–2 mm (less than ¹⁄₁₀").

VM

Coprinus atramentarius

Edible/Caution!

Atramentarius means "inky," describing the mushroom's tendency to digest its gills into a black, inklike fluid. But this species is best known for the fact that it can make one very sick when ingested along with alcoholic beverages.

Description: This mushroom typically fruits in dense clusters, often appearing on buried, decaying wood, with gray caps that darken to nearly black in age. The caps have radial lines running from near the center to the edge. The gills are white when young, darkening rapidly as the spores mature, and deliquescing into a black, inky liquid. The stalks are white and have a ring that forms a zone of fine fibers near the base. The spore print color is black, but the self-digestion occurs so quickly that it may be difficult to obtain a spore print.

Comments: This is a delicious edible mushroom, but the would-be mycophagist should take caution not to imbibe alcoholic beverages with the meal, or the day after. The mushroom contains a chemical substance much like the drug Antabuse, which causes violent vomiting when alcohol is taken. Clusters often fruit from buried wood under new asphalt walks and driveways, uplifting or turning over pieces of asphalt.

Season: Spring, fall, and mild winters.

Habit, habitat, and distribution: Several to numerous, often prolific, on decaying wood, usually buried, or on mulch, wood chips, and so forth.

Cap diameter: 5–7.5 cm (2–3″).

Stalk height: 7.5–15 cm (3–6″).

Stalk diameter: 1–2 cm (⅓–⅔″).

OM

Family Boletaceae: The Boletes

This family of mushrooms, often referred to as "boletes," is typified by having "pores" under the cap rather than gills, which make the underside look much like a well-used pincushion. The species are fleshy, the stalk single and central, and they are found on the ground. They might be confused with the polypores (which are woody rather than fleshy, grow on wood, and usually lack a stalk) if these characteristics are not observed.

The major genera of the family Boletaceae covered in this book include the following:

Boletus, having smooth spores and giving an olive brown spore print; no scabers (fine hairs on the stalk that mat into scales) and never slimy.

Tylopilus, having pink pores and a pink spore print, often tasting bitter, with no scabers and never slimy.

Suillus, with a brown spore print, may or may not have a ring on the stalk, a slimy cap, and/or radially arranged pores.

Strobilomyces, having brown to black pores, a black spore print, and a very shaggy cap and stalk.

Boletinellus, having an olive brown spore print and very thin, radially arranged, yellow pores that often are connected by crosswalls.

Boletellus, with highly ridged spores that are olive brown in deposit, but otherwise resembling *Boletus.*

Pulveroboletus, with olive brown spores and a yellow powdery covering over cap and stalk.

Leccinum, with brown spore print and brown to black hairs that mat into scales (scabers) on the surface of the stalk.

Gyroporus, having a pale yellow to yellow spore print, without scabers, not slimy capped, and the pores are never radially arranged.

1. General appearance: These mushrooms have a fleshy cap and central stalk, and on the underside of the cap is a layer of tubes rather than gills. The tube layer is best observed by cutting the mushroom longitudinally through the cap and stalk.

2. Pores: In boletes, the spores are produced along the inner surface of the tubes or pores. The tube layer may be thick or thin, and the tubes may be uniform and round like cylinders. The pores may be lined up in radial rows (this arrangement is called *boletinoid*) or may be nonuniform and angular—the exact shape and alignment of the tubes is an important characteristic to observe in

determining the genus and species of a specimen that you find. As with gilled mushrooms, the color of the pores is important to note, and in many species there is a color change as the spores mature.

3. Spore print: As with all mushrooms, you should determine the color of the spores in deposit, since the spore print is a major differentiation between genera. To take a spore print of a bolete, cut the stalk across so that it extends about ¼ inch below the pore surface and will hold the pore surface above the sheet of paper on which the spores will fall. Place a paper cup over the cap to preserve the moisture. After six to twelve hours, the spores should be deposited in sufficient number to determine their color. One note: boletes contain a great deal of water and often will "drip" onto the paper, especially in muggy weather. So we recommend taking your spore print in a dry place (we put ours on the water heater) for best results. The color of the spores will help you determine your specimen's genus, according to the list above.

4. Ecology: Boletes are mycorrhizal (associated with roots of a higher plant), found on the ground, and many are associated with specific tree hosts. Therefore, once you know what tree(s) host particular boletes and the best times to look for them, you can pick them year after year. In Texas, most boletes are summer species; others are found in the fall. We recommend that you make careful notes as to the date, location, and habitat whenever you find them.

Some of the most delicious edible mushrooms are found in this family. Fortunately, it is also one of the safest groups for beginners to eat. The edibility rule to follow is this: Nick the pores or cap with your fingernail or a knife and look for a blue stain to develop in a few seconds. If this occurs, and the tube mouths are also red or orange, consider it nonedible. If the tube mouths are some color other than red or orange or if no staining occurs, take a small piece of the cap and taste it, letting it touch all parts of your tongue. (You may wish to spit it out, rather than swallow it.) If it is bitter or tasteless, pass it up. But if it tastes sweet and nutlike, gather it for the table. Pick young and prime specimens only, and check carefully for small insects, usually maggots (fly larvae that look like tiny white "worms"). Cut them out if you find any, refrigerate until ready to cook, and, preferably, eat your mushrooms the same day or soon after you find them.

All over the world, boletes are considered among the best edible wild mushrooms. This is certainly true in Texas, also. Unfortunately, in many cases, the study of cellular and spore characteristics using a microscope and additional technical references (Alexander Smith and Harry Thiers's *Boletes of Michigan* is a standard work) may be required to identify your specimen accurately. Even then, an exact identification may be difficult or impossible, as a great deal of work remains to be done in the study of southern boletes. Some of the same species occur in parts of Texas as in other places across the United States and the world, but our version may be smaller or larger, slightly differently colored, with larger or smaller pores, or with a different ratio of cap width to stalk height. There is also a large group of boletes that we call "Murrill's southern boletes," which were first described early in this century by William A. Murrill, a mycologist working in Florida. Murrill published written descriptions of the microscopic and macroscopic characteristics of the species, but many of them have never had their photographs published in field guides.

Boletes are a fascinating and complex group. We are including photos and descriptions of many of the common species. Wherever possible, any characteristics that can be used to differentiate one species from another have been pointed out. In working with this group, we recommend that you first determine what genus your specimen belongs to, and then begin to try to put a species' name on it. If your specimen doesn't match any in this book, you may want to consult some other books, or content yourself with recognizing the genus. By following our "rules" for edibility, you can still eat it with impunity, and we hope that your interest in mushrooms will lead you to continue to study and enjoy wild mushrooms!

TABLE 11. Common Genera of Boletes in Texas

Family	Boletaceae			
Genus	*Boletus*	*Tylopilus*	*Suillus*	*Strobilomyces*
Spore Print	Olive brown	Purple-brown to deep pink	Olive brown	Gray to black
Cap	Usually dry; colors vary; texture varies	Varied, usually smooth	Often with a slimy texture; some are dry	Gray to black and covered with black tufts
Pores	White, yellow, or red pores	White to gray, aging to dull pink	Elongated pores, arranged in radial rows	White when young, darken to black in age
Stalk	Many have a net-like pattern that may be raised; others smooth	Generally thick, and may have a netlike pattern; others smooth	The stalks may be smooth or covered with fine black "dots"	White, covered with black hairs; veil leaves zones along stalk
Ring	No ring	No ring	Usually present	No ring
Base, habit, habitat	Frequently bulbous. Usually scattered on the ground	Thick, but not bulbous	Not bulbous; some taper at the base; a common genus	White, same diameter as the stem (not bulbous)
Color Reactions	Many stain blue instantly when bruised	Generally not staining	Generally not staining	Stains red, then black, on bruising
Comments	Under mixed conifers and hardwoods	Varied hosts: mixed oak and conifers; very common	Usually under pine; smaller in size than other genera	Under mixed conifers and hardwoods
Edibility	Many delicious species; others are unpalatable	Bitter to very bitter—unpalatable	Many are edible if the slime layer on the cap is removed	Edible, though not very tasty

TABLE 11

Boletaceae				
Boletinellus	*Boletellus*	*Pulveroboletus*	*Leccinum*	*Gyroporus*
Olive brown	Olive to brown	Olive brown to brown	Dark brown to black	Pale yellow
Brown and feltlike	Dry or moist, sometimes scaly	Covered with yellow powdery veil material	White, brown, red, black; smooth	Typically dry; most are brown
Bright yellow, staining greenish-blue	Usually yellow, some bruise blue	Yellow in youth, brown in age	White or gray, free from stalk	Pores white to yellowish
Very short, not bulbous	Long, slender, deeply jagged or ridged	Bright yellow, usually smooth	Standing; dark tufts of hairs may be present	Hollow to partly hollow
No ring	No ring	Usually present	No ring	No ring
Not bulbous; found on ground under ash trees	Not bulbous	Not bulbous	Not bulbous	Not bulbous
Pores bruise greenish-blue on bruising	Some bruise blue	No bruising reactions	Flesh may stain reddish or blue	Either no reaction or deep blue
Under ash trees	Preferred host is usually pines	Very visible due to bright yellow color	Under birch and poplar	Under oak; rarely common
Edible and good, though somewhat mushy when cooked	Not generally eaten, due to bland taste	Edible, but not recommended	No toxins in this group; many are delicious	Edible and good

Boletus pinophilus

Edible/Choice

The name *pinophilus* means "pine loving" and reflects its preferred habitat. It is a truly choice edible that is large enough to be spotted from the road.

Description: The robust caps of this mushroom are brick red, smooth and dry to the touch, and often 5 inches (12.5 cm) across. The pores are yellow with green tints at maturity, and in youth they are stuffed with a white, cottony material so that it appears as if the underside of the cap is white and smooth. The stalk may be an inch or more (2–3 cm) in diameter, and the surface has a distinct netlike pattern called a *reticulum.* If this mushroom is cut or bruised, the flesh will remain white. The color of the spore print is olive brown.

Comments: A single mushroom can easily weigh in at half a pound, and if one is lucky enough to find them fruiting in a pine plantation, they can be collected by the bushel. This is the Texas "cousin" to *Boletus edulis* ("king bolete"), which has a brown cap and is prized around the world. We believe *B. pinophilus* tastes even better!

Season: Summer and fall.

Habit, habitat, and distribution: Several to often numerous, mycorrhizal with and under long-leaf pine forests; found in large concentrations usually about every 18–24 months.

Cap diameter: 10–15 cm (4–6″).

Stalk height: 7.5–15 cm (3–6″).

Stalk diameter: 25–50 mm (1–2″).

VM

Named for C. C. Frost (1805–1880), this bright red bolete that stains blue is one of the easiest boletes to learn to identify.
Description: The bright red cap is slightly sticky when young. The tube mouths and stalk are also red. There is a very shaggy, deep, netlike pattern on the stalk, which may be yellow or red. All parts of the mushroom stain blue very quickly when cut or bruised. The color of the spore print is olive brown.

Comments: The "rule" for eating boletes is to avoid those that have red tube mouths and bruise blue, but this is an edible species. (The species of *Boletus* are so numerous that they are subdivided into sections, and this rule is intended to prevent you from eating *B. satanus, B. luridus,* and related species in the section *Luridi.*) We do not recommend eating it, however, unless you are absolutely certain of your identification!
Season: Summer and fall.
Habit, habitat, and distribution: Single to several, mycorrhizal with and found under hardwoods, especially oaks and beech.
Cap diameter: 4–7.5 cm (1½–3″).
Stalk height: 4–6 cm (1½–2½″).
Stalk diameter: 20–40 mm (¾–1½″).

VM

Boletus campestris

Not recommended

Campestris means "of the fields," but this bolete is commonly found in suburban areas—lawns and parks, in grass, and under oaks.

Description: This bolete has a dry, red, velvety cap, rounded in youth and almost flat in age. In age, cracks in the cap may have a yellowish coloration. The pores are yellow and even in size, enlarging as the cap expands. The stalk is slender, tapering toward the base, yellow at the top, and deepening in color to red at the base. A coating of bright yellow mycelium (the cottony vegetative part of the fungus) covers the base, and there is no netlike pattern on the stalk. On handling, the flesh of the stalk, pores, and cap rapidly bruises a blue color. The spore print color is olive brown.

Comments: The yellow mycelium at the base is the best field identification characteristic. This species is a member of a large group of boletes that have dry red caps, yellow flesh and pores, and rapidly stain blue on bruising. Often, exact identification requires study of microscopic features, as the species are distinguished by differences in pore size, spore size, and microscopic differences in the cellular structure of the cap. This difficulty of exact identification is the reason we don't recommend members of this group for the table—besides, in our experience, they are bland and don't have that firm texture we look for in boletes.

Season: Summer.

Habit, habitat, and distribution: Single to several, under hardwoods, especially oak, on watered lawns and shady, well-mulched grass. They are mycorrhizal with oak.

Cap diameter: 5–7.5 cm (2–3").

Stalk height: 4–7.5 cm (1½–3").

Stalk diameter: 8–16 mm (⅓–⅔").

AB

Boletus fraternus group

Edible

Fraternus means "closely allied" or "brotherly" and refers to the fact that there are several boletes that are very similar in features to this one.

Description: The mushroom has a dry, red cap that opens in age until it is nearly flat. The cap flesh is yellow, as are the pores. In older specimens the cap cracks into patches along the surface so that the yellow flesh shows through. The stalk is slender and yellow, with a light red netlike pattern over it, especially along the lower half. All parts of this mushroom stain blue on injury. The spore print is olive brown. There are several similar species in this group, and generally, microscopic determination is required for an accurate species identification.

Comments: The yellow flesh showing through cracks in the caps of mature specimens is the best field identification characteristic. The mushroom lacks the yellow cottony fibers (mycelium) over the stalk base so typical of *B. campestris.* These are common inhabitants of parks and lawns, where we find them associated with large, old oaks. They are not especially good eating, being rather bland and with a mushy texture, so we don't recommend them. The best thing about these boletes is that they are commonly found alongside chanterelles.

Season: Summer.

Habit, habitat, and distribution: Single to numerous, on the ground under and mycorrhizal with hardwoods, especially oaks. They are often prolific after early summer rains.

Cap diameter: 4–7.5 cm (1½–3″).

Stalk height: 5–7.5 cm (2–3″).

Stalk diameter: 8–16 mm (⅓–⅔″).

DG

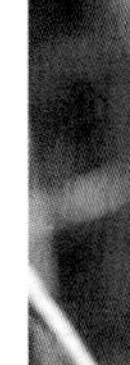

Boletus sensibilis
Not recommended

This is the largest species of a group of boletes that are similar in having reddish caps and yellow flesh and staining blue instantly. The difficulty of distinguishing among these very similar species is part of the challenge and frustration of trying to identify Texas and southern boletes.
Description: The caps are rounded, dry and unpolished, brick red or darker red, fading to a dull cinnamon brown in age. The flesh of cap and stalk is pale yellow, instantly changing to blue when cut, then slowly fading back to yellow. The pores are bright yellow, about ⅝ inch (1.5 cm) deep, and in age may be reddish on old bruised areas. The stalk is long and even, and the top is covered with a faint netlike pattern. The spore print is olive brown.
Comments: The rapid color change back to yellow on the stalk flesh after bruising blue is the best field identification characteristic, along with the fine netlike pattern over the top of the stalk near the pores and the lack of cracks in the cap surface. Use a hand lens to observe the faint netlike pattern on the upper part of the stalk. That, and the instant blue color change, will distinguish it from *B. miniato-olivaceus,* which is smaller and shows a more gradual color change to blue when cut. *Boletus bicolor* looks similar but very slowly stains blue when cut. This group of mushrooms is not recommended for the table due to the difficulty of making a definite species' identification.
Season: Summer and fall.
Habit, habitat, and distribution: Scattered to gregarious on sandy open woods under beech, oak, and other hardwoods.
Cap diameter: 6–15 cm (2½–6").
Stalk height: 8–12 cm (3¼–5").
Stalk diameter: 10–30 mm (⅜–1¼").

AB

This bolete was first described by William Murrill (1869–1957), a Florida mycologist. Murrill named this one for its red (*rubri-*) cap and yellow (*-citrinus*) flesh.
Description: This bolete's cap is a rosy red when young, often darkening to a more bricklike color in age. The dense flesh and pores are a bright yellow and stain a deep blue when cut or injured. The pores are small in youth, opening in age, and the pore surface is depressed at the stalk. The size of the pores varies, with some larger or smaller than others. In youth, the center of the stalk is almost as wide as the cap, tapering at the top and at the base, dense and yellow, with a very slight reddish netlike pattern at the top and white to pale salmon-colored cottony fibers (mycelium) over the base. Also, red stains are often present at the base. The spore print color is olive brown.
Comments: The very rounded, thick stalk in youth of this mushroom is the best field characteristic. It is near *B. rubellus* in appearance but lacks the yellow basal mycelium and is much larger in size. Use a hand lens to see the reddish netlike pattern at the top of the stalk. This mushroom is one of a group we refer to as "Murrill's southern boletes", a little-known and less-studied group of southern species that are rarely pictured in common mushroom field guides. This is, however, a very delicious mushroom, and the blue quickly disappears on cooking.
Season: Summer and fall.
Habit, habitat, and distribution: Single to numerous, scattered along the root lines, and mycorrhizal with oak and pine, usually along slopes where the two types of trees are mixed.
Cap diameter: 5–13 cm (2–5").
Stalk height: 5–10 cm (2–4").
Stalk diameter: 25–50 mm (1–2").

VM

Boletus rubellus

Edible

Rubellus means "rusty red" or "almost red" and is an accurate description of this brick red–capped common bolete that is a member of the *fraternus* group of the *Boletus* genus.

Description: This is one of the smaller members of the *fraternus* group of boletes; with a dry, velvety brick red cap that becomes cracked in age. The flesh of the cap is yellow, as are the pores. The pores and flesh of this mushroom quickly show a blue color when injured. The stalk is even and slender, yellow at the top, red below, and the flesh of the stalk is yellow with yellow cottony fibers surrounding the base. The spore print is olive brown.

Comments: The especially slender stalk that is not covered with a netlike pattern and its small size are the best field characteristics for identification. The blue bruising color doesn't fade quickly as in *B. sensibilis,* and this mushroom is smaller than *B. campestris* and doesn't have the bright yellow flesh showing in the cracks in the cap as in *B. fraternus.* This is an edible species but tends to have a bland and slimy texture when cooked.

Season: Summer.

Habit, habitat, and distribution: Single to several under oak, with which it is mycorrhizal, through the summer.

Cap diameter: 2.5–5 cm (1–2″).

Stalk height: 4–7.5 cm (1½–3″).

Stalk diameter: 6–8 mm (¼–⅓″).

DL

Edible

Tenax is from the Latin for "tenacious," a reflection of the tenacious hold it has on the substrate—that is, it is tough to pull up!

Description: The cap is rounded, in youth with a dull brick red color with an olive-tinted sheen, then losing the olive tints and becoming red to reddish brown in age. The flesh of the cap is yellow. The pores are deep, broad (1–3 mm), and arranged radially, bright yellow becoming dingy yellow in age, and turning slightly reddish brown to orange when bruised near the stalk. The stalk is thick and pale cream to tan, with a very wide, distinctive dark brown netlike pattern covering the upper half. The spore print color is olive brown.

Comments: This bolete is easily recognized due to the deep netlike patterns around the upper half of the stalk and its broad pores, which are radially arranged. Alexander Smith described it from Michigan, saying that it "seems to fruit in the early fall if the weather is exceptionally wet"; in Texas we find it in the early fall, but during relatively dry periods. (Smith also says it is "gregarious among poison ivy," but fortunately, we haven't experienced that!)

Season: Fall.

Habit, habitat, and distribution: Single to several, on ground under oak.

Cap diameter: 4–10 cm (1½–4").

Stalk height: 3–9 cm (1¼–3¾").

Stalk diameter: 10–30 mm (⅓–2¼") at top; 8–12 mm at base (⅓–½").

AB

Boletus luridellus

Edible

This bolete, first described by William Murrill (1869–1957), a Florida mycologist, was named *luridellus,* which means "an indefinite, dingy color."

Description: This is one of the larger boletes; the cap is brown, often streaked with shades of cinnamon and tawny brown, dry, and in age discolors to a lighter tawny brown. The dense flesh and pores are bright yellow and stain deep blue when cut or injured. The pores are minute and even-sized in youth, enlarging as the mushroom matures. The stalk is thick and yellow, becoming red at the base. The spore print color is olive brown.

Comments: The red coloration at the base of the yellow stalk and the comparatively large size are the best field characteristics. *B. fraternus* has a light red netlike pattern over the stalk base, but the ground color is yellow. *Boletus rubellus* has a reddish base but is a slender, small species. It is a commonly seen mushroom in the South; we refer to it and some others as "Murrill's southern boletes," a little-known and less-studied set of species that are rarely pictured in most mushroom field guides. This is a very meaty and delicious mushroom and cooks up with a nice firm texture. It is similar in appearance to the European species *B. appendiculatus,* though microscopically it is not closely related.

Season: Summer and fall.

Habit, habitat, and distribution: Single to numerous, scattered along the root or on the root zone of, and mycorrhizal with, oak, often on lawns and other grassy areas.

Cap diameter: 5–15 cm (2–6″).

Stalk height: 5–13 cm (2–5″).

Stalk diameter: 25–50 mm (1–2″).

VM

This common summer bolete gets its name from its olive brown spores; it was named by William Murrill and described from Florida.

Description: This mushroom has a brown to reddish brown, dry cap. The flesh of the cap is a yellowish olive color, as are the pores, and both parts quickly show a blue color when injured. The stalk is even and slender, yellow at the top, and often with a reddish band below. This band on the stalk does not have a netlike pattern but is made up of distinct red wooly spots that stand out over the yellow color of the stalk. The spore print is olive brown.

Comments: This is a medium to large member of the *Boletus luridus* group. The reddish stalk that lacks a netlike pattern is distinctive. Fortunately for the mycophagist, it is edible and delicious, with a firm texture when cooked. North of Texas this species could be confused with *Boletus luridus,* which is poisonous. Remember, the pores of *B. oliveisporus must be yellow* with no hint of orange or red.

Season: Summer and fall.

Habit, habitat, and distribution: Single to several under oak, with which it is mycorrhizal, through the summer and warm months of the fall.

Cap diameter: 6–15 cm (2¼–6″).

Stalk height: 7.5–12.5 cm (3–5″).

Stalk diameter: 25–50 mm (1–2″).

VM

Boletus pulverulentus

Not recommended

Pulverulentus means "powdery"—here it refers to the dry, powdery surface of the cap.

Description: The cap is dull brown to dark brown, rounded to broadly rounded, dry, dull, and appearing powdery on the surface. The cap slowly becomes sticky, shiny, and tacky to the touch, making this a very variable species. The flesh is yellow but changes so quickly to blue when cut that it is often difficult even to see the yellow context. The pores are medium deep, yellow, and also bruise instantly blue. The stalk is equal, bright yellow to orange-yellow at the top, reddish brown and slightly fuzzy at the base, and appearing covered with a fine powder. Raised lines, but not a true netlike pattern, can be observed on the stalk. The spore print color is olive brown.

Comments: The powdery covering on the cap and base of the stalk is the best field character to identify this species, which is one of many similar-appearing species. Due to the difficulty of making a positive identification, we do not recommend eating any of the yellow-fleshed, blue-bruising species, though none are known to be toxic.

Season: Summer and early fall.

Habit, habitat, and distribution: Solitary to scattered, often on moist soil on slopes, in mixed deciduous and coniferous woods.

Cap diameter: 4–8 cm (1½–3¼″).

Stalk height: 4–8 cm (1½–3¼″).

Stalk diameter: 10–25 mm (⅓–1″).

AB

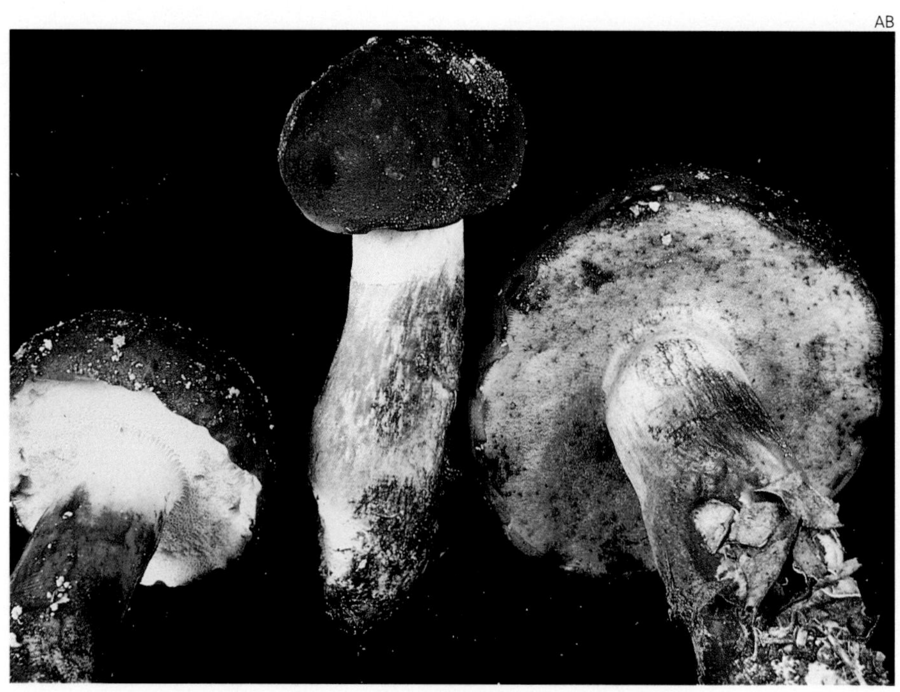

Communis is from the Latin word for "hair" and describes the slightly hairy cap of this brown-capped bolete.

Description: The cap is brown to rosy brown in color and slightly hairy. There is typically a reddish layer just under the surface. The flesh is whitish to yellow and rapidly bruises blue on cutting or bruising. The pores are dull greenish yellow, darkening to brown on aging, and they bruise blue when wounded; the pores are irregular and are not stuffed when young. The stalk is equal or slightly enlarged just above the base, minutely covered with fine hairs in places, and is not covered with a netlike pattern, varying in color from dull yellow with reddish mottling to deep red. The flesh of the stalk is solid, yellow, and bruises blue when handled. The spore print color is olive brown.

Comments: The presence of a red layer just under the brown cap cuticle (outer layer) is the best field characteristic. Cut the cap in half to observe it. It is closely related to *B. rubellus,* which is smaller, but the two are easily confused in the field. This mushroom, like the other reddish-capped, yellow-fleshed, blue-staining boletes, is not recommended for the table. It is often confused with *B. subtomentosus,* which lacks the red layer under the cap cuticle and does not show the staining reaction.

Season: Summer.

Habit, habitat, and distribution: Single to several on ground in deciduous woods, or in grassy areas. Often found in relatively dry woods.

Cap diameter: 5.5–12 cm (2¼–5").

Stalk height: 4–10 cm (1½–4").

Stalk diameter: 9–17 mm (⅓–⅔").

AB

Boletus affinis var. *maculosus*

Edible/Choice

This mushroom has a complex name, which translates to "spotted member of the family," but it is so delicious it is worth learning to remember and pronounce!

Description: The cap of this mushroom has a velvety yellow-brown, dry skin that is often pitted or spotted, revealing meaty yellow flesh below. The pore mouths are white when young, darkening to the olive brown color of the spores as it ages. The stalk is white to brown, equal in diameter or sometimes with an enlarged base. The spore print color is olive brown.

Comments: In our opinion, this is one of the best edible boletes. Clean it gently and sauté it in a little butter, and it has a taste and texture of the most tender, juicy steak you have ever eaten! We find it in the wooded areas around golf courses; but, unfortunately, rarely do we find a great quantity.

Season: Summer and fall.

Habit, habitat, and distribution: Single to several, mycorrhizal with and found under deciduous trees, especially oak and beech; usually found in mixed woods (rather than pure stands) containing these trees.

Cap diameter: 3.5–10 cm (1⅜–4").

Stalk height: 3–10 cm (1½–4").

Stalk diameter: 10–20 mm (⅜–¾").

VM

Boletus curtisii
Edible

This southern bolete was named for botanist-mycologist M. A. Curtis (1808–1872) and is very distinctive with its lemon yellow cap and stalk.

Description: The overall color of this mushroom is bright yellow: cap, stalk, and young pores. Both the stalk and cap are slimy, as if covered with a mucous coating. The stalk is long and slender, and the base is white and cottony and often extends an inch (2.5 cm) or more into the ground. The spore print color is olive brown.

Comments: Edible, but not especially tasty. Common under pines during the summer. W. A. Curtis was a pioneer in mycology in the South, collecting throughout North Carolina, finding many species he could not identify. He became an advocate of mycophagy, believing that better knowledge of the wild species could have done much to alleviate hunger and starvation during the Civil War. *B. retipes* is similar but is orange to orange-yellow overall, is not slimy, and has a stalk that has a distinct netlike pattern.

Season: Summer and early fall.

Habit, habitat, and distribution: Single to several under pines, with which it is mycorrhizal. Most often found following the first fall rains.

Cap diameter: 4–7.5 cm (1½–3").

Stalk height: 10–15 cm (4–6").

Stalk diameter: 4–8 mm (⅙–⅓").

AB

Boletus viridiflavus

Edible

Viridiflavus is from the Latin roots for "green" and "yellow," which is an apt description of this bolete with its olive tinges in the cap and bright golden yellow pores.

Description: This bolete has a velvety surface, which may be slightly slimy to the touch under moist conditions, and a red-brown to yellow-brown cap that may have an olive tinge. In youth it is rounded; as it ages, it opens out until nearly flat. The pores are bright golden yellow, darkening to olive as the spores mature, and are even in size, enlarging slightly as the cap expands. The stalk is rose to red, long and slender, and equal in diameter. It is the same color as the pores at the top and is often covered with white cottony fibers at the base. There is no color change on handling. The spore print color is olive brown.

Comments: This mushroom is known from throughout the South, from Florida to Texas; north to Vermont, and even from China. Some older works refer to this mushroom as *B. auriporus.* A similar but poorly understood species, *B. caespitosus,* occurs in clusters and has an enlarged base, but it is seldom found in Texas. All these species are edible but reported as bland and mediocre in flavor. The fruiting bodies are on the small side, and rarely can enough be found at one time for a meal.

Season: Late spring through summer.

Habit, habitat, and distribution: Single to several, rarely in quantity, under hardwoods and conifers, with which this species is probably mycorrhizal.

Cap diameter: 2–7.5 cm (¾–3").

Stalk height: 5–7.5 cm (2–3").

Stalk diameter: 6–12 mm (¼–½").

AB

Separans means "notable" or "distinct" and is the name of another member of the genus *Boletus;* this one is somewhat like it—thus the name *pseudo.* It is one of the most delicious of all Texas (and southern) boletes.

Description: This bolete has a dry, purple, velvety cap, with a distinct rounded shape. The pores are pure white and equal in youth, darkening to olive as the spores mature, enlarging slightly as the cap expands. The stalk is thick and equal in diameter, white to tan at the base and covered with a distinct pink netlike pattern. The stalk darkens to purplish brown on the upper half in age. There is no color change on handling. The spore print color is olive brown.

Comments: From above, this mushroom looks a lot like *Tylopilus plumbeoviolaceus,* but the olive brown rather than pink spore print, the netlike pattern on the stalk, and the delicious nutty flavor distinguish it. It is our very favorite edible Texas bolete—the wonderful, meatlike texture and delicious flavor make it well worth braving the chiggers to get it. Look for this one early in the day, before the bugs beat you to it!

Season: Summer.

Habit, habitat, and distribution: Single to several, occasionally in quantity, under hardwoods and conifers, with which this species is probably mycorrhizal.

Cap diameter: 5–10 cm (2–4").

Stalk height: 5–10 cm (2–4").

Stalk diameter: 12–37 mm (½–1½").

DL

Boletus albisulphureus

Edible/Choice

Sulphureus means "yellow, like sulfur," and *albi-* means "white," and this is a white bolete with a yellow netlike pattern on its white stalk.

Description: This bolete has a dry cap that is chalk white and rounded. The pores are sulfur yellow when young, darkening to olive as the spores mature, and are equal in size, enlarging as the cap expands. The stalk is thick and bulbous at the base, covered at the top with a yellow netlike pattern that looks like a thick, open netting over the white stalk. There is no color change on handling. The spore print color is olive brown.

Comments: This southern species is a member of the *B. edulis* group, sharing the bulbous base and thick stalk, the very rounded cap, and even more important to the mycophagist, the delicious taste and firm texture. It is not as large as *B. edulis* but is just as delicious!

Season: Late spring through summer.

Habit, habitat, and distribution: Single to numerous, occasionally in quantity, under hardwoods and conifers, with which it is probably mycorrhizal.

Cap diameter: 4–10 cm (1½–4").

Stalk height: 5–7.5 cm (2–3").

Stalk diameter: 25–50 mm (1–2").

AB

Edible

Griseus means "gray," the predominant color of the fruiting bodies of this common bolete.

Description: The caps are pale gray to brownish gray, thin fleshed, and nearly plane at maturity, with a dry, feltlike surface. The pores are pale gray when young, darkening to gray-brown as the spores mature. The stalk is white to creamy tan, with a distinct brown netlike pattern along it, and shows yellow coloring at the base in age. The color of the spore print is light olive brown.

Comments: The raw flesh of this bolete has a mild flavor; cooked, it is considered quite good. The novice could mistake a bitter *Tylopilus* species for this bolete—always check the spore print color to make sure it is olive brown and not pink as in *Tylopilus*.

Season: Summer and fall.

Habit, habitat, and distribution: Several to numerous, often abundant, on ground and generally associated with oak species.

Cap diameter: 5–12 cm (2–5").

Stalk height: 4–11 cm (1½–4¼").

Stalk diameter: 10–24 mm (⅓–1").

VM

Tylopilus ballouii

Not edible

This mushroom was named after W. H. Ballou, an amateur mycologist who first collected it. When young, it is very pretty, with its cap of fluorescent orange tinged with pink.

Description: These mushrooms are small but are quite noticeable when young because the cap is a bright pinkish orange color. In age, the caps darken to dull orange to brown. The tube mouths are white, deepening to pink as the spores mature. A brown stain appears if the tube mouths are injured. The stalk is white and covered with a fine netlike pattern. The color of the spore print is tan.

Comments: This species has been reported as edible, but some people find it bitter even when thoroughly cooked. Others find it merely insipid. A northern species, *Tylopilus felleus,* also has a netlike pattern on the stalk and bitter taste but usually grows from very old decayed stumps. It is under hardwoods, especially oak.

Season: Summer and fall.

Habit, habitat, and distribution: Single to several on ground in mixed woods, often under pine. Rarely numerous.

Cap diameter: 5–12 cm (2–4¾").

Stalk height: 2.5–12 cm (1–4¾").

Stalk diameter: 5–25 mm (¼–1").

JL

Tylopilus "purple cap group A"

Not edible

This is a common summer bolete that has not yet been named and described in the literature. It is found in East Texas woods and eastward through Mississippi.

Description: This is a large and meaty mushroom, and it is not unusual for a specimen to weigh upwards of a pound. The height averages 6 inches, and the cap is often as broad. The deep wine red–colored cap is smooth and dry, with light-colored pores that deepen to brown as the dark pink spores mature. The stalk is smooth and thick—a truly magnificent and handsome specimen with white flesh that does not change color when bruised. The spore print color is pink.

Comments: Unfortunately, this bolete is inedible and bitter, a great disappointment to mushroom hunters whose first glance leads them to believe they have found *Boletus edulis,* a well-known edible bolete found in other parts of the country (but rarely in Texas). Also unfortunately, this is one of the most common species found in southern mixed woods. *Tylopilus plumbeoviolaceus* also has a violet-purple cap but has a violet stalk and shows netlike reticulations at the top of the stalk.

Season: Summer.

Habit, habitat, and distribution: Several to numerous in mixed woods throughout East Texas, Louisiana, and Mississippi. At times, extremely common.

Cap diameter: 10–20 cm (4–8″).

Stalk height: 10–15 cm (4–6″).

Stalk diameter: 20–37 mm (3/4–1 1/2″).

VM

Tylopilus chromapes
Edible

This mushroom gets its name from the striking bright yellow color at the base of the stalk, and *chromapes* translates to "yellow foot."

Description: The cap is rounded at first, opening until it is nearly flat in age, dry, and bright pink to rose colored when fresh, often fading to tan in age. The pores are very small, white when young, and deepening to a dingy pink as the spores mature. The stalk is fairly thick and white, with a bright yellow base. The flesh of the base is also bright yellow. The spores are a wine-red to pinkish brown.

Comments: Reported edible, but having had bitter experiences (pun intended) with other *Tylopilus* species, we have not had the fortitude to try it.

Season: Fall.

Habit, habitat, and distribution: Single to several, occasionally numerous, under conifers and hardwoods.

Cap diameter: 5–10 cm (2–4″).

Stalk height: 4–12 cm (1½–5″).

Stalk diameter: 8–16 mm (⅓–⅔″).

AB

Edible

Suillus is from the Italian meaning "pertaining to or belonging to swine"; here it refers to the genus of boletes that have either slimy caps or boletinoid pores (arranged in radial rows) and often have "dots" that contain "resin" (often referred to as *glandular dots*) along the stalk. *Hirtellus* means "hairy" and refers to this species' fine hairs on the cap.

Description: These boletes are easily overlooked due to their small stature. The caps are small, pale tan to reddish brown, and covered with tiny hairs. These hairs are pale yellow to tan in youth, darkening to a cinnamon brown in age when they become matlike and imbedded in a layer of slime. The pore mouths are very fine, pale yellow in youth, darkening to an olive brown in age. The pores become boletinoid in age. The stalks are equal, pale in color, and covered with the resinous glandular dots along their length. The spore print color is olive brown.

Comments: Members of the genus *Suillus* are often slimy, which is due to microscopic features of the cells of the cap. If you peel off the slime layer (or cuticle) of the cap before cooking, these can be quite palatable; if you neglect to do that, they will be quite slimy. If you like okra, you will likely be quite fond of *Suillus* species.

Season: Summer and fall.

Habit, habitat, and distribution: Several to many under two- and three-needle pine species with which they are mycorrhizal. It is often abundant and is widely known throughout the eastern half of the United States.

Cap diameter: 2.5–6 cm (1–2½").

Stalk height: 4–7.5 cm (1½–3").

Stalk diameter: 4–6 mm (⅙–¼").

AB

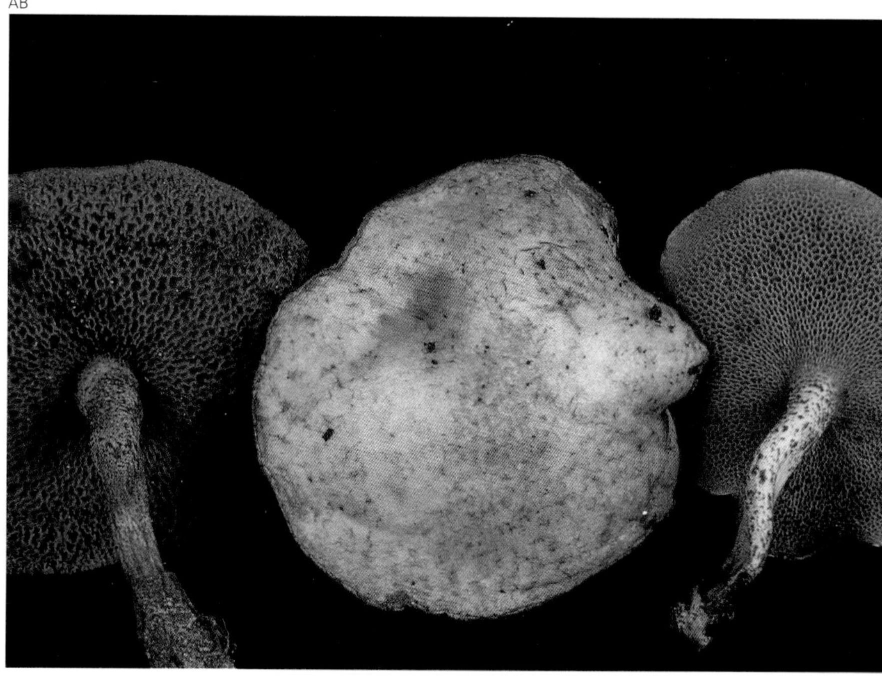

Suillus decipiens
Edible

Decipiens means "deceiving," indicating that this mushroom superficially resembles another—in this case, *Boletinellus meruliodes.*
Description: These are small boletes with yellow-tan to pinkish caps covered with dry fibers and scales. The caps are not slimy. The pore mouths are yellow, quite large, and boletinoid in age. The stalks are short with a distinct ring at the top and lack glandular dots. The spore print color is olive brown.
Comments: Many members of the genus *Suillus* are often slimy, but this one is not. It is edible but not very memorable. At times it is so common that you can't resist trying some. It does tend to get slimy during cooking, so we recommend "field trimming" (cutting away any dirty spots at the time of collecting) so that you can minimize washing. The pore layer is at least 8–10 mm thick, which clearly separates it from the very thin pores (1–3 mm) of *Boletinellus meruliodes.*
Season: Summer and fall.
Habit, habitat, and distribution: Several to many in dry pine woods. It is often found along roadcuts and is frequently the first mushroom spotted when entering the woods. It is often abundant and is widely known throughout the eastern half of the United States.
Cap diameter: 2.5–5 cm (1–2").
Stalk height: 2.5–5 cm (1–2").
Stalk diameter: 4–6 mm (1/6–1/4").

AB

Strobilomyces confusus

Edible

Strobilomyces means "resembling a pine cone" and *confusus* means "confusing," referring to the similarity of this species with *S. floccopus.* This mushroom (and others of the *Strobilomyces* genus) is often referred to as "old man of the woods."

Description: The cap is easy to recognize because it is covered with grayish-black to black, soft, downy scales. The margin of the cap is shaggy as well. The pores are white when fresh, gradually darkening in age. If bruised or cut, the white flesh turns dull red and then black. The stalk is also covered with black wooly fibers. The spore print color is black.

Comments: Two species, *S. confusus* and *S. floccopus,* both occur in the South; microscopic characteristics are required to separate the species. In our experience, *S. confusus* is much more common. Reported edible but not remarkable; often recommended due to the ease of positive identification. A convenient field character is the soft downy fibers of *Strobilomyces confusus* while *S. floccopus* has stiff erect fibers.

Season: Summer and fall.

Habit, habitat, and distribution: Single to several, under mixed woods and hardwoods; rarely abundant.

Cap diameter: 2.5–7.5 cm (1–3").

Stalk height: 7.5–15 cm (3–6").

Stalk diameter: 8–16 cm (⅓–⅔").

AB *Strobilomyces floccopus.*

AB

Boletinellus merulioides

Edible

This mushroom's name means "like the bolete, like the merulius" and refers to the unusual pore structure, which resembles gills with crosswalls rather than typical round pores that are arranged in radial rows.
Description: This mushroom is found under ash trees, which have been planted by the hundreds all across Texas for their drought resistance and rapid growth. The caps are light brown, dry, and feltlike when young, darkening in age. The decurrent (running down the stalk) pores are bright yellow and bruise a greenish blue. The pore layer is only 2–3 mm thick. When young, the pores are very small and close, becoming larger as the cap expands. The stalks are short, yellow to deep brown, and frequently off-center. The color of the spore print is olive brown.

Comments: This is a common urban mushroom, found throughout the summer months. It is edible, and we consider the taste to be pretty good, especially in spaghetti sauce. Over half a bushel were collected under a single tree when we took this photo. If you look around the base of the stalk you will often see small black balls called sclerotia. These can germinate and produce new hyphal growth.
Season: Summer and fall.
Habit, habitat, and distribution: Several to many, associated closely with and found only under ash trees throughout the state. In warm weather, when rainfall is sufficient, they can be prolific.
Cap diameter: 5–15 cm (2–6″).
Stalk height: 3.7–5 cm (1½–2″).
Stalk diameter: 8–25 mm (⅓–1″).

VM

Boletellus is the genus name given to a group of boletes that have heavily ridged spores. (Members of the genus *Boletus* have smooth spores.) *Ananus* is the plant genus that contains the pineapples; the name was given to this species because the pattern of scales on the cap looks much like the pattern on a pineapple.
Description: This mushroom is found at the base of or very close to pine trees. The cap is purple to a dull pinkish red and covered with fiberlike hairs that compact into large scales. These hairy scales are often found hanging from the edge of the cap. The pore mouths are yellow in youth, darkening to deep olive brown in age. Both pores and flesh stain blue when handled or injured. The stalk is white to pale tan and smooth. The color of the spore print is olive brown.
Comments: This is an easy mushroom to learn to recognize, with its reddish to purple cap and heavy scales on top. It is reported edible, but we do not recommend it (anyway, it's quite tough!). This is not a rare mushroom but is only occasionally found in any quantity.
Season: Summer and fall.
Habit, habitat, and distribution: Single to several in mixed oak pine woods often at the base of living conifers. This is a warm temperate to tropical species, worldwide in distribution, and is to be expected during very warm, humid summer months.
Cap diameter: 5–15 cm (2–6″).
Stalk height: 5–10 cm (2–4″).
Stalk diameter: 8–25 mm (⅓–1″).

AB

Pulveroboletus hemichrysus

Edibility unknown

Pulver- is from the Latin for "powdery" and indicates the powdery outer covering. This genus of boletes features a universal veil that surrounds the embryonic fruiting body and breaks up into powdery areas that remain on the cap of the mature mushroom. *Hemichrysus* means "half-yellow."

Description: This is a large bolete with a dry, bright yellow cap. In youth, the cap is covered with powdery veil remnants, though these may wash off. The cap is rounded, thick and meaty, and the pore mouths are brown or reddish brown. The stalk is short and thick, yellow, tinged with red, and the tube mouths descend down the stalk. The spore print color is olive brown.

Comments: This mushroom is found near pines and pine stumps and is to be found wherever pines are common. We don't know about its edibility.

Season: Late spring into fall.

Habit, habitat, and distribution: Several to numerous, occasionally in quantity, around conifer stumps and under living conifers.

Cap diameter: 5–12.5 cm (2–5").

Stalk height: 5–7.5 cm (2–3").

Stalk diameter: 25–50 mm (1–2").

AB

Pulveroboletus (from the Latin *pulver-* meaning "powder" or "dust") is the genus of boletes that have a powdery universal veil. This one is named for W. H. Ravenel, a botanist and mycologist who lived and worked in the South during the 1800s. More than fifty species of plants and fungi have been named for him.

Description: In youth, the entire mushroom is covered by a cobweblike veil that is bright sulfur yellow. In age, the cap expands to nearly plane, darkens to pinkish, orange, or reddish brown, and the remains of the veil may be left as matted remnants on the cap center. The pores are bright yellow when fresh, darkening to olive yellow in age, and on handling bruise bluish green and later darken to brown. The stalk is rather long, bright yellow when young, and equal in diameter. Remnants of the cobweblike veil often remain on the stalk and are visible only because the dark olive brown spores often stick to it.

Comments: This bright yellow mushroom looks almost fluorescent when young—you can't miss it! It is reported edible.

Season: Summer and fall.

Habit, habitat, and distribution: Single to numerous, on the ground under conifers and hardwoods, often appearing during dry spells, and prolific in wet weather.

Cap diameter: 2–8 cm (¾–3¼").

Stalk height: 6–15 cm (2½–6").

Stalk diameter: 5–15 mm (¼–½").

JL

Leccinum albellum

Edible

Leccinum is an Italian word for fungus; it has been assigned as a genus name for the group of boletes that have small tufts of hairs along the stalk. These tufts, called scabers, form scales that are often darker than the lighter context of the flesh under them. *Albellum* means "little white one," an appropriate name for this white species.

Description: The caps of this mushroom are white to pale tan, dry to the touch, and the pore mouths are white when young, darkening to brown as the spores mature. The stalks are white, long and thin, and the scabers on the stalk are tan to brown. The spore print color is brown.

Comments: This species is edible but has very little flavor. It is often common in mixed hardwood forests during summer and fall. It is a very variable species, and its forms include one with brownish gray spots on a white background and one with a coarse grayish brown netlike pattern over the cap.

Season: Summer and fall.

Habit, habitat, and distribution: Single to several (rarely numerous) on ground under conifers and in mixed hardwoods. Common in wooded areas in fall throughout the state.

Cap diameter: 2.5–5 cm (1–2").

Stalk height: 5–10 cm (2–4").

Stalk diameter: 4–8 mm (1/6–1/3").

AB

Rugosiceps derives from the Latin roots for "rough" and "head"; thus, this mushroom would be expected to have a rough or wrinkled cap.

Description: The caps of this mushroom are yellow-brown to dull brown, smooth when young, but by maturity developing a notably wrinkled or cracked surface. The edges of the cap often crack as the cap expands. The pores are yellow, deepening to olive brown in age. The stalks are tan to brown with dark brown to black scales, especially in the middle and lower thirds. The spore print color is brown.

Comments: This species is reported edible but flavorless. It is often common on oak-shaded lawns and among oaks throughout the summer.

Season: Late spring into fall.

Habit, habitat, and distribution: Single to several (rarely numerous) on ground under oaks. Common in partially wooded areas during warm, wet summers.

Cap diameter: 2.5–5 cm (1–2″).

Stalk height: 5–10 cm (2–4″).

Stalk diameter: 6–12 mm (¼–½″).

CO

Leccinum crocipodium

Edible

Crocipodium translates roughly to "saffron foot," obliquely referring to the somewhat enlarged, bulbous base of this mushroom.

Description: The brown and yellow, cracked and mottled, uneven pitted surface of the cap of this mushroom is the best identification feature. The pore mouths are yellow in youth, darkening in age. The stalks are tan and smooth, covered with very fine dark brown scales, and are enlarged at the base. The spore print color is brown.

Comments: This species is reported edible but flavorless. It is often common wherever oaks are found; throughout the Coastal Plain and the Hill Country.

Season: Summer and fall.

Habit, habitat, and distribution: One of our most common boletes, found in a wide range of habitats and shows much variation. Common in partially wooded areas during warm, wet summers.

Cap diameter: 2.5–5.5 cm (1–3").

Stalk height: 5–10 cm (2–4").

Stalk diameter: 6–18 mm (¼–¾").

AB

Not recommended

Gyroporus (which translates to "round pores") is the genus name given to the boletes that have pale yellow spores, small, nearly circular pores, and a stalk that is often hollow in age. *Subalbellus* means "somewhat white," an apt description for the "dirty white" color of the mushroom.

Description: The caps of this mushroom are smooth, white, and thin, often with a small area that is pinkish, tan, or yellow. The tube layer is thin, and the tube mouths are white and darken to a dull yellow-tan in age. The stalks are thick and white, often darker than the caps, and hollow in age. The spore print color is pale yellow.

Comments: This is a rather drab mushroom, with little to recommend it. Although it is reported to be edible, it is seldom found in sufficient quantity for eating.

Season: Late spring into fall.

Habit, habitat, and distribution: Single to several, usually in sandy soil, it is widely distributed throughout the Coastal Plain. It is often found under oaks and pines and is to be expected during dry weather.

Cap diameter: 5–15 cm (2–6").

Stalk height: 5–10 cm (2–4").

Stalk diameter: 12–25 mm (½–1").

VM

Order Aphyllophorales

Family Cantharellaceae: The Chanterelles

This is a very well-known mushroom family that is often referred to as the "chanterelles." Variously known as the *girolle* of France and the *pfifferling* of Germany, it is one of the most delicious edible species and is found in abundance in Texas. Chanterelles can be found under oaks throughout the summer and fall given sufficient rainfall.

1. General appearance: These are brightly colored mushrooms—most are golden yellow or bright red-orange—and are highly conspicuous against the dark soil where they appear. At maturity, the mushroom resembles a filled funnel with the spore-bearing surface along the outer sloping sides.

2. Ridges: The spore-bearing surface of these mushrooms is composed of shallow, blunt, raised ridges, unlike the sharp-edged gills found in the gilled mushrooms. These ridges are often forked, or folded over, or with veins between the ridges, and in some species are like raised veins yielding a nearly smooth spore-bearing surface.

3. Spore print: The color of the spores in deposit is white to buff, yellow, cream, pinkish, or tan. To take a spore print of members of this group, lay a cap on its side on white paper. Six to twelve hours later, a spore print should be visible.

4. Ecology: These mushrooms are mycorrhizal with various trees, including primarily oak species, and are found prolifically during the warm summer and fall months. We have found them almost all over Texas, from the Hill Country to East Texas, and even at Lost Maples State Park in the High Plains (we didn't pick them; collecting is forbidden in state parks!). They are slow-growing mushrooms and often dry out and remain for several weeks, as they seem to be impervious to insects. During wet months, under the right conditions, we have collected them by the bushel.

As you look at the photos and read the descriptions in this section, make careful comparison with the specimens you find. It is important to read the descriptions with care and study the pictures since there are "look-alikes" that can confuse the beginner, and this is a group that you are very likely to try for the table. For recipes and information about cooking chanterelles safely, consult the cooking chapter.

Cantharellus cibarius

Edible/Choice

Cibarius means "resembling food," and this mushroom, often referred to as the "golden chanterelle," is among the best-known edibles and is one of the most common species found in mixed Texas woods in summer and fall.

Description: These bright mushrooms are egg-yolk yellow to golden yellow over the entire fruiting body and can resemble a field of golden flowers when fruiting in quantity. The caps are smooth and golden, with a depressed center. When young, the edges are rolled under, and as the mushrooms enlarge, the edges unroll and open until they are wavy and often extend above the center so the mushroom appears to have turned itself inside out. The smooth ridges running down the flaring stalk are not sharp and distinct as in the gilled mushrooms. The spore print color will be pale yellow. To confirm your identification, pinch off a chunk of the cap and rub it between your thumb and index finger, then smell it. It will smell sweet, like apricots, not at all "musty." By the time you've filled your bag or basket, the aroma will permeate your hands.

Comments: This choice edible species is prolific, occurring throughout the state on watered lawns, in forests, and almost anywhere there are oak trees. The prime place to look for them is along sloping ground under hardwoods in summer and early fall. For eating, pick firm, young, golden specimens and trim away and discard any brown or "mushy" spots before cooking. (Throw your cleanings out under oak trees near your house—and start looking there for chanterelles!) Be careful not to confuse *Omphalotus olearius* (the jack-o'-lantern) with chanterelles; make sure your specimen has blunt ridges, a sweet aroma, and egg-yolk yellow coloring described and pictured here. Remember, *no chanterelle fruits in clusters on wood*! See the cooking chapter for cooking instructions and recipes.

Season: Early summer through late fall, whenever moisture is sufficient.

Habit, habitat, and distribution: Several to numerous, on ground, under oak and other hardwoods, with which it is mycorrhizal. Known from wooded areas and lawns across East Texas and in elevated areas of Central and West Texas.

Cap diameter: 5–15 cm (2–6").

Stalk height: 5–10 cm (2–4").

Stalk diameter: 8–12 mm (⅓–½").

VM

Cantharellus lateritius

Edible/Choice

This chanterelle's species' name translates to "bricklike," referring here not to the color (it is more yellow to orange-yellow) but to the fairly smooth underside. This is a common edible species and is closely related to the golden chanterelle. It is distinguished by its more fragile aspect, lighter color, and the nearly smooth underside.

Description: The cap of this mushroom is pale egg-yolk yellow, with a depressed center. In youth, the edges are rolled under, and in age they open out and become wavy. The spore-bearing surface is almost smooth, or at most only slightly wrinkled, and this surface descends down the stalk and extends nearly to the base. The spore print color is yellow.

Comments: This mushroom is edible and just as good as others in the chanterelle family but is a tropical to subtropical species and therefore has a more narrow, Gulf Coast distribution. It is distinguished from *C. cibarius* by its paler color and smoother underside.

Season: Summer and fall.

Habit, habitat, and distribution: Several to many, on ground, under hardwoods and in mixed woods. It is commonly prevalent along sloping creek banks.

Cap diameter: 2.5–10 cm (1–4″).

Stalk height: 2.5–10 cm (1–4″).

Stalk diameter: 5–25 mm (¼–1″).

VM

Taking its name from cinnabar (a bright red ore containing mercury), this diminutive member of the chanterelle family is common and easy to identify.

Description: The cap of this mushroom is a bright reddish orange, with a depressed center. The edges are inrolled at first, turning upwards at maturity. The spore-bearing surface under the cap consists of pinkish, thick-edged ridges that descend along the stalk. The stalk is slender, and the overall proportion of cap width to height is usually about 1:4. The color of the spore print is pinkish cream.

Comments: This is a good edible for beginners because it is so easy to identify. It may take a good collection to have enough to eat, but they are so prolific under oak and pine that many can be collected quite easily. When cooked (thoroughly!), it has a delightful peppery flavor. The biggest problem with this mushroom is that since it is so small, it may be a chore to clean. We always "field trim" our collections by pinching off the dirty end before putting them in the bag.

Season: Early spring through late fall; often found during unseasonably warm winters.

Habit, habitat, and distribution: Several to numerous under oak and pine; often prolific.

Cap diameter: 1–5 cm (3/8–2").
Stalk height: 2–6 cm (3/4–2 3/8").
Stalk diameter: 1.5–15 mm (up to 5/8").

AB

Craterellus fallax
Edible

This trumpet-shaped fungus, a cousin of the chanterelle, is called "trumpet of death" in France—but for its somber appearance rather than its edibility. The species' name *fallax* means "deceptive."
Description: The mushrooms closely resemble pale to dark gray trumpets on the forest floor, usually less than an inch (2.5 cm) across and no more than 3 inches (7.5 cm) tall. The fruiting bodies are trumpet shaped, with inrolled edges, and the spore-bearing surface consists of low ridges and veins along the outer edges of the stalk. The spores are salmon colored.
Comments: This is a good edible and not easily confused with anything dangerous—it just requires a sharp eye to see it against the similarly colored forest floor. It is black when cooked, and unscrupulous cooks occasionally chop it up and pass it off as truffles! It is closely related to *Cantharellus cornucopiodes,* differing only in spore print color.
Season: Fall and winter.
Habit, habitat, and distribution: Single to several in mixed woods, often under oak and conifer. Found throughout the Coastal Plain and in forested areas.
Cap diameter: 1.8–5 cm (¾–2″).
Stalk height: 5–10 cm (2–4″).
Stalk diameter: 3–18 mm (⅛–¾″).

AB

Cantharellus minor

Edible

This scientific name has an obvious meaning—this species is a much smaller version of the golden chanterelle.

Description: These tiny chanterelles are easy to spot because they are a bright fluorescent yellow. The caps are very small and nearly translucent, with bright ridges along the underside. The smooth, equal stalk is quite long compared to the cap diameter. The spore print color is pale yellow.

Comments: These can be difficult to distinguish from "baby" versions of the larger chanterelles. The difference is that these don't get any bigger, and the color is more translucent. They are still edible and good, and the best we can say is that they generally herald the arrival of summer and their larger cousins.

Season: Early summer to late fall.

Habit, habitat, and distribution: On slopes, under oaks.

Cap diameter: 0.8–1.2 cm (⅓–½″).

Stalk height: 5–10 cm (2–4″).

Stalk diameter: 3–6 mm (⅛–¼″).

AB

Family Clavariaceae: The Coral and Club Fungi

The coral and club fungi comprise a rather large family of fungi that resemble sea coral or small clubs emerging from the forest floor. They were once considered to be one large genus, but new studies have caused the group to be divided into more than thirty genera. In many cases, these distinctions are made on the basis of microscopic characteristics and chemical reactions. In addition, some are parasites, others decomposers, and still others are mycorrhizal fungi, so they are different in both their microscopic characteristics and ecology.

1. General appearance: Members of this family will usually be found on the ground and are of two types. The club fungi, as the name implies, look like small (usually 3 inches or less) clubs or straight spindles standing on end (these are considered "unbranched" corals). The corals look very much like sea corals, with medium to large bodies made of a fleshy base or stalk that repeatedly branches, narrowing to fine tips. As a group, corals are easy to recognize, but an exact identification may be more difficult. When looking at a coral, it is important to note the branching pattern: is it bilateral or symmetric? Are the branch tips blunt, pointed, or divided?

2. Spore print: The spores of corals are borne along the branches rather than just at the tips of the fungus. Spore prints are generally white or buff to brown.

3. Ecology: Most of the coral and club fungi derive their nutrients from dead wood, humus, and well-decayed organic matter or are mycorrhizal (living in association with the roots of a higher plant). One genus is parasitic on grasses and is not included here. They are most frequently found on the ground or on well-decayed moss-covered wood.

As for edibility, several species are toxic; some are bitter or tough; and some are edible and choice. Our experience is that when corals are abundant enough to consider eating them, other, safer, more delicious fungi are also prolific (and easier to clean!). For us, these tiny sculptures on the forest floor present more of a photographic challenge. The species of *Ramaria* which do not bruise brown or have translucent gelatinous tissue, are edible, and one of these is included here.

In this general introduction to the fungi, only those members that are identifiable according to visible characteristics will be fully named; for the rest, it is enough to be able to identify them as "corals."

The names *Clavulina* (small club) and *cristata* (crested, like a cock's comb) describe this fungus well. When the fruiting body is young and still translucent, these members of the coral family are especially delicate and lovely.

Description: This is an extremely variable coral fungus. The average fruiting bodies are white when young, with many smooth branches that darken to gray in age. Some specimens may be sparsely branched, while others have many branches; most are smooth, but some are wrinkled. At the tips, the branches are short, finely toothed (cristate) and pointed (until they look almost like feathers), giving the typical fruiting body its "cock's comb" appearance.

Comments: Reported edible, though difficult to clean, especially if found in a soil with a high component of sand. These are commonly found in Texas under mixed woods and are associated with pines.

Season: Late summer and fall.

Habit, habitat, and distribution: Single to several in groups under mixed woods, found on the ground, and probably mycorrhizal.

Fruiting body diameter: 2–7 cm tall × 4–5 cm across (¾–3″ × 1½–2″).

JL

Ramaria botrytis
Edible

The species' name of this fungus translates to "a bunch of grapes," which describes its form rather well, but the best characteristic is reflected in a name that is often used: "pink-tipped coral mushroom."

Description: The fruiting body can be six or more inches in diameter, with a thick, fleshy stalk that is white when young and tan to brown in age. There are many crowded branches, which are white and relatively undifferentiated when young. The tips of the branches are pink to purple, or wine colored, with the colors fading in age. This is one of the easiest corals to identify, due to the white body with pink to lavender tips. The flesh does not bruise brown and is not gelatinous in the center.

Comments: This is the safest coral mushroom for the beginner to eat, with the caution that here we are definitely describing the Texas form! (There are several sickeners among the *Ramaria,* but they are not pink tipped.)

Season: Fall and winter.

Habit, habitat, and distribution: Single to several in groups or rings on ground among hardwoods or conifers, widely distributed.

Fruiting body diameter: 5–15 cm tall × 4–12 cm across (2–6″ × 1½ × 5″).

DL

Not edible

This coral fungus has straight, upright branches (*stricta* means "straight") and resembles clusters of tiny organ pipes on the forest floor.

Description: The fruiting body consists of many compact, straight, parallel branches that are grayish orange at the base, becoming paler toward the tips, where the color is a pale yellow.

Comments: This is a common coral fungus in the forested areas of East Texas. There are several similar forms that also grow on wood (often buried), and microscopic differentiation is required for accurate determination of the species. The taste is bitter, and there is often an unpleasant odor; we do not recommend it for the table.

Season: Late summer and fall.

Habit, habitat, and distribution: Several to many in groups or rings on well-decayed, often moss-covered logs or wood litter; widely distributed.

Fruiting body diameter: 5–10 cm tall × 2.5–7.5 cm across (2–4″ × 1–3″).

Individual stalk diameter: 0.15–0.5 cm (up to ¼″).

VM

Clavicorona pyxidata

Edible

This lovely fungus is one whose Latin name is very appropriate—it means "small, crowned coral." The "crown" part of the name refers to the tiny branched tips that resemble a crown at the end of each branch.

Description: This is a small coral fungus, white with a yellowish tinge. It has a short sterile base from which the many tiers of branches arise and branch in pairs. The branches are white to pale yellow when young, and the lower parts of the branches darken to brown or gray brown in age. This multiple, usually dichotomous branching habit and the many crownlike tips around the edges at the end of each branch are the best characteristics for identification. The taste of the raw fungus is mildly peppery, and the spore print color is white.

Comments: This is an edible coral, and the peppery taste, which makes it easy to identify, is not overpowering when cooked.

Season: Summer and fall.

Habit, habitat, and distribution: Single or several fruiting bodies on decayed hardwood litter. It is occasionally common.

Fruiting body diameter: 5–12 cm tall × 2–8 cm across (2–5″ × ¾–3″).

JL

Clavariadelphus ligula

Not edible

Ligula is Latin for "little tongue," and they look like little cat's tongues sticking up out of the ground. A troop of them can be quite a sight!

Description: The fruiting bodies of this fungus look a lot like flattened wooden spatulas, narrow at the base and rounded or occasionally lobed at the top. They are light yellow to tan or reddish brown, and the spores, which are borne all along the fruiting body surface, are white.

Comments: These fungi are of no value for eating, due to the very small size. Thus, we consider them inedible, though not harmful. They can be very common, fruiting in large numbers in cool weather in damp areas under conifers.

Season: Fall and winter.

Habit, habitat, and distribution: Several to many, on humus, under hardwoods; occasionally common.

Fruiting body diameter: 2–7.5 cm tall × 0.3–1.5 cm across (¾–4″ × ⅙–½″).

VM

Clavaria zollingeri

Edibility not reported

The species' name of this fungus honors Heinrich Zollinger (1818–1859), an early mycologist who worked with the *Clavaria* family.

Description: This is a common violet to amethyst-colored coral fungus, with clustered branches. The sterile base is short, and the branching begins a very short distance above the ground. The tips of the branches are blunt. The spores are borne along the branches, and the spore print color is white.

Comments: There are three common lavender to violet corals commonly found in the South. *Clavulina amethystinoides* has multiple branching patterns so that it looks almost toothed, and *Clavulina amethystina* is only distinguishable using microscopic characteristics (the basidia of *Clavaria* have four spores each; *Clavulina* basidia have only two). *Clavaria vermicularis* has a similar growth habit but is pure white and rarely branches. See description.

Season: Late summer to fall.

Habit, habitat, and distribution: Usually single to several, on ground or in grassy places under hardwoods.

Fruiting body diameter: 5–10 cm tall × 4–7 cm across (2–4″ × 1½–3″).

DL

Not edible

The species' name of this fungus, *byssiseda,* translates roughly to "pertaining to a mass of fine threads or filaments." The name refers to fine, white threads of mycelium, or cottony fibers, at the base of this interesting coral. It is sometimes referred to as the "bird of paradise."

Description: The fruiting body of this fungus is made up of a slender, pliant, tough stalk giving rise to a network of thin branches. The base is nearly white, while the spore-bearing branches are pinkish buff. One of the best identification points for this fungus is the delicate pea green flush at the tips and the pliant, tough nature of the fruiting body. The spore print is white.

Comments: This is a tropical genus that is widespread throughout the United States. It is not worth eating.

Season: Summer and fall.

Habit, habitat, and distribution: A decayer of conifer logs occurring singly or several together and in rich humus. Rarely found in any abundance.

Fruiting body diameter: 5–7.5 cm tall × 2.5–6 cm across (2–3″ × 1–2½″).

JL

Clavaria vermicularis

Not edible

The name of this fungus translates roughly to "clubs that resemble worms," another very descriptive Latin name.

Description: The fruiting bodies are white, unbranching, and almost translucent, occurring in dense clusters. They emerge from the ground, closely resembling a toothpick, barely tapering or perhaps curving at the top. These little fungi are so fragile that they are difficult to gather without breaking them. The spores are borne along the stalk, and the spore print color is white.

Comments: These tiny forms are considered edible, but why bother? They are said to be flavorless, and you'll spend the day gathering a handful. They are so ephemeral that they are usually gone by midday.

Season: Summer.

Habit, habitat, and distribution: Several to many, often in tufts or clusters, on ground or in grassy places under hardwoods.

Fruiting body diameter: 6–12 mm across (¼–½").

Height: 4–7 cm (¾–3").

VM

Family Hydnaceae: The Tooth Fungi

The "teeth" of this family of fungi are tiny spines along which spores are formed and released. Some of these species resemble mushrooms, that is, they have a cap and stalk (with the teeth underneath the cap); others have no distinct cap or stalk and resemble a mass of dainty icicles emerging from a crack or split place on a tree.

1. General appearance: The most distinctive feature of tooth fungi is, as one might suspect, the presence of tiny teeth, usually a few millimeters long, on which the spores are produced. The *Steccherinum* species resemble polypores in that they grow, stalkless, on downed wood, and form overlapping tiers of thick semicircular caps, with the teeth along the undersides. The *Hydnum* and *Sarcodon* species resemble the common mushrooms in having a rounded cap and central stalk, but with teeth under the cap where gills or pores are normally found. And the *Hericium* species have no cap or stalk, but simply emerge like icicles or corals from a dead tree.

2. Spore print: The spores of these fungi are formed along the "teeth," and those of most of the species described in this section produce either a white or brown spore print.

3. Ecology: Those *Hydnaceae* that resemble mushrooms are mycorrhizal with the trees under which they fruit and can be found there year after year. The other species are decayers of dead and downed wood and cause a white pocket rot on living trees.

This family of fungi contains several easily identified types, such as *Hericium* species and *Hydnum repandum,* which are delicious edibles. The brown-spored species of *Hydnellum* (not covered here) are bitter, tough, and toxic. As with all wild fungi, the mycophagist should prepare for the table only young and firm specimens since old specimens often become bitter and can harbor bacteria that can cause stomach upset.

Hericium erinaceus

Edible/Choice

Erinaceus means "pertaining to a hedgehog," and some people call this the "hedgehog mushroom" because it looks like a ball covered with spiny teeth.

Description: This fungus has no cap or stalk; it consists of "iciclelike" teeth that can be an inch or more long and emerge from a ball of tissue in an injured part of a living tree. The spores are borne on the iciclelike spines. The clusters of spines form a dense surface reminiscent of a hedgehog, all hanging down in the same direction from a thick, fleshy base.

Comments: You may have to look up for this one since it is often on wounds on trees well above ground. The white masses are easy to spot. Delicious when fresh; trim away any parts that are discolored or tough, and sauté in butter with onion. This delicately flavored fungus is one of our favorites.

Season: Winter.

Habit, habitat, and distribution: Usually in a single body on a dead or living tree, emerging from a hole, crack, or dead stub. Found on pine and oak.

Fruiting body diameter: 8–20 cm (3–8″).

Spine length: 2–5 cm (3/4–2″).

JL

Edible/Choice

The reason this fungus was named *coralloïdes* ("resembling coral") is not hard to guess; it is also often called the "bear's head" because the masses of rounded clusters of teeth resemble the contours of an animal's face.

Description: This fungus has no cap or stalk; it consists of very short "iciclelike" teeth in clusters along the underside of the branches. The white spores are borne on the iciclelike spines. The "icicles" in "bunches," hanging on an open framework, with the tips of the spines often pointing in different directions, are typical of this fungus. The spores are produced along the spines, and the spore print color is white.

Comments: A typical fruiting body of this fungus leaves you with the impression that this one is full of dirt and hard to clean. We find this frequently in winter but seldom eat it for that reason. It is edible when young but gets bitter and tough in age. This white fungus is often seen on dead logs, limbs, or stumps of maple, beech, and birch. It is often fruiting inside hollow logs or stumps where snakes may also seek shelter, so look before you reach!

Season: Winter.

Habit, habitat, and distribution: Single bodies fruiting on (and inside) decaying trees and dead logs.

Fruiting body diameter: 8–12 cm (3–5").

Spine length: 3–10 mm (⅛–⅓").

DG

Hericium americanum

Edible/Choice

The derivation of the scientific name for this tooth fungus is easy to guess and reflects where it was first collected.

Description: This fungus consists of medium-length "iciclelike" teeth in smooth clusters at the tips of the branches; it has no cap or stalk. The spores are borne on the iciclelike spines. The smooth tufts of "icicles," like spines on a framework, with the tips of the spines pointing in one direction, are typical of this fungus. Short spines (averaging half an inch long) grouped in rounded clusters forming a solid mass are the identifying characteristics. The spore print color is white.

Comments: Young, fresh, tender specimens are delicious when slowly sautéed in butter. The shorter teeth of this fungus distinguish it from *H. erinaceus.* The fruiting body is more dense and lacks the open branches with rows of spines so typical of *H. corralloides.*

Season: Winter.

Habit, habitat, and distribution: Individual masses on wounds and dead branches on living hardwoods and on or in dead logs and stumps.

Fruiting body diameter: 8–20 cm (3–8").

Spine length: 10–15 mm (⅓–⅔").

DG

Edible/Good

This tooth mushroom has a spreading, wavy edge to the cap, which is the meaning of the species' name, *repandum* ("wavy edge").

Description: From the top, this looks like an "ordinary" mushroom, with a smooth cinnamon to pale orangey tan cap. But turn it over, and you will reveal white teeth underneath the cap. Yellow stains quickly appear when the flesh is injured. The stalk is short and smooth, ringless, and white to tan or colored like the cap, growing on the ground. The flesh is soft and mild tasting. The spore print color is white.

Comments: This mushroom (called *Dentinum repandum* in some books) tastes mildly peppery when raw but delicious and definitely nutlike when cooked. It is a prime edible with a firm texture and is one of our favorite mushrooms.

Season: Summer through early winter.

Habit, habitat, and distribution: Single to scattered or even gregarious on ground under both hardwoods and conifers, with which it is mycorrhizal.

Cap diameter: 2–7.5 cm (¾–3").

Stalk height: 2–7.5 cm (¾–3").

Stalk diameter: 6–18 mm (¼–¾").

VM

Sarcodon imbricatum

Edible/Fair

Imbricatum designates the "bricklike" scales on the caps of this common tooth mushroom.

Description: The surface of the cap is white to gray, but it is covered with heavy, dark, raised scales that resemble thick "shingles" above the smooth surface. On the underside of the cap, fine gray to brown spines hang like little "teeth." The teeth extend down the broadly tapered stalk, which is then smooth at the bottom half-inch. The flesh is firm but not tough. The spore print color is brown.

Comments: This mushroom was called *Hydnum imbricatum* in older guides. The scaly cap and gray spines make this an easy mushroom to recognize. Found in summer and fall in all parts of the state, especially in sandy soils under oaks. As a bonus, it is edible, with a firm texture (and increasing bitterness with age). We frequently forego the pleasures of eating it when our friends who dye wool using dyes made from fungi beg us for these specimens. Our "dyeing" friends achieve a lovely green color from this species found in Texas. Tough stalked *Hydnellum* species may be encountered. They are bitter tasting, require effort to cut them in two, and have a zoned flesh. These brown-spored species tend to surround and include small sticks and seedlings as they grow.

Season: Summer and fall.

Habit, habitat, and distribution: Several to numerous, scattered on the ground under oaks and conifers, occasionally plentiful.

Cap diameter: 7.5–12.5 cm (3–5″).

Stalk height: 2.5–7.5 cm (1–3″).

Stalk diameter: 15–35 mm (½–1½″).

VM

Not edible

The species' name *pulcherrimum* means "appearing beautiful"; an interesting description of this fungus, which resembles a polypore growing shelflike on wood, but with "teeth" on the underside.

Description: The caps are white when fresh, darkening to light buff in age, with fine hairs on the cap and lacking a stalk. The cap thickness is about an inch (2.5 cm) at the attachment to wood, tapering to very thin at the edges. The caps are tough but pliable, and when fresh, a milk-colored, sticky sap can easily be squeezed from them. On the underside are many white, dense, crowded, slender spines. The spines darken to a pale pinkish buff and finally to reddish in age. The spore print color is white.

Comments: This is a commonly seen fungus, often found on rotting wood. It is not edible. The pliant, hairy cap and white spines are the best field characters.

Season: Fresh during summer and fall, but old specimens may be found year round, and the white sap is only seen on young specimens.

Habit, habitat, and distribution: Usually single on dead or downed oak, hickory, birch; occasionally reported on pine.

Cap diameter: 6–15 cm (2½–6″).

Cap height: 2–2.5 cm (¾–1″).

Spines: 2.5–5 mm (⅛–¼″).

AB

Family Polyporaceae: The Polypores

This is a very large family of fungi and includes some of the most common specimens to be found in the woods. Many polypores (a general term that can be used to refer to any member of this diverse group of fungi) are of great economic importance because of their ability to degrade (rot) organic material. This role is considered beneficial when the nutrients in downed wood are released for use by the next generation of plants, and detrimental when houses, fences, ships, and other products are victims of the same process. We regret that we cannot include a simple chart to help you distinguish between genera in this family; the genera are divided on the basis of microscopic characteristics, and field identification is often impossible. Thus, we include a dozen or so of the most common and distinctive species, hoping that you will learn to recognize them and enjoy the rest for their beauty.

1. General appearance: The name "polypore" translates to "many pores," referring to the spore-bearing surface, usually on the underside of the cap, which consists of a large number of tiny holes, or pores. Most of the polypores have little or no stalk, and if one is present, it is usually lateral (at the side of the cap). Thus, most polypores have a "shelflike" appearance, as they tend to fruit in parallel rows on dead wood or stumps. Most are woody or leathery (though some are soft and fleshy), often so tough a knife is required to remove them from the dead wood. Some species are annual; others are perennial, adding new layers each year.

2. Pores: The pores of most species are located on the underside of the cap, are usually very small, and often are very short. However, true polypores will develop pores along the margin of new growth, but often the older pores become toothlike. The exact size and shape of the pore mouths is an important characteristic (e.g., diamond shape, mazelike, round, etc.) in their identification. The spores are borne within the pores and are forcibly discharged into the air from them.

3. Spore print: Originally, the genus *Polyporus* was defined as containing members with smooth, colorless spores. A spore print may be important for confirmation of identification, but spore print color is not as important in identification of polypores as it is for other groups of fungi. Many times, a spore print is very difficult to obtain—the specimen may be old, with all the spores

having been released; and in some cases the spores are released too slowly.

4. Ecology: Members of the polypores fill several important roles. First, there are the *saprophytes,* those that break down dead material and release the nutrients back into the ecosystem for reuse by other living organisms. Second, there are those that are *parasitic* and take their nourishment from living organisms, and in the process, kill the host.

Generally, polypores are inedible, due to the toughness of the fruiting bodies rather than toxic chemicals. Determining the exact name of any given specimen frequently requires microscopic examination looking for complex cell characteristics. For these reasons, we have included only the most common and a few edible species. We admire them for their beauty but realize that few people are interested in identifying them much beyond the general grouping: "polypore."

Trametes versicolor

Not edible

The "many-colored polypore," this must be the most common fungus in the world! It has had a number of names as taxonomists (those who classify fungi) have moved it from one genus to another, including *Polyporus versicolor, Coriolus versicolor,* and others. We often hear it referred to as "turkey tails."

Description: The cap of this thin, shelflike fungus has many alternating zones of bright and dull colors. Large clusters emerge from a dead log, limb, or stump. The pore surface underneath the cap consists of very fine, barely visible white pores. There is no stalk present, and the caps grow on wood, often forming long, parallel, and shelving rows. During wet weather, the fruiting bodies are often bright and firm, turning dull and curling under when dry. The spore print color is white.

Comments: We have seen blue, orange, lavender, brown, tan, gray, and yellow colors alternating with tans and white (though usually any given fruiting body has only one or two of the colors mentioned). This fungus is universally present wherever there is dead wood and is of great ecological importance for its role in breaking down dead wood. If the pores are easily seen with the naked eye and the zonation is somewhat obscure, your specimen is likely to be a closely related species, *Trametes ochracea.*

Season: All year, especially summer and fall.

Habit, habitat, and distribution: Several to numerous, on downed, dead wood, and stumps, nearly always found, but bright, firm, and prolific following periods of warm, wet weather.

Cap diameter: 2–5 cm (¾–2").

Cap thickness: 3–6 mm (⅛–¼").

Pore size: 3–5 per mm.

JL

Laetiporus sulphureus translates literally to "the bright-spored, sulfur-colored (yellow) fungus." The top sides of the shelves are orange and the margins are a bright lemon yellow, making it hard to miss and easy to recognize.

Description: The thick, fleshy shelves with their bright yellow and orange colors, growing on dead tree trunks, are readily identifiable. The fruiting bodies emerge knoblike or fingerlike and soon spread until they are semicircular or shelflike. The shelves are thick, and the upper surface is composed of bands of bright yellow-orange to orange colors. The flesh is pale yellow, and the pore surface is composed of fine yellow pores. The spore print color is white.

Comments: Known as the "chicken mushroom" because of the meaty consistency of the cooked flesh, which closely resembles chicken breast, this is considered a delicious edible. Some stomach upsets have been reported, however, so exercise moderation and be sure to cook it thoroughly! This is a very safe mushroom for beginners to eat, as there are no similar toxic species. We often find it on burned stumps, where it can occasionally be gathered by the basketfuls. A closely related species, *Laetiporus persicinus* (or *L. semialbidus* in some books) occurs in large rosettes on the ground and has the usual orange cap surface but the pores are white. It is also edible and good and could be found throughout the area covered by our guide.

Season: Summer and fall.

Habit, habitat, and distribution: Arising solitarily or in large clusters from recently dead hardwood, most often oak or willow. It causes a rot of the tree's center, until the tree becomes hollow.

Cap diameter: 5–50 cm (2–20").

Cap thickness: 2–4 cm (¾–1½").

Pore size: 2–4 per mm.

VM

Pycnoporus sanguineus

Not edible

Pycnoporus means "close pores"; *sanguineus,* from the Latin root for "blood," indicates a bright red color. This polypore, common on oak and sweet gum, is easily identifiable from the red color of the "shelves" and pores.

Description: These thin shelf fungi are a brilliant red-orange over both the cap and pores. The caps are solid colored rather than having bands of color. There is no stalk, and the shelves, which are often less than 0.5 mm thick, emerge directly from the wood. When young, the shelves are quite pliable, but they become tough when dry. The spore print color is white. The bright red color doesn't readily fade but remains quite bright.

Comments: When dried, these "shelves" can be used in arrangements. It is a beautiful fungus, even though it is far too tough to eat.

Season: All year.

Habit, habitat, and distribution: Growing in single shelves or in clusters, emerging from dead limbs and downed wood; common on tallow and other soft trees. A closely related but less commonly encountered species in Texas, *P. cinnabarinus* is thicker and fades considerably on drying.

Cap diameter: 2–12 cm (¾–5").

Cap thickness: 0.6–1.5 cm (¼–¾").

Pore size: 2–4 per mm.

Pycnoporus cinnabarinus. AB

VM

Not edible

Lucidum translates to "shiny," "clear," or "glossy," an apt description of these woody polypores, which often have a shiny surface that appears varnished.

Description: The caps of these mushrooms are shiny, appearing varnished, and colorful, with gold, yellow, white, and even lavender hues on the caps. The white pore surface quickly stains brown on bruising. The stalk is lateral (at one side of the cap rather than in the middle), a smooth brown color, and often "ropelike" rather than even in diameter. The spore print color is brown.

Comments: Due to the brown bruising of damaged pore mouths, this species of *Ganoderma* is often called "artists' conks," since they make a long-lasting and unusual drawing surface. They hold their color well on drying and are also nice in dried arrangements, even though they are too tough to eat. In ancient oriental culture, this mushroom was considered to be health giving. It is raised commercially in Japan and Korea. A hot drink is made, much the same as tea, and it is said to have curative properties. This mushroom is also raised commercially in San Antonio, Texas, and is sold in tablet form.

Season: All year.

Habit, habitat, and distribution: Single to several on ground under deciduous trees, often growing along the roots.

Cap diameter: 5–20 cm (2–8″).

Cap thickness: 2–4 cm (¾–1½″).

Pore size: 4–7 per mm.

VM

Trichaptum biformis

Not edible

This small, violet-toothed polypore is very common, often covering the entire surface of dead logs and trees. The name "*biformis*" means "two forms," referring to the two differently colored sides. It was formerly known as *Polyporus pergamenus*.

Description: Viewed from above, the caps of this tan to white, dull-colored polypore are quite nondescript. But from below, the lavender tint of the pore surface is quite striking. In age, the pores become tooth-like, but true pores can be seen along the newly formed margin. There is no stalk, and the overlapping caps often cover the side of a tree or stump. The spore print color is white.

Comments: This polypore is known to occur on at least sixty-five types of trees, totally decomposing them. It is much too tough to be of value for food, but it is seen on almost every TMS Annual Mushroom Foray and brought to the identification table.

Season: Year round.

Habit, habitat, and distribution: Numerous caps, overlapping each other, on dead trees.

Cap diameter: 1–2.5 cm (½–1″).

Cap thickness: 1–3 mm (up to ⅛″).

Pore size: 2–5 per mm.

VM

Not edible

Perennis translates to "perennial" or "year-round," and this tiny polypore can be found at almost any time of year.

Description: The fruiting bodies are small (less than an inch across) on slender tough stalks, and from the top they resemble an ordinary mushroom with a cap that appears zoned and pleated. The most notable characteristic is the distinctly zoned, velvety cap, which commonly has bands of alternating cinnamon, brown, and orange, with an outer band that is white. The stalk is dark brown and very slender, but tough and leathery, often emerging from well-decayed wood or leaves. The spore print color is white.

Comments: Not edible; the best use for this mushroom is as an addition to dried arrangements. It is one of the first mushrooms to appear after a rain.

Season: Year round.

Habit, habitat, and distribution: Single to several on the ground or on decaying wood debris. Its role in nature is not known, but it may be one of a series of polypores that are mycorrhizal, or it may be decaying roots underground.

Cap diameter: 2–5 cm (¾–2").

Cap thickness: 0–2 mm (up to ⅒").

Pore size: 5–6 per mm.

VM

Gloeophyllum saepiarium

Not edible

This common shelving mushroom takes its name from its common habitat—hedges and other soft-centered trees. It is also common on fence posts and pine trees.

Description: The cap of this shelflike mushroom is thin, dry, smooth to nearly hairy, and banded with bright orange and yellow colors, especially when fresh. (When old and dry, the colors fade appreciably.) The pore surface is made up of irregular pores to gill like structures, often with crosswalls. The spore-bearing surface is yellow-brown to rusty brown, darkening to brown in age. It is sessile (without a stalk), and the caps grow in rows directly from wood. The color of the spore print is white.

Comments: This is a common species, which can be found year round. During dry or cold weather, the dried out conks can often be found, without the bright colors, usually looking like hairy dark shelves with the cross-walled gills beneath. It is too tough to eat.

Season: All year.

Habit, habitat, and distribution: Several in groups of overlapping rows on dead conifers and hardwoods. It also attacks wood in service such as fence posts, telephone poles, docks, and house and bridge timbers. It was found once on the wooden frame of an old Ford beach wagon!

Cap diameter: 2–12 cm (¾–5″).

Cap thickness: 1–5 mm (up to ¼″).

Pore size: 1–2 per mm.

VM

Phaeolus schweinitzii

Not edible

This polypore honors Lewis D. de Schweinitz (1780–1834), an early American mycologist from South Carolina. It is sometimes referred to as the "dyer's polypore" due to pigments it contains.

Description: The oval-shaped fruiting body of this mushroom usually consists of several thick caps rising from a common base, but it can occasionally be shelflike or consist of just one cap. The top is fan-shaped, hairy, usually a drab orange to ochre or brown, notably hairy in youth, smoother in age. The pore surface is mustard yellow to greenish when young but darkens to brown or black in age. The stalk may not be present; if present, it is the same color as the cap. When fresh it is very watery; if squeezed, water will ooze from the surface. The spore print color is white to greenish yellow.

Comments: This mushroom is a common cause of root rot of conifers and is found on the ground around the base of living or dead conifers. Trees with roots infected by this fungus are subject to windthrow and could damage nearby buildings. The best way to identify it accurately is to pinch a cap. If your fingers show yellow stains, the mushroom is probably *P. schweinitzii.* In the dye pot it imparts yellow, orange, and brown hues to wool that has been treated with various mordants.

Season: Fall and winter.

Habit, habitat, and distribution: Arising in clusters on dead or dying conifer roots, usually pine in Texas, it is a serious threat to conifer species. It is found throughout East Texas in the pine forests as well as throughout the rest of North America.

Cap diameter: 5–30 cm (2–12").

Cap thickness: 1.2–3.7 cm (½–1½").

Pore size: 1–3 per mm.

AB

Inonotus quercustris

Not edible

Quercustris means "growing on oak"; this species was recently described from Baton Rouge, where it was found on water oak trees.

Description: Growing from wounds on living trees, this sessile polypore is at first golden yellow on top, darkening to a deep rusty brown in age. The upper surface is covered with matted, stiff hairs. The pore surface is bright golden yellow, darkening to dark yellowish brown, and the pores are angular. When fresh, the fruiting body is soft and spongy, with a high moisture content. The spore print color is pale golden yellow.

Comments: This species causes a heart rot on water oak and can be spotted, often quite high, on living trees. It does not kill the tree, and fresh specimens appear year after year. Trees infected for many years are weakened and more susceptible to wind damage. It is not edible.

Season: Late summer and fall.

Habit, habitat, and distribution: Single specimens, appearing on wounds of water oak (*Quercus nigra*) trees; first reported from Louisiana, but probably found throughout the Coastal Plain.

Cap diameter: 15–20 cm (6–8″).

Stalk height: 5–10 cm (2–4″).

Pore size: 3–5 per mm.

VM

Not edible

The genus name of this mushroom is easy to translate: *schizo-* means "split" and *-phyllum* means "gills," and when you look at the underside of the caps, the paired gills are clearly visible. *Commune* means "communal" or "in groups," reflecting the growth habit.

Description: The caps are shelflike and without a stalk or with a minute base, white to gray, and quite hairy on top. On the underside, you will see pairs of hairy gills, radiating from the point of attachment to the wood. These are not true gills but are folds in the spore-bearing surface. The spore print color is white.

Comments: During dry weather, these distinctive caps curl up and darken to deep gray. Then, when moisture is sufficient, they open up again and are more visible. They are not edible but are often seen on downed branches and limbs during moist weather. If the fruiting body is cross-sectioned, one can discover that it is composed of a series of tightly clustered cups unlike either a polypore or a gilled fungus.

Season: All year.

Habit, habitat, and distribution: Several to numerous, on downed hardwood limbs or logs, especially oak, usually present well after the tree has died. It is also common on wood in service, such as porch stairs, oak barrels, fence posts, and so forth.

Cap diameter: 1–4 cm (3⁄8–1½″).

Cap thickness: 4–6 mm (1⁄6–¼″).

VM

Miscellaneous Genera of the Order Aphyllophorales

In taxonomy (the science of classification of living things), an order is a grouping that contains several families. Each family may then contain one or more genera (sing., genus). The order Aphyllophorales contains a number of families that are considered related because of the similarity of the structures and method by which spores are produced and by the lack of a veil covering in the embryonic state and the lack of true gills or pores (Aphyllophorales means "without plates or gills"). This order contains the chanterelles, polypores, coral fungi, and tooth fungi, which are discussed in this book in separate sections. However, the Aphyllophorales contains several other families, including the Schizophyllaceae and the Stereaceae. Species in these families share similar field characteristics and will be discussed as a combined group in this guide, even though they are only distantly related by microscopic characteristics.

1. General appearance: The Aphyllophorales discussed here are generally thin, flat, tough structures, growing on visible or buried wood. The spore-bearing surface has no visible pores or gills and simply appears to be a slightly roughened surface on the underside of the caps. The species described in this section have little or no discernible stalk and often consist of individual fruiting bodies that grow together in a large cluster, often with a "shelflike" appearance.

2. Spore-bearing surface: The spores of these species are not borne on gills or pores. Rather, the individual spore-bearing structures, called basidia, line the underside of the cap.

3. Spore print: The spores are colorless or white, and often a spore print is hard to obtain since the fruiting bodies dry out and remain standing for a long while; thus, all the spores may have already been released. In other cases the spores may be released too slowly to obtain a visible deposit in twelve to twenty-four hours. Thus, generally, spore print is not as important in identification of this group as it is with other groups of fungi.

4. Ecology: Typically, members of the Aphyllophorales discussed in this book are saprophytic, which means that they break down dead material to release and reuse the nutrients.

Generally, these Aphyllophorales are inedible, due to the toughness of the fruiting bodies rather than toxic chemicals. Determining the exact name of any given specimen frequently requires microscopic examination looking for complex cell characteristics. For these reasons, we have included only the most common species.

Stereum complicatum

Not edible

This species of *Stereum,* named for its common growth habit of many caps in multiple tiers (a "complex"), often covers entire logs, stalks, and stumps.

Description: The thin, small, numerous caps of this mushroom form stalkless, leathery, fan-shaped fruiting bodies that are banded with color (orange is commonly predominant). The caps are often fused (making long wavy sheets), overlapping, and split at the margin. The pore surface is light tan colored, and the color of the spore print is white.

Comments: The tough, inflexible, leathery texture and zoned surface of this small species distinguish it from other species of *Stereum.* It is one of the most commonly seen mushrooms on downed hardwood in eastern North America and elsewhere. It is too tough to be edible.

Season: Year round.

Habit, habitat, and distribution: Several to numerous, in rows or tiers on downed hardwoods and conifers, but most commonly on oak.

Cap diameter: 1.3–3.7 cm (½–1½").

Cap thickness: 1–3 mm (up to ⅛").

Pore size: 5–6 per mm.

VM

Not edible

The largest and most colorful of the *Stereums,* this is a very common wood-rotting fungus. It gets its name from its oyster-shell shape.

Description: The fruiting bodies range from the size of a fingernail to several inches across and are about the thickness of a flower petal. The tops are banded with tan, white, and orange colors and are finely hairy on the upper surface. The stalk is usually absent or very short. The spore-bearing surface is cream colored, and the spore print is white.

Comments: The lack of pores and the tough, flexible fruiting bodies with a zoned cap surface are characteristic of the genus *Stereum.* It is too thin and tough to eat. It is one of the most common fungi in the world and can be found at almost any time of year.

Season: Year round.

Habit, habitat, and distribution: Several to numerous, arising from downed wood, especially oak.

Cap diameter: 1–5 cm (½–2″).

Cap thickness: 2–4 mm (up to ⅙″).

Pore size: 4–10 per mm.

VM

Merulius incarnatus

Not edible

You'll know this one when you see it—nothing else has the pink color and fleshlike texture that caused it to be named *incarnatus*.

Description: The color of the cap of this mushroom is vivid coral pink when fresh but very quickly fades to a dull pink when aged or dried. The cap is slightly hairy to fleshy to leathery (depending on moisture content), and several caps are often overlapping. The cap is rubbery, pliable, and lacks a stalk. The pore surface has irregular pits divided by blunt ridges, is a dull pink, and the spore print color is white.

Comments: This inedible fungus has one of the prettiest colors of any you'll find!

Season: Fall.

Habit, habitat, and distribution: Single to several decomposing downed wood, especially white oak and beech; widely distributed in eastern North America.

Cap diameter: 5–12 cm (2–5″).

Cap thickness: 3–12 mm (⅛–½″).

Pore size: 2–3 per mm.

JL

Not edible

The name translates roughly to "torn into spatulalike pieces," an apt name for this mushroom that most closely resembles a white head of leaf lettuce. It is related closely to the coral fungi, but because of its similarity in appearance to the smooth, woody members of the Aphyllophorales, it is discussed in this section.

Description: This fungus is composed of a number of branches, or "leaflets," that resemble large flower petals. The "leaflets" are each about 3–4 inches (7.5–10 cm) wide and ½–1 inch (1.2–2.5 cm) tall and emerge in whorls from a common base. Each "leaflet" is banded with white and pale tan colors, and the white spores are produced on the white, smooth surfaces of the "leaflets." The spore print color is white.

Comments: This fungus is inedible; it is tough and bitter even when quite young and fresh. Compare it to *Sparassis crispa,* which has smaller "leaflets" and is tender and edible. Dried pieces or entire fruiting bodies can be lovely in arrangements. It is also known as *S. herbstii.*

Season: Summer and fall.

Habit, habitat, and distribution: Usually single, on stumps and at the base of trees where they are found growing on organic matter.

Fruiting body diameter: 10–20 cm (4–8").

Branch thickness: 0–3 mm (up to ⅛").

JL

Sparassis crispa

Edible/Good

This *Sparassis* species gets its name from the "crisped" or "curled" shape of the "leaflets." It is occasionally referred to as the "cauliflower mushroom," due to the overall shape of the fruiting body cluster.

Description: This fungus is composed of a number of branches, or "leaflets," that resemble distinct flower petals. The "leaflets" are each about an inch (2.5 cm) wide and 2–3 inches (2.5–7.5 cm) tall, emerging in whorls from a common base. Each "leaflet" is banded with white and pale tan colors, and the spores are produced along the white underside. The spore print color is white.

Comments: *Sparassis crispa* is generally more abundant in the western United States; *S. spathulata* is known from the East. Both are found in Texas and are best distinguished by comparing the width of the "leaflets," which in this species are much narrower than the 3–4 inch (7.5–10 cm) width of the latter species. In *S. crispa*, the "leaflets" are tender, sweet, and edible when young (our rule is to trim the leaves with a pair of scissors; any parts that do not cut easily are too tough to eat). It is delicious when dipped in a batter and quickly fried. Dried pieces or entire fruiting bodies can be lovely in arrangements. This fungus is also called *S. radicata* in older works.

Season: Summer and fall.

Habit, habitat, and distribution: Usually single, on stumps and at the base of trees where they are found growing on organic matter.

Cap diameter: 1.5–2.5 cm (3/5–1").

Cap thickness: 0–3 mm (up to 1/8").

Pore size: 5–6 per mm.

VM

Orders Tremellales, Auriculariales, and Dacrymycetales

The Jelly Fungi

The commonly seen larger fungi in these three orders are often referred to as "jelly fungi," due to their gelatinous to rubbery texture and more-or-less amorphous shape. Members vary in shape and size, often resembling brains, ears, or leaves. At least one species is edible and choice, and no members are known to be poisonous.

1. General appearance: The primary characteristic for these fungi is their texture, which may be soft to stiff and gelatinous to rubbery; thus, the common name, "jelly fungi." Some are brightly colored orange, yellow, or red; others are dark brown to black; some are transparent. The shapes of these fungi range from bloblike and amorphous to those that look like ears, brains, horns, and other shapes.

2. Spore print: The spore prints of these fungi are generally white to yellow. In some species, the spores are formed on the lower surface; in others the spores may be formed over the entire surface.

3. Ecology: The species covered in this section derive their nourishment from decaying wood. Most are found on downed or dead limbs or twigs and often on those that are well into the decay stages.

The best edible in this group is *Auricularia auricula,* an ear-shaped fungus that is common and plentiful in the spring. Most of the other species described here are too small to be of value for the table.

Auricularia auricula

Edible / Good

Both the genus and species' names mean "ear" and indicate the common shape as well as the texture of this fungus. It is a favorite in oriental cooking, where it is often called "cloud ears."

Description: The fruiting body is often the size and shape of a light pinkish tan to reddish brown "ear." When mature, the edges can flare and become wavy, lessening the "ear" resemblance. The tops of the caps are slightly hairy, and these stalkless fungi are found emerging directly from dead and downed wood. The color is uniform (the top and the underside are the same hue, though the edges will darken if they dry out), and they are easy to distinguish. Pinch an ear, and if it has the same kind of cartilaginous feel as your earlobe, you've got it! The spore print is white, and the spores are borne on the lower surface.

Comments: This is an excellent edible fungus for the beginner: it is common and plentiful, grows almost year round, and is unmistakable for anything poisonous. We are often able to collect it in good quantity. When we do, we collect only firm, young specimens that have no discoloration on the edges, and we "field trim" the ears by cutting off the tough connective tissue where the mushroom was attached to the tree. We refrigerate it until we are ready to use it, then soak it in water to rehydrate, and slice it into strips to add to a stir-fry. This fungus is often available in dried form at specialty and oriental grocery stores.

Season: Any time of year, but most common in spring and fall.

Habit, habitat, and distribution: Several to numerous, emerging from dead (and usually downed) hardwoods and conifers in humid, forested areas.

Cap diameter: 2–15 cm (¾–6").

Cap thickness: 3–8 mm (⅛–⅓").

VM

Edibility unknown

This jellylike white fungus has many "leafy lobes" emerging from a single point of attachment. The species' name, *fuciformis,* means "leaf form."

Description: The fruiting body consists of several lobes or convoluted sections, emerging from a single point of attachment. When fresh, this fungus is white to clear, translucent and plumply jellylike, but on drying, it becomes thin and rigid with a pale tan color. The white spores are produced on the underside of the "lobes," and the spore print is white.

Comments: A very similar species is raised commercially in Taiwan and imported into this country, where it is sold as "white jelly fungus" and used in much oriental cooking. We have no information on the edibility of the American version.

Season: Warm, wet months, especially in summer.

Habit, habitat, and distribution: Single to several on dead and downed wood, widespread, including the tropics, and the coastal areas of Texas and the Gulf.

Fruiting body diameter: 2.5–10 cm (1–4″).

Fruiting body thickness: 2–6 mm (1/12–1/4″).

VM

Tremella mesenterica

Edible

Mesenterica derives from the Latin meaning "middle intestine" and is an apt description of this fungus's form.

Description: The fruiting body of this bright yellow to orange jelly fungus looks like a translucent "squeeze cheese" being extruded from a crack in a dead log or limb, forming many convoluted lobes. The texture is gelatinous when fresh and quite tough when dry. The spores are produced along the lobes, and the spore print is pale yellow.

Comments: Several species of yellow jelly fungi have been referred to as "witches' butter." This is the largest and most often encountered of them. It is edible and has been used as a flavoring in soups. However, we recommend confirmation of your species' identification before eating this fungus.

Season: Fall and winter.

Habit, habitat, and distribution: Single or occasionally several on hardwood sticks and logs. It is very common and widespread.

Fruiting body diameter: 1–10 cm (⅜–4").

Fruiting body height: 6–25 mm (¼–1").

OM

Inedible

This has an intermediate form between the jelly fungi and coral fungi families. This fungus has the gelatinous, tough texture of a jelly, but its form resembles a coral. *Pallidum* means pale or white.

Description: The fruiting body is small (1–2 inches [2.5–5 cm] tall) and white, and it looks much like a sea coral or a coral fungus. The fruiting body emerges from the ground like a tiny tree trunk, then branches again and again, always symmetrically, and with the branches upright. The spores are borne along the "branches," and the spore print is white.

Comments: This fungus is very common in the Big Thicket forests. It is considered edible, but its leathery texture and "rancid-butter" taste do not recommend it.

Season: Summer and fall.

Habit, habitat, and distribution: Single to several on ground under mixed conifers and hardwoods; occasionally numerous.

Fruiting body diameter: 1.2–5 cm (½–2").

Stalk height: 2.5–10 cm (1–4").

Stalk diameter: 3–6 mm (⅛–¼").

AB

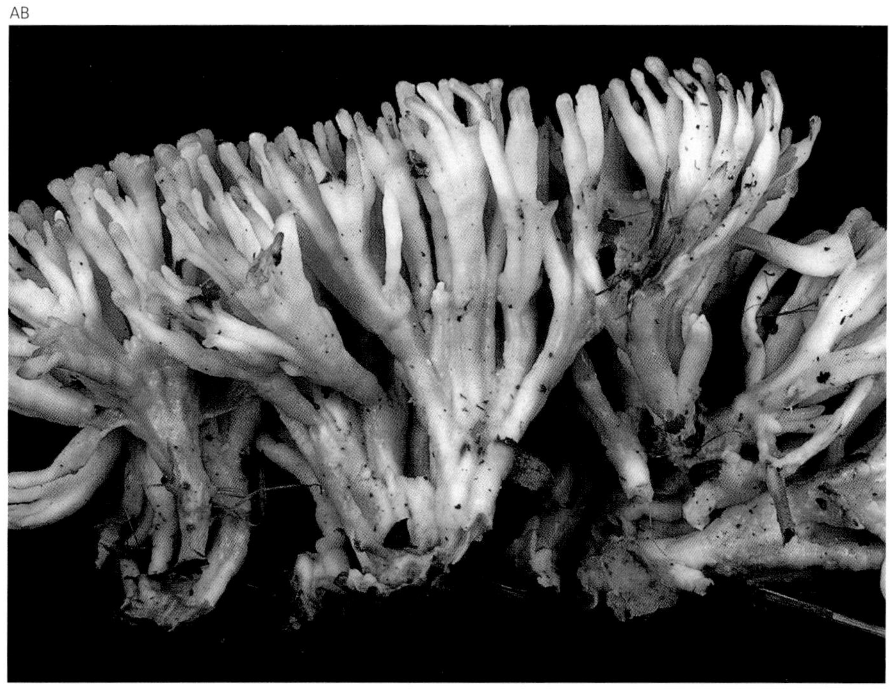

Calocera cornea

Inedible

This brightly colored member of the jelly fungi takes its name from its beautiful (*calo-*) horns (*cornea*).

Description: The fruiting body of this fungus looks like tiny horns made of yellow translucent jelly extruding from the bark of fallen wood. The little structures are about ½ inch long and about the diameter of a kitchen match. At the tips are tiny "horns" from which the yellow spores are discharged.

Comments: These fungi are too small to be of concern for eating. They are fairly common (and always noticed by children!) in the wet winter months.

Season: Winter and early spring.

Habit, habitat, and distribution: Several to numerous on decaying wood; often common. Widespread and to be expected in wet, cool weather all across the state.

Fruiting body diameter: 2–4 mm (1/12–1/6").

Fruiting body height: 6–12 mm (¼–½").

DG

Not recommended

The species' name "*glandulosa*" means "glandular," referring to the glandlike appearance and texture of these odd-looking jelly fungi.

Description: The fruiting bodies consist of reddish black to brownish black or black, shallow, jellylike cups attached directly to dead wood without a stalk. They resemble blisters on the wood at first, then deflate to form the cuplike shape. Many of these tiny cups can fuse together so that the entire fruiting mass resembles an amorphous blob more than individual bodies. The spores are produced along the wrinkles in the cups, and the color of the spore print is white.

Comments: These jelly fungi are considered inedible. They can, at times, be quite common.

Season: Most common in the fall, but they can appear at any time of year.

Habit, habitat, and distribution: Several to numerous on downed wood, often with the individual fruiting bodies fused into a sheet. Widespread, and to be expected all over the state.

Fruiting body diameter: Individual: 3–6 mm (⅛–¼"). Fused: Up to 25 cm (10") or more.

Fruiting body thickness: 2–4 mm (1⁄12–⅙").

VM

Class Gasteromycetes

The class Gasteromycetes consists of a series of orders within the subdivision Basidiomycotina. "Gastero-" means "stomach" and indicates that the spores of this class are produced internally, often in a saclike, membranous structure. In the gill fungi and boletes, for example, the spore-producing basidia are external to the mushroom (on the gill or pore surfaces), and the spores are forcibly discharged into the air. In this class, the basidia mature within a spore mass called a *gleba,* which at maturity is dispersed in various ways by wind, rain drops, insects, or by animals.

1. General appearance: The class includes a number of commonly seen fungi, among them the puffballs (so called because they look like balls, and the spores "puff" out at maturity), the earthstars (which resemble a puffball sitting on a platform that is star shaped), the very small birds' nest fungi, the earthballs and false earthstars (*Scleroderma* and *Astraeus*), which are the only mycorrhizal order, and the stinkhorns (many of which are shaped like horns, and which are also quite aromatic!).

2. Spore print: The spores of these fungi are not forcibly discharged, and so it is not possible to take a spore print as we did with the mushrooms and the boletes, but the color of spores in deposit at maturity is still important to know. Instead, the spores mature inside the fruiting body, and later, the outer membrane disintegrates, and the spores are dispersed.

3. Ecology: Members of this class are either decayers of dead organic matter, or mycorrhizal with pines, oaks, and other trees. They are a very common class and are often seen even in arid areas and on dry hot open slopes within Texas. In arid regions they commonly fruit following the yearly rainy season. They can appear quite quickly, and the spore mass can remain, dispersing the spores for a long time.

Many members of the puffballs are edible. The stinkhorns and earthstars are generally considered inedible. The earthballs are either inedible or toxic. They resemble puffballs but have colored spore masses at first and do not puff their spores out through an opening.

In this, as with all the groups described in this book, read the descriptions carefully and examine the photos for the characteristics mentioned in the descriptions. Then, compare your specimens to those in the photos, and be certain of your identification. If you are still uncertain, seek the advice of an expert, but don't eat the fungus until you do!

Order Lycoperdales

The Puffballs and Earthstars

The true puffballs grow on the ground or in dead wood, are oval to pear shaped, and are enclosed within one or more membrane layers that split open or are shed to release the mature spores.

1. General appearance: The fruiting bodies of puffballs range from the size of marbles to that of a baseball or larger; one species is often larger than a basketball. The overall shape is oval or pear shaped, and the outer skin is usually white to tan in youth and may darken to brown in maturity. Earthstars have a thicker external layer that splits into rays that curve backward, forming a starlike appearance. The puffball has three distinct parts: a base that does not produce spores, a spore mass that takes up most of the body of the puffball, and an outer membranous covering. This outer layer is pliable enough to tear easily if you pull the puffball apart, and if left in place, a hole or tear in the top center will develop, allowing the spores to be released when the puffball is squeezed.

2. Spore print: In the *Gasteromycetes,* the spores are not forcibly discharged; thus, a true spore print cannot be obtained. However, the color of the mature spores is important to determine and may be necessary for correct identification. Brown, olive, and purple spore masses may be found in this group.

3. Ecology: Members of this order are found worldwide, and a number of species are found in temperate and tropical climates, including all areas of Texas. Most species are decomposers of plant material and are commonly found on wood, leaf mulch, and grass clippings. Puffballs are often found along the drip line of trees, where drops of rain water shed by the leaf canopy

strike them with sufficient force to disseminate the spores.

There are a number of species that are edible and good, and this is a good group for the beginner to experiment with tasting—with the following caution: Always cut puffballs longitudinally through the center to make sure that the spore mass is white, firm, and has the consistency of a thick cottage cheese. If the spore mass has started to darken (a sign that the spores are maturing) or if the spore mass is yellow or stains bright yellow, do not eat it! Also, check carefully to be sure that your "puffball" cannot be an immature *Amanita*—in this case, the outline of a cap and stem will be discernible in cross-section.

OM

Lycoperdon pyriforme

Edible/Good

This commonly seen puffball is one of the smaller species, seldom as large as a golf ball, and takes a definite "pear" shape; hence the name *pyriforme* from the Latin *pyri-* (pear) and *-forme* (form).

Description: The outer skin of this puffball is smooth and with only a few scaly patches in youth, usually pear shaped or rounded, and pale tan in color. As it ages, the outer sac becomes increasingly rough and patchy until it finally falls away, revealing the inner skin with a preformed pore, through which the spores are released. The sterile base is more tapered and thin than other similar species, and the spore mass is yellow when young, becoming olive brown and powdery at maturity.

Opposite page: *young puffballs;*
Below, *mature puffballs.*

Comments: Edible when very young and white throughout, this mushroom can be bitter even when still fairly fresh. Slice it through the middle, and be certain it is pure white and uniform, and also that it is *not* a developing *Amanita* button (in which case the outline of an embryonic mushroom cap is visible). It is a bit bland for our taste but is a safe mushroom for the beginner to eat, keeping in mind the cautions mentioned here.

Season: Summer and fall.

Habit, habitat, and distribution: Several to numerous, often in great clusters on dead and decaying wood or on straw. It arises from a complex, rootlike system of white fibers called *rhizomorphs.* It is quite common and can be found in almost any part of the state, given enough rain to thoroughly soak dead wood.

Fruiting body diameter: 2–4 cm (¾–1½″).

Fruiting body height: 1.5–5 cm (⅝–2″).

OM

Lycoperdon perlatum
Edible/Good

The most frequently seen puffball, this one commonly occurs in vast numbers, so many that they often resemble a string of pearls (*perlatum* means "like pearls"). It is often called the "gemmed" puffball.
Description: Look on downed and well-decayed, even moss-covered, logs for this puffball, and you will frequently see a mass of individual balls, just larger than marbles. The outer skin is white with many well-formed, conelike warts over the surface, which leave tiny circular spots when they are rubbed and removed. When young, the spore mass is a uniform, cheeselike white substance. In age, the central darker zone opens to form a pore at the top, and the maturing spores are extruded. The spore mass is olive brown to chocolate brown at maturity; paler in youth.
Comments: Edible (slice, and fry lightly in butter) when young, but always be certain (by slicing down the center and checking for the outline of an embryonic mushroom) that you don't have a button of an *Amanita*! The gregarious habit and distinctive conelike warts of this fungus are good characteristics for identification.
Season: Summer and fall.
Habit, habitat, and distribution: Several to numerous on well-decayed wood; often common after soaking rains and cool weather.
Fruiting body diameter: 1.5–6 cm (½–2½").
Fruiting body height: 3–7 cm (1¼–3").

OM

Edible

Marginatum means "having a border or margin," referring to this puffball's outer skin, which comes apart and peels away in large pieces to reveal the inner membrane and the characteristic pore.

Description: The fruiting body of this puffball is round to flattened, with a pale, white to buff skin when young. The outer layer of this skin is covered with short tiny fine fibers that peel off in layers to expose the dark brown inner skin and the pore through which the spores are released. The spore print is olive brown to chocolate brown at maturity, but paler in youth.

Comments: Edible (slice, and fry lightly in butter) when young, but it is not very tasty. As with all puffballs, make certain (by slicing down the center and checking for the outline of an embryonic mushroom) that you don't have a button of an *Amanita*.

Season: Summer and fall.

Habit, habitat, and distribution: Several to numerous in dead grass, mulch, or on decaying wood; often common after soaking rains on golf courses or athletic fields.

Fruiting body diameter: 1–5 cm (3/8–2").

Fruiting body height: 2.5–6 cm (1–2½").

DG

Geastrum saccatum

Not edible

A typical member of the group called "earthstars" because of their "starlike" shape. The species' name *saccatum* means "with a sac" and describes the rounded, saclike structure in the middle, from which the spores are released.

Description: The young fruiting body closely resembles a puffball, looking much like a rounded, rooted ball, but as it matures, the outer skin splits along radii and curves backward gracefully, so that the pieces resemble the rays of a star, "framing" the fruiting body and elevating it to accommodate the release of its spores. A pore develops in the center of the spore sac, and a slightly depressed white circular zone surrounds it. In this species, the outer skin and inner skin remain after the "puffball" is completely spent. The spore mass is brown at maturity.

Comments: Members of the earthstar group can range from less than half an inch (1.25 cm) across to three or more inches (7.5 cm). They are not edible. A closely related species, *Geastrum fimbriatum,* forms delicate fibers that arise from the well-formed circular "mouth," or stoma, and lacks the depressed white circular zone. These features are best seen with a hand lens.

Season: Summer, fall, and winter.

Habit, habitat, and distribution: Several to numerous on well-decayed downed logs and organic litter, usually in conifer or mixed woods.

Fruiting body diameter: 1–10 cm (½–4").

Fruiting body height: 1–2.5 cm (½–1").

JL

Calvatia bovista

Edible

This is a common puffball that gets its name from the Latin root for cows and pastures, *bovista,* probably because these mushrooms were so commonly found in pastures.

Description: This pear-shaped puffball can be as broad as a dinner plate. The outer skin is white to tan or pale brown, with a large sterile (not spore-bearing) rooted base that can be half as large as the entire fruiting body. The spore mass is enlarged and flattened along the top. When young, the developing spore mass is white, with a creamy texture like goat cheese. As the spores mature, it becomes powdery, the outer skin cracks and falls away, and the spores are slowly blown away until only the sterile base remains. The spore mass is yellow or olive to dark brown at maturity.

Comments: Edible when eaten young and fresh (before the spore mass has turned yellow-brown). To prepare, slice in half-inch slices and dip in an egg and milk batter and quickly fry in hot butter.

Season: Summer and fall, usually following heavy rain and humid weather.

Habit, habitat, and distribution: Several to numerous on grass litter in pastures and lawns, old fields, and in woods.

Fruiting body diameter: 5–25 cm (2–10″).

Fruiting body height: 10–20 cm (4–8″).

VM

Calvatia cyathiformis

Edible/Good

This baseball-sized puffball takes its name from the fact that when it has completely released its spores, the sterile base remains in the shape (*formis*) of a cup (*cyathis*).

Description: This large (4 inches [10 cm] or more) pear-shaped puffball has a sterile base (an attachment that does not produce spores) and a brown outer covering that cracks into patches or scales to release the spores. The spore mass is white when very young, soon becoming powdery and changing to yellow, then light purplish brown, and finally deep purple.

Comments: This puffball is edible and quite good when firm and white inside (when very young). It is found on exposed soil in open woods and on pasture lands. *Calvatia craniformis* is similar but usually craniumlike, and the mature spore mass is yellow-olive. It is also a delicious edible and may be encountered on occasion though it is much more common farther north.

Season: Summer and early fall.

Habit, habitat, and distribution: Single to several on decaying wood or grass, widespread, and often seen in pastures and grasslands after good rains.

Fruiting body diameter: 7–18 cm (2¾–7").

Fruiting body height: 9–20 cm (3½–8").

Young specimen. JL

Cut specimen. Note white interior. VM

Order Nidulariales

The Birds' Nest Fungi

The birds' nest fungi are so called because at maturity they resemble a bird's nest filled with eggs. However, the birds' nest fungi are very tiny, usually no larger than the tip of your finger, so you will have to look closely for them—try looking in your garden or near shrubs.

1. General appearance: These fungi are very small, usually less than ½" (12 mm) across, but they often occur in large clusters. At first, they may look like tiny cones on the ground. When the humidity is high, the top of the cone will split open or lose its cover, revealing the tiny "eggs" inside. Each of the eggs is embedded in a gelatinous pad or attached to the "nest" by a tiny, coiled cord. The maturing spores are contained inside the eggs. Rain water falling into the nests splashes the eggs out, and when they break open, the spores are disseminated.

2. Spore print: Because the spores are contained inside the "eggs," a true spore print cannot be obtained from these fungi. Instead, you will have to use the characteristics of the shape, size, and color of the nest and eggs to make your identification.

3. Ecology: These fungi are found on decaying wood, leaf or bark mulch, and on the rich soil found in lawns and gardens. They are most commonly in circular patterns in the open, resulting from the random distribution of the splashed-out "eggs." These tiny fungi are inedible but not toxic. Enjoy them for their delicate beauty and for the challenge of photographing them!

Cyathus stercoreus

Not edible

Stercoreus means "growing on dung," and that's exactly where you can expect to find these common members of the Gasteromycete class that are often referred to as "birds' nest fungi."

Description: The birds' nest fungi got their name because they resemble tiny birds' nests, filled with miniature eggs. This species consists of tiny tan to brown cups, each about the size of a pencil eraser and filled with dark gray to black "eggs." The "eggs" are called *peridioles,* and the spores are borne inside of the peridioles. The peridioles are attached to the bottom of the cups by a coiled, threadlike cord. Each of the cups is large enough to hold a drop of water. The peridiole is splashed out of the cup by rain drops. The cord uncoils and catches on blades of grass or tiny bits of wood anchoring the peridiole. The peridioles split open and release the very thick-walled spores.

Comments: These can be found in almost any mulched, well-watered garden, usually in the open or occasionally under low-hanging branches of plants throughout the summer, growing on bits of wood. They are also common in openings in woods on debris.

Season: Summer and fall.

Habit, habitat, and distribution: On small pieces of wood, woody mulch, or the organic plant parts usually present in cattle or horse dung.

Fruiting body diameter: 0.4–1 cm (⅛–⅜").

Fruiting body height: 0.5–1 cm (⅕–⅜").

JL

Not edible

Sphaerobolus translates to "sphere thrower," and *stellatus* means "like a star"; thus, these are star-shaped fungi that actually throw their entire sphere-shaped spore mass—often as far as several yards! No wonder it has been called the cannonball!

Description: These are like small earthstars that resemble tiny yellow-orange globules set inside star-shaped cases. The entire fruiting body is about the size of a pencil eraser. The dark yellow-brown globules (peridioles) actually contain spores and are shot out from the cases, which turn inside out, so that they look like minute transparent bubbles.

Comments: On release, the spores sail for several feet! They are said to make a "popping" sound when released. These fungi are too small to be edible.

Season: Fall and winter.

Habit, habitat, and distribution: Several to numerous on pieces of wood, cellulose, horse dung, sawdust, or well-decayed woody organic matter. It is common, but small and easily overlooked. If you try to take a close-up, the flash from your camera will usually cause the mushroom to discharge at your lens!

Fruiting body diameter: 0.1–0.3 cm (up to ⅛").

Fruiting body height: 0.1–0.3 cm (up to ⅛").

OM

Order Sclerodermatales

The Earthballs

The earthballs get their common name from their hard, ball-like appearance and their habit of being half, or more, buried in the soil. They differ from the puffballs in that their outer layers are thick, tough, and hard, and in many species only the top sticks out above the soil.

1. General appearance: These balls are round to oval and range in size from about Ping-Pong ball size to as large as a baseball. When cut longitudinally in half, the outer layer is shown to be a very thick, rindlike skin, and the spore mass is contained inside. The spore mass of earthballs may be white when very young, but it quickly changes to brown, reddish brown, or purple before it matures. In the false earthstars, the thick outer rind splits into rays that curve backward to form an earthstar.

2. Spore print: As in the other Gasteromycetes, a true spore print cannot be obtained, but it is important to determine the color of the mature spore mass for identification. The spore mass may be white or tan in youth, but it quickly darkens to cinnamon brown, dark brown, or purple at maturity.

3. Ecology: These species are mycorrhizal with pine, beech, and other hardwood trees and are often found in sandy or poor soil. None of the members of this group are considered edible, and toxins are contained in several species, so mark this group "not edible." One species, *Pisolithus tinctorius,* is of interest to those who might like to use mushroom pigments in dyeing wool. *Pisolithus* is also grown commercially for use as a mycorrhizal partner in forestry.

Not edible

Pisolithus means "pea stone"; *tinctorius* translates to "used for tinting"—together, an appropriate name for this puffball made up of peridioles that are pealike compartments embedded in a blackish gelatinous material that stains anything it touches to a yellow-olive color.

Description: Look closely for this fungus—in the "wild" it resembles a dirty tennis ball, half buried in dry sand. The outer layer is gray-brown and pitted and has a narrow, rooted base. When you dig it up and cut it down the center, the inside reveals bright yellow, pea-sized spore-bearing compartments separated by black material. When mature, the outer skin cracks and flakes off, and the inner membranes burst, releasing the spores. The fruiting bodies can remain for months, with layer after layer slowly blowing away until nothing is left but the sterile base. The spores are dark brown.

Comments: This mushroom is drought resistant; we find it during dry summers in high, dry, sandy areas. It is considered inedible—save it for the dye pot, where it yields black and brown pigments. Lumber companies frequently inoculate this fungus on the roots of conifers because its mycorrhizal relationship is highly conducive to the reforestation of hot open areas.

Season: Summer to winter.

Habit, habitat, and distribution: Single to several on sandy soil under conifer trees, with which it is mycorrhizal.

Fruiting body diameter: 4–20 cm (1½–8").

Fruiting body height: 5–30 cm (2–12").

AB

Astraeus hygrometricus

Not edible

The rays of the false earthstar open up when wet and close back down in dry weather, as if the fungus were "measuring the water," which is a rough translation of the species' name *hygrometricus.*

Description: Like other earthstars, this one resembles a puffball when unopened and young. However, the young spore mass is divided into small chambers with white walls and brown contents. As it matures, the outer skin of this fungus splits into seven to fifteen pointed rays, which open up and flatten out when ample moisture is present. The exposed rays are light in color (darkening in age) and show distinct dark cracks on the white exposed surface, yielding a checkered appearance. When the humidity is low, the rays curl back up over the spore sac, and this opening and closing can repeat a number of times. The inner spore sac *splits open* (rather than forming a pore as in the true earthstars, from which the spores are released). The spore sac is covered with fine hairs, and if cut in two, it does not have the sterile area in the bottom of the spore sac. The species in *Geastrum* (true puffballs) all have the sterile area and a preformed pore.

Comments: This false earthstar is common on sandy soil and will be found in cool, wet weather. It is one of a number of fungi that can be found in moist as well as arid and semiarid areas. However, it is mycorrhizal with pines and hardwoods.

Season: Fall and spring.

Habit, habitat, and distribution: Single to several, usually on sandy soil near or under pines and hardwoods.

Fruiting body diameter: (Opened) 5–10 cm (2–4").

Fruiting body height: 1–1.8 cm (⅓–¾").

VM

The name *Scleroderma* is a combination of *sclero-* for "hard" and *-derma* for "skin." The earthballs are distinguished from the common puffballs by their very thick, hard outer rind. This species is common in cow pastures; hence, the name *bovista.*

Description: These earthballs are often overlooked since they resemble pale-colored rocks, often bulging up from sandy soil or ground. They are generally the size of small limes, with the thick outer rind cracking into small scales that may slough off, totally exposing the spore mass. When cut open, the spore mass is white when young, darkening to purple-black, and composed of small chambers with white walls and purple contents. The spore mass is fairly uniform at maturity, though one may see the chamber walls in the darkening spore mass. The mature powdery spore mass is totally exposed as the skin, or peridium, peels back.

Comments: Caution! This earthball can cause vomiting, nausea, and diarrhea. The adage that all earthballs are edible when the spore mass is white does *not* apply to *Sclerodermas.* When young, the spore mass is off-white, but very soon the deep purple pigments develop throughout.

Season: Summer and fall.

Habit, habitat, and distribution: Single to several, on soil and sand. This earthball is mycorrhizal with conifers and hardwoods and is widespread, but it is often partially hidden in the litter and overlooked.

Fruiting body diameter: 1.5–8 cm (½–3¼").

Fruiting body height: 1.2–7 cm (⅜–3").

OM

Scleroderma polyrhizon

Toxic

Polyrhizon means "many roots" and refers to the mycelial "root" of tough fibers that anchor the fruiting body to the ground.
Description: When fresh, this earthball resembles a light-colored to brown tennis ball that has been lost for some time. The spores mature very quickly from off-white to purple-black (but still firm). Very fine white-walled chambers are visible, which soon break up into a brown to purple-brown powder, and the outer skin splits open into uneven rays that spread open like a large, ungainly earthstar. However, there is no inner skin surrounding the spore mass. When the spores are dispersed, the outer rindlike skin remains, looking like a blackened piece of orange peel.
Comments: Toxic and not edible! The outer rind is often seen on the ground among the young, new fruiting bodies.

Season: Summer and fall.
Habit, habitat, and distribution: Single to several on sandy soil, and when excavated from sandy soil, large clusters of rootlike fibers (rhizomorphs) are present. We often find this along the edges of trails through wooded areas. It is mycorrhizal with both pines and oaks in Texas.
Fruiting body diameter: 4–15 cm (1½–6").
Fruiting body height: 3–12 cm (1½–5").

DG

Scleroderma texense

Toxic

Where do you suppose this hard-skinned earthball was first described?
Description: Another of the "dirty tennis ball" fungi, this earthball can be distinguished from others by its very thick skin (at least ¼ inch thick when cut) and the very scaly outside surface. The spores mature from white to purple-black. The spore surface appears marbled but on close inspection is composed of chambers with white walls. These chambers with the spore mass are very obvious when the fungus is young, as you see in the photo. Later, the naked spore mass becomes dry and powdery and lightens in color to a gray-black, as the spores slowly blow away, leaving the "rind" behind.

Comments: Again, inedible and toxic! Even small pieces can cause severe stomach upset. The good news is that you'll quickly recover after you have vomited up what you ate, but you may lose your zeal for eating wild mushrooms for a while.
Season: Summer and fall.
Habit, habitat, and distribution: Single to several on sandy soil, mycorrhizal with hardwoods and conifers.
Fruiting body diameter: 2.5–7.5 cm (1–3").
Fruiting body height: 2–7 cm (¾–2¾").

VM

Order Phallales

The Stinkhorns

Members of the Phallales order are among the most fascinating of all the fungi. They are often generically referred to as "stinkhorns" for reasons that will become obvious as you study first the photos and descriptions in this section and then examine the specimens you find in the woods. This order gets the prize for "most-suggestive fungus" and certainly indicates that Mother Nature has a sense of humor or that humans have a vivid imagination! Historically, stinkhorns have been credited with causing and curing a plethora of ailments from cancer to rheumatism, and they have inspired many folktales in different cultures.

Interestingly enough, stinkhorns are one of the few fungus groups that have been extensively studied in Texas. Mycologist William H. Long received a bachelor's degree from Baylor University in 1888 and spent the next twenty years pursuing graduate degrees and studying fungi near Waco, Austin, and Denton, ultimately making considerable scientific contributions to our knowledge of gasteromycetes (including the stinkhorns). Long recorded nineteen species of stinkhorns in Texas.

1. General appearance: Stinkhorns can be of many different forms. Some actually resemble horns, while others look like an open lattice. Still others look like a lattice at the end of a horn. All of them arise from a pliant, egglike, gelatinous embryo (the cup, or volva), and they all stink! The aroma has been variously described as "fetid," "putrefying," and "as of something dead and well into decay." This odor is emitted from the mature green spore mass, is quite strong, and carries for some distance. We recommend that when you find stinkhorns, don't try to carry them unwrapped in your car or inside a building; this is to protect your good standing among your friends!

2. Spores: The spores of stinkhorns are small, rodlike or narrowly elliptic, and covered with a slime layer. They are found in the mass of olive to dark olive black "goo" that may cover the apex of the fruiting body or line the inside of the chambers. This spore mass gives the stinkhorns their offensive odor, which has an unusual function: it is an attractant for many insects, especially flies, which provide a uniquely effective transport mechanism to disperse the stinkhorn's spores. When the

flies come, they eat the spore slime and get it on their feet. The spores are then spread everywhere the fly goes!

3. Cup: The cup is an egglike, membranous structure in which the spores mature and from which the stinkhorns emerge. The cup remains at the base of the fungus very much like the cup in Amanitas. Incidentally, if you find stinkhorn eggs, you may be able to hatch them. As with many mushrooms, the saclike "egg" contains the fully formed "button," ready to expand, like a sponge, into full size when the water it needs is available. To "hatch" stinkhorns, select large eggs that appear to be splitting at the top and dig them up carefully, so that you remove eggs from the soil with the rootlike rhizomorphs and mycelium intact. "Replant" the egg in some soil or sawdust, or place it on a wad of paper towels in the lid of a mayonnaise or similar jar, and thoroughly wet the medium the egg sits on. If you use a jar lid, you may want to place the jar upside down on top of the lid over the stinkhorn egg. Then, watch for the egg to hatch. Once the stinkhorn emerges, it can take as little as an hour for the fungus to attain full height.

4. Ecology: The stinkhorns are decayers of grass, straw, wood chips, and mulch, and they play an important role in releasing nutrients for use by other organisms. They are common in gardens, along wood-chip jogging trails, and in loose soil in forested areas, where they are of benefit to the organisms present.

The stinkhorns themselves are not considered edible (with that odor, who would want to eat them?) but the immature eggs of many species can be eaten (though none have been reported as choice!). Slice open an immature "egg" and you will see the gelatinous inner skin that protects a perfectly formed diminutive button.

We are especially pleased to find stinkhorns and to undertake the challenge of photographing them, even if we have to hold our noses! We hope it reflects our sense of humor, too!

Phallus ravenelii

Not recommended

It is easy to see why this mushroom is placed in the genus *Phallus;* less obvious is that the species' name *ravenelii* honors W. H. Ravenel, (1814–1887), an early southern mycologist.

Description: Generally 4 to 5 inches tall, the fungus emerges from a saclike, pinkish lavender-colored egg to reveal a white stalk and a cap covered with the greenish gray spore mass, with a circular white opening at the apex. This opening is the top of the stalk and is hollow and translucent. In a young specimen (as shown here), the apex appears emerald green, shiny, and smooth. Actually, the cap has a grainy surface that is covered with a slime containing spores. As flies remove the spore-bearing slime, the cap color fades to a dull gray-green, revealing the wrinkled surface. The pinkish lavender color of the eggs and the attached rootlike rhizomorphs are characteristic.

VM

Comments: Common in Texas during cool, wet weather. These specimens were along a jogging trail. We spotted the eggs popping up through the loose mulch and predicted this species from the eggs' lilac coloring. The eggs are reported edible (after hatching, the aroma would discourage even the most ardent mycophagist!), but we don't recommend it, due to the danger of confusing these eggs with those of the *Amanita.* It just isn't worth the risk. *Phallus hadriani* is similar but has a *pitted* olive brown head, or apex. It is found in similar habitats but much less frequently.

Season: Fall and winter.

Habit, habitat, and distribution: Single to several in loose, rich soil. Often found in lawns, gardens, and in mulch and compost piles.

Fruiting body diameter: 2–4 cm (¾–1½").

Stalk height: 7.5–15 cm (3–6").

Not recommended

Dictyophora translates to "net bearer"; the name refers to the prominent net below the green apex.

Description: This is among the largest (and stinkiest) of the stinkhorns, averaging 5 inches (12.5 cm) tall, and emerging from a membranous, paperlike egg-shaped structure, the cup or volva. The stalk is white, with a green slime layer at the top, and just below the cap is the white net.

Comments: The specimen in the photo is a particularly nice example, having been found in its prime, with the skirt white and clean looking. The more commonly seen specimens will have a droopy, dirty, torn "skirt," called the indusium. It is theorized that the function of the indusium is to increase the surface area on which the spore-bearing "goo" drips, thereby accommodating more flies. One may encounter a pure white specimen after the flies have removed all of the green spore mass!

Throughout history, these fungi have captured imaginations. They have been reputed as cures for impotence, baldness, rheumatism, gout, epilepsy, and gangrenous ulcers. The late Alexander Smith told the story of an older man who carried one in his cap. When the astonished Dr. Smith asked why, he said it helped ease his rheumatism! In China, the eggs of a related species are eaten in a soup that is considered a delicacy.

Season: Summer and fall.

Habit, habitat, and distribution: Single to several on mulch and decaying wood.

Fruiting body diameter: 2–3.5 cm (¾–1½").

Stalk height: 5–12 cm (2–5").

VM

Linderia columnatus

Not recommended

The scientific name translates to the "columned" stinkhorn; the columns are the "arms" that rise from the egg and are connected at the top. This fungus is so common that we are frequently asked about it. The best descriptions we have heard are "The one that looks like a bright pink Chinese lantern," and "It looks like four crab legs emerging from an egg and joined at the top."

Description: This fungus has bright pink arms emerging from a pale lavender to white, paperlike egg-shaped membrane. The arms join at the top, and the insides of the arms are coated with an olive black slime. The foul odor is quite noticeable.

Comments: This stinkhorn is common in gardens, along jogging trails and paths, and in well-mulched areas. Note the stages of growth in the photo—the odor appears after the color, so if you *want* to eat it, do so before the colors appear. Remember that the deadly *Amanita* also arises from a very similar egglike structure, so cut your "eggs" through the center, from top to bottom, to be certain you don't have an *Amanita*! To confirm your identification, watch a school-age child look at a mature one, and listen to his/her comment: "Yuck!" On a serious note, the stinkhorn egg will have a gelatinous inner skin and a small greenish spore mass. *Amanita* buttons have neither but do appear to be minute mushroom buttons.

Season: Summer into winter.

Habit, habitat, and distribution: Single to numerous on well-mulched soil that is loose enough to allow the egg to grow and expand.

Fruiting body diameter: 5–7.5 cm (2–3″).

Stalk height: 5–10 cm (2–4″).

VM

Not recommended

Blumenau is an area in Brazil, and Angola is a country in Africa, and this stinkhorn was named for the two places because it was first described from collections in those countries.

Description: This stinkhorn looks much like the *Linderia columnatus* illustrated previously, except that the fruiting body is entirely white, and the egglike structure from which it emerges is very dark gray. The almost black egg "cracks" into large scales to reveal the white color underneath as the fruiting body arises. The slimy spore mass coats the inside of the lattice formed by the fruiting body.

Comments: This photo documents a first sighting in North America for this fungus, which had previously been known only from Africa, Brazil, and Trinidad. Incidentally, the photo was taken at the Aline McAshan Arboretum at Memorial Park in Houston, Texas. Stinkhorn spawn is easily transported in mulch or soil with exotic plants and probably arrived at the arboretum by this method.

Season: Summer.

Habit, habitat, and distribution: Single to several on fertile ground or mulch.

Fruiting body diameter: 5–7.5 cm (2–3").

Stalk height: 5–10 cm (2–4").

DG

Mutinus elegans
Not recommended

The Latin name translates to the "elegant" stinkhorn—an interesting appellation. It is common throughout the eastern United States.

Description: The fruiting body consists of a slender stalk that arises from a white, paperlike, egg-shaped membrane and tapers from about halfway to the blunt tip. The stalk is bright pink, making this stinkhorn very striking but hardly "elegant." The green spore mass covers the newly emerged upper ⅓ of the stalk. Flies have usually removed the green slime layer from older specimens. The putrescent odor is quite pronounced.

Comments: This stinkhorn can be quite common, especially in well-manured gardens. Imagine the surprise of the gardener when a crop of these pops up overnight! A similar species is *Mutinus caninus,* which differs mainly in having a white stalk and a differently shaped head and is common in Europe and North America. The common name "dog stinkhorn" is a literal translation.

Season: Summer and fall.

Habit, habitat, and distribution: Single to numerous on decaying wood debris, grass cuttings, and leaf litter.

Fruiting body diameter: 1.3–2 cm (½–¾").

Stalk height: 5–10 cm (2–4").

DG

Not recommended

The species' name describes the clawlike fused tips at the top. This is the most common of a group of stinkhorns colorfully called the "lizard's claw stinkhorns" in Texas.

Description: The fruiting body is white, forming a simple, straight column. At the top it divides into four arms (the "lizard's claws"), which are fused at the top and covered with an olive black spore mass. The stalk arises from a white, papery, egg-shaped membrane. The aroma is quite noticeable.

Comments: This is a warm-temperate to tropical species found throughout the Gulf Coast area. We do not recommend it for the table, especially since the eggs are quite small. Also, while it is often found, it is rarely found in number. *L. borealis* is another name for it.

Season: Summer.

Habit, habitat, and distribution: Single to several on loose, manured, mulched soil.

Fruiting body diameter: 1–2 cm (⅓–⅔").

Stalk height: 5–10 cm (2–4").

VM

Lysurus periphragmoides

Not recommended

"Fenced in all around" is a rough translation of the species' name for this stinkhorn and nicely describes the distinct head. In older works it is often called *Simblum sphaerocephalum.*

Description: This stinkhorn resembles a hollow stalk with a closed lattice structure at the top. The spore mass is the dark colored area that coats the "windows" between the walls of the lattice. The stalk and cap can be a deep bright pink, yellow, or white (though the pink is the most common). The "egg" from which the stinkhorn arises is white and papery. This is one of the less offensive-smelling stinkhorns.

Comments: This stinkhorn was named *Simblum texense* by W. H. Long in 1907 from collections made in Austin, but this earlier name replaced his according to the rules of botanical nomenclature. Incidentally, in his rationale for *S. texense* as a separate species, Long claimed that it smells "sweet" rather than foul like other stinkhorns! Actually, the foul smell intensifies as the spore mass is exposed to air; when very fresh, the odor may often be described as "sweet."

Season: Spring, late fall, and winter.

Habit, habitat, and distribution: Single to numerous on fertile ground or on mulch, following spring rains.

Fruiting body diameter: 1–2 cm (⅓–⅔").

Stalk height: 5–10 cm (2–4").

DG

Note "egg" remnants at base.

DS

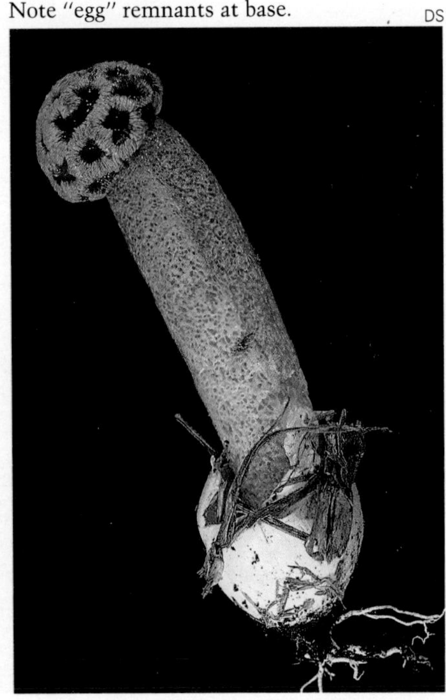

Other Gasteromycetes

One additional species is included here from another order of the Gasteromyces. It is a "stalked puffball," and species in this group are separated from the other Gasteromycetes by having a stalk on which a structure much like a puffball sits.

Calostoma cinnabarina

Not edible

This stalked puffball, with its aspic-jelly layer around it, is fairly common and easily recognizable. The species' name *cinnabarina* reflects the cinnabar red color of the spore sac and gelatinous layer.

Description: When young, this stalked puffball is covered with a translucent red gelatinous layer. At maturity, the stalk elongates and the spore sac is revealed when the gelatinous layer falls away, leaving red pieces of jelly that look like seeds along the stalk. The spore sac at the top of this stalked puffball is bright red, as are the little "teeth" at the top of the sac. The white to buff-colored spores are emitted through the "teeth," which open at maturity.

Comments: When young, the entire body looks like a mass of cherry jelly. Look for these along road cuts in wooded areas. We have at times found them by the hundreds! It is too small to be considered for the table, and the jellylike consistency has never appealed to us. A very similar species is *Calostoma ravenelii,* which has no gelatinous layer, is yellow to clay colored and slightly smaller in size, with cinnamon-colored "teeth." This stalked puffball is a member of the order Tulostomatales within the Gasteromycetes.

Season: Summer through winter.

Habit, habitat, and distribution: Single to numerous on fertile soil and humus in woods.

Fruiting body diameter: 1–3 cm (¾–1½").

Fruiting body height: 2.5–10 cm (1–4").

JL

SUBDIVISION ASCOMYCOTINA: The Ascos

In the classification of fungal groups, a major division is made between those fruiting bodies that produce their spores on basidia and those that produce their spores inside a special saclike structure called an ascus (plural asci). The Ascomycotina, or sac fungi, is the larger of the two groups and includes some yeasts and powdery mildews. The class also includes a number of macroscopic fungi (large enough to be seen with the naked eye), such as the morels, truffles, some cup fungi, and others. In this book, we will discuss only the groups that are large enough to be seen without a microscope, and only the more common species of those. Two classes are represented here: the Pyrenomycetes, or flask fungi, and the Discomycetes, which includes the cup, brain, and sponge fungi.

1. General appearance: Determining the type of structure that produces the spores of a fungus requires a microscope, but that doesn't mean that you can't distinguish a member of the class Ascomycetes in the field. This can be accomplished by studying the life forms of the larger Ascomycetes. They appear as fragile cups, saddlelike fruiting heads, rabbitlike ears, or pineconelike structures on fleshy stalks. At the same time a mental process of elimination takes place: if the fungal fruiting body you find is not a "normal mushroom" (with a distinct cap and stalk), or a bolete, polypore, other member of the Aphyllophorales, or puffball, then it is very likely an asco. The best-known family is the morels, which are widely known and sought after and considered by many to be the most delicious of all wild fungi. The morels resemble a round, spongelike structure growing above a central stalk. These, and two similar groups, the helvellas and the false morels, will have members featured in this section. Other distinct groups, including the cup fungi, so-called because they resemble small cups or bowls (with the spores forming on the inner surface), and the truffles, which resemble underground tubers, will also be discussed.

2. Spore print: Although the spores are forcibly discharged in a puff or cloud from the surface of the cup

or fruiting body, spore color is not used, and spore prints are not made in this group. The primary distinguishing feature between this group and the more commonly seen "mushrooms" is the production of the spores in a special structure called the ascus. Usually either four or eight spores are produced in each ascus, but others have more spores, usually in multiples of four.

3. Ecology: The ascos, or sac fungi, treated here are decayers of dead organic material, parasites on other fungi and insects, or are mycorrhizal fungi. The truffles will not be illustrated here as they are rarely found, although several species are present. Those truffles that are present have a lobed appearance, a thin outer "skin," and a marbled interior. Thus, most ascos are ubiquitous and can be found in the soil and on many different substrates. Many types fruit in the spring, and many also have a "translucency" and "elasticity" to their fruiting bodies.

Two of the best edible fungi are found in this class: the morels and the truffles. Among the other types, most are inedible or unpalatable, and some are toxic.

Class Pyrenomycetes

The Flask Fungi

This class of Ascomycetes is distinguished by the presence of minute "flasks" called *perithecia* that hold the spore-containing asci. The lower portion of the flasks is usually embedded in the fungus tissue, but often, the tops of the flasks can be seen causing a bumpy or "pimply" surface.

1. General appearance: This group is defined using microscopic characteristics including the form of the spore-bearing structure, the characteristics of the spores, and other features. There are many different Pyrenomycetes, and it is beyond the scope of this guide book to cover them in any detail. However, there are several unrelated groups that produce large fruiting bodies and are commonly encountered by the collector. Those covered here include members of the *Cordyceps* genus, which parasitize insects and truffles; *Hypomyces,* a genus that is found on other mushrooms; and the Xylarias, which grow on dead wood.

2. Spore print: In this group, it is often impossible to collect a spore print, and the spore print color is not used for identification. The spores are discharged through the opening at the narrow tip of a flask-shaped structure called the *perithecium.* The spores are usually examined under the microscope, where they are found to be variously shaped—some colored and others transparent; some species have threadlike spores that break apart.

3. Ecology: Most members of this group parasitize other organisms: some are found on the pupal stage of insects, such as caterpillars, or on other mushrooms; others grow on dead wood and many other plant parts as well as living plants.

This is an interesting group ecologically, but there are no species that are of value for the table.

Edibility not recorded

You're a real mushroom hunter when you can spot these small "head-shaped" caps (*capitata* means "headlike") emerging from the leaf litter!

Description: Above the ground emerges a golden yellow stalk with a reddish brown round cap that darkens to black in age. Under the surface, yellow fibers or "threads" are seen leading to an underground tuber, a species of *Elaphomyces*, a small, trufflelike ball about the size of a large marble.

Comments: This is an interesting ecological situation. An underground asco, *Elaphomyces* sp., is mycorrhizal with the roots of trees. It is often parasitized by *Cordyceps* species, which can provide the only clue to the presence of the trufflelike growth. Carefully dig up one of these mushrooms and scrape the dirt away from the ball at the base with a knife. You'll reveal *Elaphomyces granulatus*, a truffle that this fungus usually parasitizes. The edibility of the *Cordyceps* is not known, and the truffle is usually decayed or mature with purple spores. If you look at the round head with a hand lens or magnifying glass, you will see the small bumps that are tiny embedded flasks in which the sacs, or asci, that contain the spores are located.

Season: Fall and winter.

Habit, habitat, and distribution: Single to several under pines and mixed hardwood species; occasionally common. It is widespread, but not often noticed.

Cap diameter: 0.2–1 cm (up to ½").

Stalk height: 1–5 cm (½–2").

Stalk diameter: 2–4 mm (1⁄12–⅙").

OM

Cordyceps gracilis

Not edible

The species' name of this *Cordyceps* means "graceful," referring to the slim shape. This one parasitizes caterpillars.
Description: This fungus is bright golden yellow all over when fresh, with a slim stalk and slightly enlarged apex. The orange-yellow cap darkens to black as it ages. Below the ground level, the stalk extends down to the caterpillar (by this time, well decayed) on which it is growing. Look at the apex with a hand lens and note the small bumps that are the embedded flasks. The sacs, or asci, are located inside these flasks, and the spores are formed in the asci.

VM

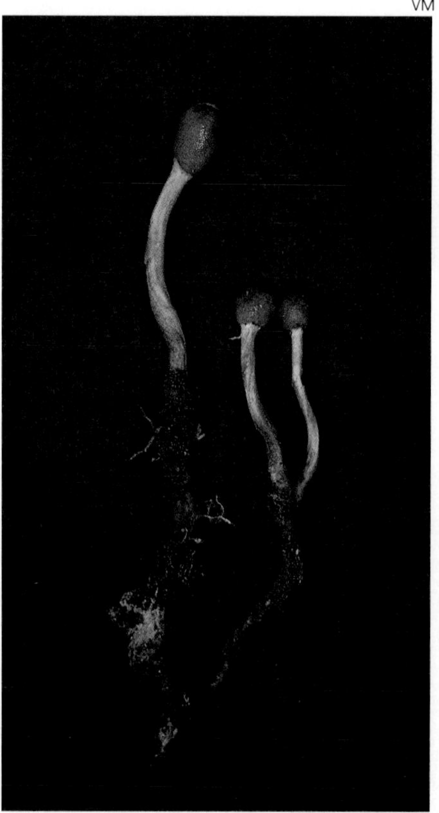

Comments: With this Clavaria-like genus, color and shape alone won't give a positive identification. To identify a *Cordyceps,* always dig it up completely (at least 4 inches below the ground surface) to get the object on which it is growing. When we collected these specimens, we were able to find the pupal case of the caterpillar visible on only one. Look closely at the photo; you may be able to make out the body segments and feet. (Hint: the *Cordyceps* is emerging from the caterpillar's head.)
Season: Fall.
Habit, habitat, and distribution: Single to several, arising from butterfly larvae. Seldom numerous.
Cap diameter: 0.3–1 cm (up to ½").
Stalk height: 1–4 cm (½–1½").
Stalk diameter: 1–4 mm (up to ⅙").

Not edible

This common fungus often fruits in large numbers, and the evenly spaced, reddish orange bodies with darker heads may remind one of the military men they were named after.

Description: This fungus is bright orange to red all over when fresh, with a slim stalk and slightly enlarged, elongated "head." This orange-yellow cap darkens to black as it ages, and it appears to have many small bumps due to small embedded flasks. The spores are produced in sacs, or asci, within the flasks (perithecia). Below the ground level, the stalk extends down to the parasitized caterpillar or bottle pupa on which it is growing.

Comments: This is the most commonly seen species of *Cordyceps* in the eastern United States. Perhaps that is because the large troops of fruiting bodies are much more difficult to overlook than the single specimens of other species.

Season: Fall.

Habit, habitat, and distribution: Usually several to many, arising from bottle or butterfly larvae, often in large groups. Commonly arising from well-decayed wood where the larvae are located.

Cap diameter: 0.3–1 cm (up to ½").

Stalk height: 1–4 cm (½–1½").

Stalk diameter: 1–4 mm (up to ⅙").

DL

Xylaria polymorpha
Not edible

The Xylarias (from the Latin root *xyla-* meaning "wood") are often referred to as "dead-man's fingers." The "fingers" are polymorphic (meaning "many forms") but generally resemble a pointing finger, sticking up from dead or decaying wood.

Description: The fruiting body is white to pale tan when young and covered with ash-colored asexual spores. It gradually darkens as it matures to form the sexual stage. When inspected closely, the small embedded flasks (perithecia) can be seen like black dots on the surface. The sacs, or asci, develop within the flasks and contain the spores. The surface is crustlike and minutely wrinkled. The fruiting bodies arise from rotting wood.

Comments: These "fingers," which often look as if they are gnarled from arthritis, are sometimes quite common on wood. The pale ash gray asexual stage occurs first in the spring, and the darker, fully mature stage follows in late summer.

Season: Spring and fall.

Habit, habitat, and distribution: Single to several, occasionally numerous, as decomposers on dead logs, limbs, and stumps.

Fruiting body diameter: 1–3 cm (3⁄8–1¼").

Fruiting body height: 2–8 cm (¾–3¼").

VM

Not edible

These tiny branched fruiting bodies grow only on rotting magnolia cones.

Description: The fruiting bodies consist of tiny white tough branches, upright spines, or "fingers," that emerge from magnolia cones during wet summer months. They are covered with white asexual spores. When the fruiting body matures to form the sexual stage, the embedded flasks in which the asci are found (perithecia) become black from the black color of the spores.

Comments: Many fungi require a very specific host; this one is an excellent example. Keep an eye out for it all across East Texas—it's unmistakable for any other fungus!

Season: Spring to fall.

Habit, habitat, and distribution: Several to many. They are decomposers of magnolia cones; thus, normally found under or near magnolia trees, and limited to the natural distribution of magnolia in East Texas forest areas.

Fruiting body diameter: 0–2 mm (up to 1⁄12″).

Fruiting body height: 2.5–7.5 cm (1–3″).

VM

Younger specimen.

AB

Older specimen.

Hypomyces lactifluorum

Not recommended/Caution

This bright orange-red fungus parasitizes species of *Lactarius* and *Russula* mushrooms. The species name translates to "flowers on *Lactarius*," which is an apt description of its fruiting pattern.

Description: Normally, the fruiting body of this fungus covers the fungus it parasitizes, and the shape of the mushroom can still be seen (though the host mushroom may be disfigured beyond recognition). It actually forms a bright layer of orange to red pimples over some or all of the fruiting body. When you slice through the mushroom, inside you will discover the remains of another mushroom (usually either a *Lactarius* or a *Russula,* but occasionally other species, including the possibility of poisonous ones) that has been parasitized by this fungus. The pimples are the flasks in which the sacs, or asci, that contain the spores are found.

Comments: The bright red color form (not the flavor) of this fungus has led to its often being called the "lobster mushroom." However, an orange color form is not uncommon. It is said to be edible when it fruits on an edible mushroom. However, we do not recommend it due to the difficulty of making a correct determination of the species of its host (which is often a bitter species of *Russula*).

Season: Summer and fall.

Habit, habitat, and distribution: Several to many on *Lactarius* and *Russula* species. To be expected wherever those genera are found fruiting during prolonged wet, humid weather.

Fruiting body width: Usually dependent on the host species.

Fruiting body thickness: 0.3–0.6 cm (⅛–¼").

JL

Not recommended/Caution!

This parasitic species fruits on *Lactarius* or *Russula* mushrooms. The name comes from the Latin for "yellow" (*luteo-*) and "green" (*-virens*), for its distinctive yellow-green color.

Description: This species of *Hypomyces* parasitizes only the gill surface of mushrooms, so you will have to turn the mushroom over to see it. The fruiting body forms a yellow-green, pimplelike coating over the gills of the *Lactarius* and *Russula* species it parasitizes. The spores are formed in the pimplelike structures as described for *H. lactifluorum.*

Comments: This fungus is said to be edible when it fruits on an edible mushroom, but we do not recommend it since it appears all too often on the bitter species of *Lactarius* or *Russula.*

Season: Summer and fall.

Habit, habitat, and distribution: Several to many on *Lactarius* and *Russula* species. To be expected wherever those genera are found fruiting, especially during wet, humid weather.

Fruiting body width: Usually dependent on the host species.

Fruiting body thickness: 0.3–0.6 cm (⅛–¼").

AB

Class Discomycetes

The Cup, Brain, and Sponge Fungi

The Discomycetes is a large class of fungi grouped together because of the exposed, fertile surface lined with asci, which are microscopic, saclike containers in which the spores are borne. It is a very diverse class in size, shape, and color. Because this class is differentiated from others on the basis of microscopic characteristics, field characteristics are not usually sufficient to make an accurate identification of species in some genera.

1. General appearance: The fungi in this group are often large or brightly colored and many resemble sponges, brains, cups, tongues, saddles, urns, fans, or saucers. Truffles, which grow underground and are often round, irregular, or "blob shaped," are also part of this group, although the spore-bearing surface of truffles is internal and not exposed, as it is in the other Discomycetes.

2. Spore print: A spore print can be obtained in a number of these species, but it is not used to distinguish among species or families in this class. The spores are typically colorless to brown.

3. Ecology: The ascos treated here take on one of three roles: as decayers of dead organic material, usually leaf litter or well-decayed wood; as parasites on other fungi and insects; and one group, the truffles, are mycorrhizal fungi.

Some of the most prized edibles, including the morels (*Morchella* spp.) and truffles (*Tuber* spp.), are in this group. Others are inedible.

"Morels," as this group is generically referred to, are the most avidly hunted of all wild mushrooms. This species, whose name, *esculenta,* means "good to eat," is the most common and has been spotted in a number of places in Texas.
Description: This mushroom has a yellowish to tan cap, which is oval to round or slightly elongated, with fragile flesh, and is mottled with deep pits. The stalk is white, hollow, and has a brittle, slightly gelatinous to rubbery texture. The yellow to buff spores are produced in sacs, or asci, which line the deep pits.
Comments: Several similar species of morels are known (but not often photographed; they seem to get consumed!) in Texas, and the species can vary in size and color as well as in the shape of the cap. Cut one in half to see the hollow stalk with the cross section of the pits attached directly to the stalk (not just attached at the top, as in "false morels"). The caps of true morels are never "brainlike," or lobed (see *Gyromitra caroliniana* for comparison). *Morchella esculenta* is a delicious edible and can be sautéed, fried, baked, or cooked any way you wish.
Season: Normally spring, though they have been found during other seasons, usually after unseasonable spells of cool, rainy weather.
Habit, habitat, and distribution: Single to numerous on ground, often under oaks and "cedar" (*Juniperus virginiana*), or along creek beds. They are most common on limestone soil (alkaline) but have also been found in the acid soils of East Texas. They have been reported from Big Bend, the Plateau and Hill Country, the East Texas Timber Belt, and parts of the Big Thicket.
Cap diameter: 2.5–7.5 cm (1–3″).
Stalk height: 7.5–20 cm (3–8″).
Stalk diameter: 20–40 mm (¾–1½″).

VM

HG

Gyromitra caroliniana

Toxic/Caution!

This is an American species of *Gyromitra,* and it is named for the Carolinas, where it was first found. This is a very robust "false morel."

Description: The most noticeable characteristic of this mushroom is its massive white stalk. Above it is a reddish brown cap that is deeply lobed and convoluted so that it appears "brainlike" in shape and texture. When cut down the center, the interior of the stalk is seen to be deeply furrowed or folded and not hollow as in the true morel.

Comments: Though it is not common, this species is occasionally encountered in the early spring by people who are hunting morels. Its best use is as an indicator of the start of morel season. We recommend *not eating this species,* as it is closely related to several toxic species. The toxin, if present, is apparently destroyed when boiled in water, but it's not a risk worth taking.

Season: Spring.

Habit, habitat, and distribution: Single to several, in low-lying, mixed hardwood and conifer woods. Known from East Texas and from the Hill Country and High Plains areas.

Cap diameter: 7.5–15 cm (3–6").

Stalk height: 10–20 cm (4–8").

Stalk diameter: 2–5 cm (¾–2").

VM

Not edible

Acetabulum means "the one that resembles a cup," and true to its name, this *Helvella* looks like a cup fungus.

Description: From the top, these fruiting bodies resemble medium to dark brown cup fungi, with the inner surface a deeper shade. On the outer surface of the "cups," conspicuous gray to white ribs are present running from the base of the stalk halfway or more up the outside of the cap. None of the true cup fungi have these "ribs." The spores are dark brown and are produced on the inner surface of the "cups."

Comments: This is an early spring mushroom found in calcareous soils—we find it along damp creek beds throughout the Hill Country in March and April. Edibility unknown; but the rubbery texture would discourage most from trying it. It is a good indicator of the time and place to look for morels.

Season: Spring.

Habit, habitat, and distribution: Several to numerous on ground in calcareous soil.

Fruiting body diameter: 2.5–7.5 cm (1–3″).

Fruiting body height: 2–5 cm (¾–2″).

OM

Helvella crispa

Edible

Helvella is an ancient name for a small herb, and "*crispa*" means "curled" or "wavy." This genus is often referred to as the "saddle fungi," so named because the caps resemble saddles. A common name for this species is "elfin saddles."

Description: The fragile fruiting body of this fungus resembles a stiff, almost parchmentlike mushroom with a coarsely ribbed stalk and a cap that has been folded to form a three-lobed, saddle-shaped "hat." The fruiting body is cream colored to tan with a translucent texture. The stalks are white, hollow, and the mushrooms are found growing on the ground or on well-decayed wood. The spores are produced on the upper spore-bearing surface, and the spore print color is white.

Comments: The fruiting bodies generally occur singularly or in small groups, on ground or highly decayed wood. It is an edible species, though rarely are enough found at one time to try it. We suspect it would tend to be tough and rubbery.

Season: Late summer and fall.

Habit, habitat, and distribution: Single to several on ground or on decaying wood; rarely plentiful, but widely distributed.

Cap diameter: 4–5 cm (1½–2").

Stalk height: 5–10 cm (2–4").

Stalk diameter: 12–20 mm (½–¾").

AB

Underwoodiae columnaris
Not edible

Columnaris, meaning "columned," is a natural name for these columnlike, stalked fungi.

Description: The fruiting bodies are club shaped to cylindrical and fingerlike, creamy white to tan in youth, darkening in age. Normally, several of these rubbery-textured cylinders are fused at the base. Large chambers are visible when the fruiting bodies are sliced down the center.

Comments: These strange-looking fungi appear as if they were sculpted from cake frosting by an amateur cake decorator who twirled the top as he finished each one. It is closely related to the genus *Helvella.*

Season: Summer.

Habit, habitat, and distribution: Single to several, rarely common, under hardwoods; found throughout eastern North America.

Fruiting body diameter: 1–3 cm (3⁄8–1¼″).

Fruiting body height: 5–10 cm (2–4″).

JL

Galiella rufa

Not edible

The Latin root from which *Galiella* is derived means "helmet-shaped," and *rufa* translates to "reddish"; thus, this is a reddish brown, helmet-shaped member of the cup fungi.

Description: The fruiting body is deeply cup shaped, with a very short, almost nonexistent stalk. The top is closed when young, opening to form a shallow cup with the edges inrolled. The flesh is gelatinous and tough when fresh, with a reddish to brown inner surface that fades to tan. The outer surface is brown and covered with clusters of hairy fibers. The best identification characteristics are the short stalk and the gelatinous texture. Cut a specimen in half to observe the gelatinous tissue.

Comments: This is the most common late summer to fall cup fungus and is often found growing on the bark of downed limbs and logs. It does not seem to decay the wood and is often found on the bark of logs in which shiitake, a mushroom highly prized in oriental cooking, is being cultivated. It is considered inedible.

Season: Late summer and fall.

Habit, habitat, and distribution: Widespread, usually several to numerous on the bark of recently downed oak and other wood; often common.

Fruiting body diameter: 2–3 cm (3/4–1 1/4").

Fruiting body height: 1–2.5 cm (3/8–1").

JL

Not edible

Both the genus and species' names for this tiny cup fungus are from the Latin root for "dish shaped." The most notable feature of this tiny, bright red cup fungus is the tiny black hairs around the edge, from which the common name, "eyelash cups," arises.

Description: These little cup fungi are quite small (about half an inch [1.2 cm]), but they are easy to spot due to the bright red color and fine black hairs on the edge (and along the outside) of the cups. The colorless spores are borne in sacs (asci) located on the inner surface of the cups.

Comments: Occasionally common, this is one of the earliest spring fungi. They are attractive but inedible and are too small to be of interest for the table. There are several species that look alike but differ by their microscopic characteristics.

Season: Spring.

Habit, habitat, and distribution: Several to numerous on damp soil, leaves, or decaying wood; often in creek bottoms and floodplain areas. They are widely distributed.

Fruiting body diameter: 0.2–1.5 cm (up to ½").

Fruiting body height: 0.2–1 cm (up to ⅓").

AB

Urnula craterium

Not edible

This scientific name hardly needs translating: these common "crater-shaped urns" are among the earliest fungi to appear in the spring.

Description: The fruiting body is deeply cup shaped, with a narrowed base or stalk (resembling an urn). They appear like clubs when young, then slowly open in a starlike pattern to reveal the deep brown cups, with ragged fringes around the edge. The flesh is tough and gelatinous when fresh, then becomes tough and leathery, varying in color from gray or brown to black. The best identification characteristics are the clusters of long stalks and the dark inner surfaces.

Comments: These are commonly found in the early spring, after rains. Look closely along the sides of fallen branches in shady areas. Although inedible, these are good indicators that other spring mushrooms, such as the morels, will soon be fruiting.

Season: Early spring.

Habit, habitat, and distribution: Widespread, decomposers on the branches and logs of downed oak and other wood; often common.

Fruiting body diameter: 3–6 cm (1¼–2½").

Fruiting body height: 4–10 cm (1½–4").

VM

Appendix: Spore Data Chart

Genus and Species	Spore Size (in microns)	Melzer's Reaction	Spore Shape
Agaricus campestris	5.5–7.5 x 3.5–5	inamyloid	elliptic, smooth with apical pore
Agaricus micromegathus	4.5–5.5 x 3.5–4	inamyloid	broadly elliptic, smooth
Amanita abrupta	6.5–9.5 x 5.5–8.5	amyloid	globose-elliptic, smooth
Amanita albocreata	7–9.4 x 6.3–8.7	inamyloid	globose to elliptic, smooth
Amanita atkinsoniana	9–12.9 x 5.3–7.9	amyloid	elliptic to elongate, smooth
Amanita bisporigera	7–10	amyloid	globose, smooth
Amanita brunnescens	7.8–9.4 x 7.8–8.6	amyloid	globose to subglobose, smooth
Amanita caesarea	8–12 x 6–8	inamyloid	elliptic, smooth
Amanita ceciliae	11.5–14	inamyloid	globose, smooth
Amanita cinereoconia	8.3–12.1 x 4.6–6.9	amyloid	elliptic to elongate, smooth
Amanita citrina var. *lavendula*	5.5–7 x 5.5–7	amyloid	globose to subglobose, smooth
Amanita cokeri	11–14 x 6.8–9.3	amyloid	elliptic to elongate, smooth
Amanita daucipes	8.6–11.7 x 5.2–7.2	amyloid	elliptic to elongate, smooth
Amanita flavoconia	7–9.5 x 4.5–6	amyloid	elliptic, smooth
Amanita flavorubescens	9.5–10.5 x 6–7	amyloid	elliptic, smooth
Amanita frostiana	7–10	inamyloid	globose, smooth
Amanita fulva	9.5–12.5	inamyloid	globose, smooth
Amanita komarekensis	8.2–10.2 x 5.5–7.8	inamyloid	broadly elliptic, smooth
Amanita muscaria	9.4–13 x 6.3–8.7	inamyloid	elliptic to elongate, smooth
Amanita muscaria var. *flavivolvata*	10.2–11.7 x 7–8.6	inamyloid	elliptic to elongate, smooth
Amanita mutabilis	10–14.5 x 5.5–9	amyloid	elliptic to cylindric, smooth
Amanita onusta	8.1–11.7 x 5.2–8.4	amyloid	elliptic to elongate, smooth
Amanita pelioma	9–12.5 x 6–8.1	amyloid	elliptic to elongate, smooth
Amanita polypyramis	9.2–13.6 x 5.5–9.5	amyloid	elliptic to elongate, smooth
Amanita rhopalopus	7.9–12 x 5.2–7.9	amyloid	elliptic to elongate, smooth
Amanita rubescens	7–9 x 5–7	amyloid	elliptic, smooth
Amanita spissa	8.6–10.1 x 7.3–8.9	amyloid	subglobose to elliptic, smooth
Amanita thiersii	7.5–9.5 x 7–9	amyloid	globose to subglobose, smooth
Amanita virosa	8–12 x 6.5–9.5	amyloid	globose-elliptic, smooth
Anthracophyllum lateritium	9.5–12.5 x 5.5–8	inamyloid	broadly ellipsoid, smooth
Armillaria mellea	6–9.5 x 4.5–6	inamyloid	elliptic, smooth
Armillaria tabescens	6–10 x 5–7	inamyloid	elliptic, smooth
Astraeus hygrometricus	7–11	inamyloid	globose, warted
Auricularia auricula	12–15 x 4–6	inamyloid	sausage shaped, smooth
Blumenavia angolensis	3–3.5 x 1.5	inamyloid	elliptic, smooth

Appendix: Spore Data Chart (*continued*)

Genus and Species	Spore Size (in microns)	Melzer's Reaction	Spore Shape
Boletellus ananas	16–18 x 7.5–9	inamyloid	elliptic, with longitudinal ridges
Boletinellus merulioides	7–11 x 5–7.5	inamyloid	elliptic, smooth
Boletus affinis var. *maculosus*	10–14 x 3–5	inamyloid	elliptic, smooth
Boletus albisulphureus	11–13.5 x 3.5–4.5	inamyloid	elliptic, smooth
Boletus campestris	10.5–13.5 x 4.5–6	inamyloid	elliptic, smooth
Boletus communis	10–13 x 3.8–4.8	inamyloid	elliptic, smooth
Boletus curtisii	10.5–12 x 4–5	inamyloid	elliptic, smooth
Boletus fraternus	10.5–12 x 4.5–6	inamyloid	elliptic, smooth
Boletus frostii	12–17 x 4–6	inamyloid	elliptic, smooth
Boletus griseus	9–12 x 3.5–4	inamyloid	oblong, smooth
Boletus luridellus	12.4–17 x 4.5–5.5	inamyloid	elliptic, smooth
Boletus oliveisporus	11–15 x 4–4.8	inamyloid	elliptic, smooth
Boletus pinophilus	12–15 x 4–5	inamyloid	elliptic, smooth
Boletus pseudoseparans	14–17 x 4.5–5	inamyloid	elliptic, smooth
Boletus pulverulentus	11–14 x 4.5–6	inamyloid	oblong, smooth
Boletus rubellus	10–14.5 x 4.5–5	inamyloid	elliptic, smooth
Boletus rubricitrinus	12.5–19 x 4.8–7.7	inamyloid	elliptic, smooth
Boletus sensibilis	10–13 x 3.5–4.5	inamyloid	oblong, smooth
Boletus tenax	9–12 x 4.5–5.5	inamyloid	elliptic, smooth
Boletus viridiflavus	9.2–17.7 x 4.6–5	inamyloid	elliptic, smooth
Calocera cornea	7–10 x 3–4	inamyloid	sausage shaped, smooth
Calostoma cinnabarina	14–20 x 6.3–8.5	inamyloid	oblong-elliptical, distinctly pitted
Calvatia bovista	4–6.5	inamyloid	globose, minutely warted or spiny
Calvatia cyathiformis	3.5–7.5	inamyloid	globose, with distinct spines
Cantharellus cibarius	8–11 x 4–5.5	inamyloid	elliptic, smooth
Cantharellus cinnabarina	6–11 x 4–6	inamyloid	elliptic, smooth
Cantharellus lateritius	7–9.5 x 4.5–6	inamyloid	elliptic, smooth
Cantharellus minor	6–11.5 x 4–6.5	inamyloid	elliptic to oblong, smooth
Chlorophyllum molybdites	6–13 x 6.5–8	dextrinoid	elliptic, smooth with apical pore
Clavaria vermicularis	9–13 x 5–7	inamyloid	elliptic, smooth
Clavaria zollingeri	4–7 x 3–5	inamyloid	subglobose to elliptic, smooth
Clavariadelphus ligula	8–18 x 3–6	inamyloid	elliptic, smooth
Clavicorona pyxidata	4–5 x 2–3	amyloid	elliptic, smooth
Clavulina cristata	7–11 x 6.5–10	inamyloid	elliptic to globose, smooth
Clitocybe gibba	5–8 x 3–5	inamyloid	elliptic, smooth

Genus and Species	Spore Size (in microns)	Melzer's Reaction	Spore Shape
Clitocybe nuda	5.5–8 x 3.5–5	inamyloid	elliptic, slightly roughened
Collybia iocephala	7–8.5 x 3–4	inamyloid	elliptic, smooth
Coltricia perennis	9–15 x 6–7.5	inamyloid	elliptic, smooth
Conocybe lactea	12–14 x 6–9	inamyloid	elliptic, smooth with apical pore
Conocybe tenera	11–12 x 5.5–6.5	inamyloid	elliptic, smooth with apical pore
Coprinus atramentarius	7–11 x 4–6	inamyloid	elliptic, smooth with apical pore
Coprinus comatus	13–18 x 7–8	inamyloid	elliptic, smooth with apical pore
Coprinus laniger	7–10 x 4–4.5	inamyloid	elliptic, smooth with apical pore
Coprinus plicatilis	7–10 x 4–5	inamyloid	elliptic, smooth with apical pore
Coprinus sterquilinis	17–22 x 10–13	inamyloid	elliptic, smooth with apical pore
Cordyceps capitata	14–20 x 2–3	inamyloid	cylindrical, smooth
Cordyceps gracilis	5–6 x 1.5–2	inamyloid	cylindrical, smooth
Cordyceps militaris	300–500 x 1–1.5	inamyloid	barrel shaped, threadlike, smooth
Cortinarius lewisii	5.5–6 x 6.5–7	inamyloid	subglobose with small warts
Cortinarius alboviolaceous	8–12 x 5–6.5	inamyloid	elliptic, minutely roughened
Cortinarius cinnamomeus	6–9.5 x 4–5	inamyloid	elliptic, minutely roughened
Cortinarius iodes	8–12 x 5–6.5	inamyloid	elliptic, minutely roughened
Cortinarius marylandensis	7.5–9 x 4–5	inamyloid	elliptic, minutely roughened
Cortinarius semisanguineus	6–8 x 4–5	inamyloid	elliptic, roughened
Craterellus fallax	10–20 x 7–11.5	inamyloid	broadly elliptic, smooth
Cyathus stercoreus	22–40 x 18–30	inamyloid	globose to elliptical, smooth
Dictyophora duplicata	3.5–4.5 x 1–2	inamyloid	elliptic, smooth
Entoloma abortivum	8–10 x 5–7	inamyloid	angular, smooth
Entoloma strictius	10–13 x 7.5–9	inamyloid	angular, smooth
Entoloma vernum	8–11 x 7–8	inamyloid	elliptic, angular, 6-sided
Exidia glandulosa	10–16 x 4–5	inamyloid	sausage shaped, smooth
Galerina autumnalis	8.5–10.5 x 5–6.5	inamyloid	elliptic, wrinkled
Galiella rufa	20 x 10	inamyloid	elliptical, with narrow ends and fine warts
Ganoderma lucidum	7–12 x 6–8	inamyloid	elliptic, slightly roughened, truncate
Geastrum saccatum	3.5–4.5	inamyloid	globose, spiny
Gloeophyllum saepiarium	9–13 x 3–5	inamyloid	cylindric, smooth
Gymnopilus spectabilis	7.5–10.5 x 4.5–6	inamyloid	elliptic, wrinkled
Gyromitra caroliniana	25–30 x 12–14	inamyloid	elliptic, with distinct reticulum
Gyroporus subalbellus	9.5–13.5 x 4.5–6	inamyloid	elliptic, smooth
Helvella acetabulum	18–22 x 12–14	inamyloid	broadly elliptic

Appendix: Spore Data Chart (*continued*)

Genus and Species	*Spore Size (in microns)*	*Melzer's Reaction*	*Spore Shape*
Helvella crispa	18–21 x 10–13	inamyloid	elliptic, with one large central oil drop
Hericium americanum	3–5 x 3–4	amyloid	elliptic to globose, minutely roughened
Hericium coralloides	3–5 x 3–4	amyloid	elliptic to globose, minutely roughened
Hericium erinaceus	4.5–6 x 4–5	amyloid	elliptic to globose, smooth to rough
Hohenbuehlia geogenia	5–6 x 3–5	amyloid	elliptic, smooth
Hohenbuehlia petaloides	7–9 x 4.5–5	amyloid	elliptic, smooth
Hydnum repandum	4–5.5 x 2.5–3	inamyloid	elliptic, smooth
Hygrophorus cantharellus	7–12 x 4–8	inamyloid	elliptic, smooth
Hygrophorus coccineus	7–11 x 4–5	inamyloid	elliptic, smooth
Hygrophorus conicus	8–14 x 5–7	inamyloid	elliptic, smooth
Hygrophorus miniatus	6–10 x 4–6	inamyloid	elliptic, smooth
Hypomyces lactifluorum	35–50 x 4–5	inamyloid	spindle shaped, with distinct warts
Hypomyces luteovirens	28–35 x 4.5–5.5	inamyloid	spindle shaped, with small warts
Inonotus quercustris	9–10 x 6–8	inamyloid	elliptic, smooth
Laccaria amethystina	8–10	inamyloid	globose
Laccaria laccata	7.5–10 x 7–8.5	inamyloid	elliptic to subglobose, with spines
Lactarius allardii	8–10 x 5.5–8	amyloid	elliptic with warts and ridges
Lactarius aquifluus	7–9 x 6–7.5	amyloid	elliptic with bands and ridges
Lactarius chrysorheus	6–8 x 5.5–6.6	amyloid	elipsoid with warts
Lactarius corrugis	9–12 x 8.5–12	amyloid	subglobose, with warts and ridges
Lactarius croceus	7.5–10 x 5.5–7.5	amyloid	ellipsoid with coarse bands
Lactarius hygrophoroides	7.5–9.5 x 6–7	amyloid	elliptic with small warts
Lactarius indigo	7–9 x 5.5–7.5	amyloid	elliptic, with warts and ridges
Lactarius maculatipes	7.5–9 x 6–7.5	amyloid	elliptic with warts and ridges
Lactarius paradoxus	7–9 x 5.5–6.5	amyloid	elliptic, with warts and ridges
Lactarius piperatus	6.5–9 x 5.5–6.5	amyloid	elliptic, with warts and ridges
Lactarius proximellus	7.5–9 x 6–7.5	amyloid	broadly elliptic with warts
Lactarius salmoneus	8–9 x 5–6	amyloid	elliptic, with warts
Lactarius volemus	7.5–10 x 7.5–9	amyloid	subglobose, with warts and ridges
Lactarius xanthydrorheus	8.7–10 x 7.5–8.7	amyloid	elliptic to globose, with spines

Genus and Species	Spore Size (in microns)	Melzer's Reaction	Spore Shape
Lactarius yazooensis	7–9 x 6–7.5	amyloid	elliptic, with warts and ridges
Laetiporus sulphureus	5–8 x 4–5	inamyloid	elliptic, smooth
Leccinum albellum	15–20 x 4–6	inamyloid	cylindric, smooth
Leccinum crocipodium	14–20 x 6–9	inamyloid	elliptic, smooth
Leccinum rugosiceps	16–21 x 5–5.5	inamyloid	elliptic to elongate, smooth
Lentaria byssiseda	10–18 x 3–6	inamyloid	cylindrical
Lentinus detonsus	4.5–6 x 2–3	inamyloid	elliptic, smooth
Lentinus lepideus	8.5–12.5 x 4–5	inamyloid	thin walled, cylindric, smooth
Lentinus tigrinus	6–9.5 x 2.5–3.5	inamyloid	thin walled, cylindric, smooth
Lepiota americana	9–11 x 7–8.5	dextrinoid	elliptic, smooth, with apical pore
Lepiota humei	7.5–9 x 5–6	dextrinoid	elliptic, smooth
Leucocoprinus birnbaumii	8–13 x 5.5–8	dextrinoid	elliptic, smooth with apical pore
Leucocoprinus cepaestipes	6–10 x 5–8	dextrinoid	elliptic, smooth with apical pore
Leucocoprinus fragilissimus	9–14 x 7–8.5	dextrinoid	elliptic, smooth with apical pore
Linderia columnatus	3.7–4.8 x 1.8–2.4	inamyloid	elliptic, smooth
Lycoperdon marginatum	3.5–5.5	inamyloid	globose, minutely warted
Lycoperdon perlatum	3.5–4.5	inamyloid	globose, minutely warted
Lycoperdon pyriforme	3–4.5	inamyloid	globose, smooth
Lysurus gardneri	3–4 x 1–2	inamyloid	elliptic, smooth
Lysurus periphragmoides	3.5–4.5 x 1.5–2.5	inamyloid	elliptic, smooth
Macrolepiota procera	12–18 x 8–12	dextrinoid	elliptic, smooth with apical pore
Marasmiellus albuscorticis	10–15 x 5–6	inamyloid	elliptic, smooth
Merulius incarnatus	4–4.5 x 2–2.5	inamyloid	elliptic, smooth
Morchella esculenta	20–24 x 12–24	inamyloid	elliptic, smooth
Mutinus elegans	4–7 x 2–3	inamyloid	elliptic, smooth
Mycena inclinata	7–9 x 5–6.5	amyloid	broadly elliptic, smooth
Mycena viscosa	9–11 x 6.5–8	amyloid	elliptic, smooth
Nematoloma fasciculare	6–8 x 3.5–5	inamyloid	elliptic, smooth
Omphalotus olearius	6–8 x 5.5–7	inamyloid	elliptic to nearly round, smooth
Oudemansiella radicata	14–17 x 9–11	inamyloid	elliptic, smooth
Panaeolus campanulatus	13–16 x 8–11	inamyloid	elliptic, smooth with apical pore
Panaeolus phalaenarum	14–22 x 9–14	inamyloid	elliptic, smooth
Panaeolus subbalteatus	11–14 x 7–9	inamyloid	elliptic, smooth with apical pore
Panus crinitis	6–8 x 3–4	inamyloid	elliptic, smooth
Panus rudis	4.5–7 x 2.5–3	inamyloid	elliptic, smooth

Appendix: Spore Data Chart (*continued*)

Genus and Species	*Spore Size (in microns)*	*Melzer's Reaction*	*Spore Shape*
Panus siparius	7–8 x 3–4	inamyloid	broadly cylindrical, smooth
Panus strigosus	10–13 x 3–5	inamyloid	elliptic to cylindrical, smooth
Phaeolus schweinitzii	5–8 x 3.5–4.5	inamyloid	cylindric, smooth
Phallus ravenelii	4–7 x 2–3	inamyloid	elliptic, smooth
Phlogiotis helvelloides	9–12 x 4–6	inamyloid	elliptic, smooth
Phyllotopsis nidulans	6–8 x 3–4	inamyloid	elliptic, smooth
Pisolithus tinctorius	7–12	inamyloid	globose, spiny
Pleurotus dryinus	9–12 x 3.5–4	inamyloid	elliptic, smooth
Pleurotus ostreatus	8–12 x 3.5–4.5	inamyloid	elliptic, smooth
Pluteus cervinus	5.5–7 x 4–5	inamyloid	elliptic, smooth
Psilocybe cubensis	10–17 x 7–10	inamyloid	elliptic, smooth with apical pore
Pulveroboletus hemichrysus	5.5–11 x 2.7–4.8	inamyloid	elliptic, smooth
Pulveroboletus ravenelii	8–10.5 x 5–6	inamyloid	elliptic, smooth
Pycnoporus cinnabarinus	5–6 x 2–2.5	inamyloid	cylindric, smooth
Pycnoporus sanguineus	4–5 x 2–3	inamyloid	cylindric, smooth
Ramaria botrytis	11–17 x 4–6	inamyloid	elliptic, smooth, longitudinally striate
Ramaria stricta	7–10 x 3.5–5.5	inamyloid	elliptic, minutely warted
Russula aeruginea	6–9 x 5–7	amyloid	nearly globose with warts and ridges
Russula ballouii	7.5–9.5 x 7–8	amyloid	nearly globose with warts
Russula compacta	7.5–10 x 6–8.5	amyloid	elliptic, with warts and ridges
Russula emetica group	8–11 x 6.5–9	amyloid	elliptic, with warts and ridges
Russula flavida	5–7 x 5.5–8.5	amyloid	nearly globose, with roughened warts
Russula mariae	7–10 x 6–8	amyloid	elliptic to globose, with warts and ridges
Russula ochricompacta	5.5–6.5 x 4–5	amyloid	subglobose, with warts and ridges
Russula rosacea	7–9 x 6–8	amyloid	nearly globose with warts
Russula variata	7.3–11.4 x 5.7–9.4	amyloid	broadly elliptic, with warts
Russula virescens	6–9 x 5–7	amyloid	nearly globose with warts and ridges
Sarcodon imbricatum	6–8 x 5–7.2	inamyloid	elliptic to globose, with irregular warts
Schizophyllum commune	3–4 x 1–1.5	inamyloid	cylindric, smooth
Scleroderma bovista	11–18.5	inamyloid	globose, with net pattern

Genus and Species	Spore Size (in microns)	Melzer's Reaction	Spore Shape
Scleroderma polyrhizon	6.5 x 10	inamyloid	cylindric, with net pattern
Scleroderma texense	9 x 12.5	inamyloid	nearly globose, with spines
Scutellinia scutellata	18–19 x 10–12	inamyloid	elliptic, roughened, filled with oil droplets
Sparassis crispa	4–7 x 3–4	inamyloid	elliptic, smooth
Sparassis spathulata	4–7 x 3–4	inamyloid	elliptic, smooth
Sphaerobolus stellatus	7.5–10 x 3.5–5	inamyloid	unevenly oblong, smooth
Steccherinum pulcherrimum	2.2–2.5 x 4–5	inamyloid	elliptic, smooth
Stereum complicatum	5–6.5 x 2–2.5	inamyloid	cylindric to curved, smooth
Stereum ostrea	5.5–7.5 x 2–3	inamyloid	cylindric, smooth
Strobilomyces confusus	9.5–15 x 8.5–12	inamyloid	elliptic, roughened and warted
Strobilomyces floccopus	9.5–15 x 8.5–12	inamyloid	elliptic, roughened with netlike ridges
Strobilurus conigenoides	6–7 x 3–3.5	inamyloid	elliptic, smooth
Stropharia coronilla	7–10 x 4–6	inamyloid	elliptic, smooth with apical pore
Suillus decipiens	7.5–10.5 x 3–4.5	inamyloid	elliptic, smooth
Suillus hirtellus	8–10 x 3–4	inamyloid	elliptic, smooth
Trametes versicolor	5–6 x 1.5–2.2	inamyloid	cylindric to sausage shaped, smooth
Tremella fuciformis	4.6–7.4 x 6.8–11.6	inamyloid	elliptic, smooth, with apical pore
Tremella mesenterica	7–15 x 6–10	inamyloid	elliptic, smooth
Tremellodendron pallidum	7–11 x 4–6	inamyloid	sausage shaped, smooth
Trichaptum biformis	5–6.5 x 2–2.5	inamyloid	cylindric, smooth
Tylopilus "purple cap group A"	9–10 x 3.5–4.5	inamyloid	sausage shaped, with light greenish droplets
Tylopilus ballouii	5–11 x 3–5	inamyloid	elliptic, smooth
Tylopilus chromapes	11–17 x 4–5.5	inamyloid	elliptic, smooth
Underwoodiae columnaris	25–27 x 12–14	inamyloid	elliptic, smooth at first, becoming warted
Urnula craterium	25–35 x 12–14	inamyloid	elliptic, smooth
Volvariella bombycina	6.5–10.5 x 4.5–6.5	inamyloid	elliptic, smooth
Xeromphalina campanella	5–9 x 3–4	amyloid	elliptic, smooth
Xylaria magnoliae	12–16 x 3–5	inamyloid	cylindrical, smooth
Xylaria polymorpha	20–32 x 5–10	inamyloid	spindle shaped, smooth
Xylobolus frustulatus	3.5–5 x 2.5–3	inamyloid	elliptic, smooth

For Further Study

Field Guides

Arora, David. *Mushrooms Demystified.* 2d ed. Berkeley, Calif.: Ten Speed Press, 1986.

Bessette, Alan, and Walter J. Sundberg. *Mushrooms: A Quick Reference to Mushrooms of North America.* New York: Macmillan, 1987.

Hesler, L. R. *Mushrooms of the Great Smokies.* Knoxville: University of Tennessee Press, 1975.

Lincoff, Gary, ed. *The Audubon Society Field Guide to North American Mushrooms.* New York: Knopf Press, 1983.

Miller, Orson K. *Mushrooms of North America.* New York: E. P. Dutton Press, 1981.

Phillips, Roger. *Mushrooms and Other Fungi of Great Britain and Europe.* London: Pan Books, 1981.

———. *Mushrooms of North America.* Boston: Little, Brown and Co., 1991.

Smith, Alexander, and Nancy Smith Weber. *Mushroom Hunter's Field Guide.* Ann Arbor: University of Michigan Press, 1980.

States, Jack S. *Mushrooms and Truffles of the Southwest.* Tucson: University of Arizona Press, 1990.

Weber, Nancy Smith, and Alexander Smith. *A Field Guide to Southern Mushrooms.* Ann Arbor: University of Michigan Press, 1985.

Reference Books

(For using a microscope and generally learning about fungi)

Largent, David L. *How to Identify Mushrooms to Genus III: Microscopic Features.* Eureka, Calif.: Mad River Press, 1980.

———. *How to Identify Mushrooms to Genus VI: Modern Genera.* Eureka, Calif.: Mad River Press, 1988.

Miller, Orson K., and David F. Farr. *An Index of the Common Fungi of North America (Synonymy and Common Names).* Stuttgart, Ger.: J. Cramer, 1975.

Watling, Roy. *Identification of the Larger Fungi.* Cheltenham, Eng.: Hulton Educational Pub., 1973.

Technical Books

(Additional books for those who want to concentrate on technical identification techniques or develop in-depth knowledge about a particular group of mushrooms)

Bigelow, Howard. *North American Species of Clitocybe. Part I.* Stuttgart, Ger.: J. Cramer, 1982.

———. *North American Species of Clitocybe. Part II.* Stuttgart, Ger.: J. Cramer, 1985.

Coker, William C. *Club and Coral Mushrooms (Clavarias) of the United States and Canada.* 1923. Reprint. New York: Dover Publications, 1974.

Coker, William C., and Alma H. Beers. *Boleti of North Carolina.* 1943. Reprint. New York: Dover Publications, 1974.

Coker, William C., and John N. Couch. *Gasteromycetes of the Eastern United States and Canada.* 1928. Reprint. New York: Dover Publications, 1974.

Guzman, Gaston. *The Genus Psilocybe.* Stuttgart, Ger.: J. Cramer, 1983.

Halling, Roy E. *An Annotated Index to Species and Infraspecific Taxa of Agaricales and Boletales Described by William A. Murrill.* Memoirs of the New York Botanical Gardens, vol. 40. New York, 1986.

Hesler, L. R. *Entoloma in Southeastern North America.* Stuttgart, Ger.: J. Cramer, 1967.

Hesler, L. R., and Alexander H. Smith. *North American Species of Hygrophorus.* Knoxville: University of Tennessee Press, 1963.

———. *North American Species of Lactarius.* Ann Arbor: University of Michigan Press, 1979.

Jenkins, David. *Amanita of North America.* Eureka, Calif.: Mad River Press, 1986.

Miller, Orson K., and Hope H. Miller. *Gasteromycetes: Morphological and Development Features with Keys to the Orders, Family, and Genera.* Eureka, Calif.: Mad River Press, 1988.

Moser, Meinhard. *Keys to Agarics and Boleti.* London: Roger Phillips, 1983.

Singer, Rolf. *The Boletinae of Florida.* Reprint. Stuttgart, Ger.: Lubrecht & Cramer, 1977.

Smith, Alexander H. *North American Species of Mycena.* Ann Arbor: University of Michigan Press, 1947.

Smith, Alexander H., and Harry D. Thiers. *Boletes of Michigan.* Ann Arbor: University of Michigan Press, 1971.

Smith, Alexander, Helen V. Smith, and Nancy Smith Weber. *How to Know the Gilled Mushrooms.* Dubuque, Iowa: Brown Co. Publishers, 1979.

———. *How to Know the Non-Gilled Mushrooms.* 2d ed. Dubuque, Iowa: Brown Co. Publishers, 1981.

Mushroom Cookbooks

Carluccio, Antonio. *A Passion for Mushrooms.* Topsfield, Mass., 1988.

Czarnecki, Jack. *Joe's Book of Mushroom Cookery.* New York: Atheneum, 1986.

Fischer, David W., and Alan E. Bessette. *Edible Wild Mushrooms of North America.* Austin, Tex.: University of Texas Press, 1992.

Freedman, Louise, and William Freedman. *Wild about Mushrooms: The Cookbook of the Mycological Society of San Francisco.* Berkeley, Calif.: Aris Books, 1987.

Liebenstein, Margaret, and Monika Bittman (illustrator). *The Edible Mushroom: A Gourmet Cook's Guide.* New York: Ballantine Books, 1986.

Wells, Mike, and Maggie Rogers, eds. *Wild Mushroom Cookery.* Portland: Oregon Mycological Society, 1987.

Index

Boldface type indicates species description.